PEDIATRIC HOMICIDE

Medical Investigation

PEDIATRIC HOMICIDE

Medical Investigation

Edited by Karen Griest

CRC Press
Taylor & Francis Group
Boca Raton London New York

CRC Press is an imprint of the
Taylor & Francis Group, an **informa** business

CRC Press
Taylor & Francis Group
6000 Broken Sound Parkway NW, Suite 300
Boca Raton, FL 33487-2742

Printed in the United States of America on acid-free paper
10 9 8 7 6 5 4 3 2 1

International Standard Book Number: 978-1-4200-7300-3 (Hardback)

Library of Congress Cataloging-in-Publication Data

Pediatric homicide : medical investigation / editor, Karen Griest.
p. ; cm.
Includes bibliographical references and index.
ISBN 978-1-4200-7300-3 (hardcover : alk. paper)
1. Children--Mortality. 2. Child abuse--Diagnosis. 3. Children--Wounds and injuries. 4. Homicide. I. Griest, Karen. II. Title.
[DNLM: 1. Forensic Medicine. 2. Child. 3. Homicide. 4. Infant. W 700 P371 2010]

RA1063.P43 2010
362.76--dc22 2009026889

Visit the Taylor & Francis Web site at
http://www.taylorandfrancis.com

and the CRC Press Web site at
http://www.crcpress.com

For

All my teachers, foul-weather friends, and
my spiritual light

Table of Contents

Preface

This book is dedicated to the medical investigation of homicides in infants and young children. Specifically, the goal of this book is to provide a scientific basis for the diagnoses of inflicted injury and death in infants and young children. The cause of death in infants and children is often subtle and the diagnoses difficult to establish. This is true for inflicted and accidental injury as well as for natural disease. By providing reviews of the medical literature on the more problematic causes of inflicted injury in childhood, this book will help to provide a scientific foundation for making the diagnosis of homicide or for ruling out that diagnosis. In spite of our current level of knowledge, there will continue to be many instances where an exact cause of death cannot be established.

The medical aspects are only part of the total investigation in childhood deaths and injury. The physician should not make a final diagnosis without detailed knowledge of the totality of the scene investigation and witness interviews. The physician and investigator must invest the time for not only a careful investigation, but also a careful review and exchange of information.

Not included in this book are two of the more obvious and increasingly prevalent causes of death in children, gunshot and stab wounds. These causes of injury and death are easily diagnosed and well covered in other texts.

Acknowledgments

A special thanks to Dr. Steven Karch without whose recommendation and support this book would not have been written. Thanks also to Dr. Arnold Greensher for his honest criticism and vast, freely given medical knowledge. Finally, my utmost gratitude to Dr. Ross Zumwalt whose instruction and aid over the years are the basis of my forensic career.

Editor

Karen Griest graduated from The Ohio State University in Columbus, having majored in genetics. Following graduation, she worked for The Ohio State Microbiology Department on the campus of The Ohio State University. She moved to Colorado, where she worked in human cytogenetic research, Department of Biophysics and Genetics, at the University of Colorado Medical Center in Denver. During that time she worked on the umbilical cord detection technique to screen for infants with the double-Y chromosome. She earned her M.D. from the State University at Liege, Belgium. During her studies in Liege, she worked for the Red Cross Transfusion Center Mobile Donor Unit and the University Department of Microbiology and Parasitology. Following graduation from medical school, she studied surgery for one year at Good Samaritan Hospital in Cincinnati, Ohio and completed a residency in anatomical pathology at the University of Cincinnati Medical Center. These were followed by a Fellowship in Forensic Pathology at the Hamilton County Institute of Forensic Medicine, Toxicology and Criminalistics in Cincinnati, Ohio. A second Fellowship in Pediatric Clinical and Research Pathology was completed at The Children's Hospital in Denver, Colorado. She was employed by the Office of the Medical Investigator (the Medical Examiner's Office) in New Mexico and was a member of the faculty of the New Mexico School of Medicine, Department of Pathology, for two years before establishing the Center for Medicolegal Research and Consultation in order to concentrate predominantly on pediatric forensic cases.

Dr. Griest is the editor and major contributor to *The Pediatric Trauma and Forensic Newsletter*, established in 1993. In addition to forensic teaching while employed at the Office of the Medical Investigator of New Mexico, she continued to teach forensic medical investigation to police officers and other criminal investigators, as well as pediatricians, attorneys, forensic nurses, forensic pathologists, and other forensic investigators. She is the author of articles on forensic pediatric issues as well as other forensic pathology-related topics.

Dr. Griest is a member of the American Academy of Forensic Sciences, the National Association of Medical Examiners, the Children's Division of the American Humane Association, the American Professional Society on the Abuse of Children, and the American Board of Forensic Examiners.

Dr. Griest has consulted on hundreds of child injury and death cases. She has testified in state and federal courts around the United States.

Contributors

Kim A. Collins
Fulton County Medical Examiner's Office
Atlanta, Georgia

Karen J. Griest
Center for Medicolegal Research and Consultation
and
The Pediatric Trauma and Forensic Newsletter
Cedar Crest, New Mexico

Steven B. Karch
Las Vegas Fire and Rescue
Las Vegas, Nevada
and
City and County of San Francisco
San Francisco, California
and
The Forensic Drug Abuse Advisor
Berkeley, California

Helen Whitwell
West Midlands Forensic Centre
Sandwell General Hospital
Lyndon, West Bromwich
West Midlands, United Kingdom

Intentional Head Injury in Infants and Young Children

1

HELEN WHITWELL

Contents

1.1 Introduction

Intentional head injury in infants and young children is the major cause of death in the field of pediatric homicide.[1–4] In addition, it is a major cause of long-term morbidity, with survivors showing variable patterns of brain injury. The mortality rate ranges from 15% to 35%. The long-term morbidity varies from 50% to 78%.

The true incidence is difficult to determine. This is due in part to the variable histories obtained from the caregivers as well as, in many cases, the nonspecific nature of the presenting features. In the United Kingdom, the incidence varies between 11.2 and 24.6 per 100,000 children under 1 year of age. In a recent study from Pennsylvania, the rate was higher in the first year of life, with an incidence of 26 cases per 100,000 person-years and 3.4 cases per 100 person-years.[5–8]

In terms of head injury, there are many age-dependent phenomena. Of particular interest is the issue of the so-called "shaken baby syndrome."

In older infants and children, there are many difficult problems related to the diagnosis of head injury, including correlation of a given history with the clinical and pathological findings as well as issues relating to timing and dating of the injuries. In addition, in some cases there may be considerable difficulty in differentiating accidental injury due to a fall from inflicted injury.

Significant numbers of head injury cases in children are due to traffic accidents, as occupants of vehicles, pedestrians, and cyclists. Other accidental causes include sports-related accidents.

1.2 Investigation of Suspected Pediatric Non-Accidental Injury Cases

From the pathological aspect, as is true in the clinical setting, investigation of these deaths may be difficult and prolonged, and even when all of the evidence has been assessed, ultimately it may not be possible to come to a firm conclusion. It is important that the pathologist, while taking into account other evidence, in particular clinical and radiological evidence, not be tempted to stray outside of his or her field of expertise.

Clinically, a child with inflicted head injury typically presents with immediate loss of consciousness, although this is not necessarily a reliable feature. Aside from immediate loss of consciousness, other manifestations of head injury include irritability, vomiting, focal neurological signs, and bulging of the anterior fontanelle.

In abuse cases, there is frequently a discrepancy between the physical findings and the explanation given by the caregivers. In a child with multiple injuries, not only of the head and neck but also elsewhere, and who may have other findings associated with abuse, the diagnosis is relatively straightforward. However, even in these cases issues such as timing of injury may be important, particularly if there is more than one caregiver. The essential issue in many of these cases is: "Does the explanation given explain the findings?"[9]

In a child where the sole presentation is a head injury, or more controversially in the presence of the "triad" of subdural hematoma, brain swelling, and retinal hemorrhage, it may be extremely difficult if not impossible to come to a firm conclusion as to cause.

The pathologists' responsibilities vary between jurisdictions in the United States and elsewhere. In some jurisdictions, the forensic pathologist will have sole responsibility for the postmortem examination and delivering the evidence. In other jurisdictions there is more of a multidisciplinary approach, utilizing the services of not only forensic pathologists but also pediatric pathologists, neuropathologists, ocular pathologists, osteopathologists, and potentially other pathological specialties. In some jurisdictions, joint examinations are undertaken utilizing a forensic pathologist and pediatric pathologist. This is particularly true in the United Kingdom.[10]

Irrespective of the jurisdictional structure, it is essential that the forensic pathologist take the lead in the recording and interpretation of any injuries.

1.3 Autopsy Examination

Prior to any examination, full clinical details must be available, in particular details of any therapeutic intervention including neurosurgical intervention. In addition, radiological input with review of various neuroradiological investigations is essential. This should be undertaken by a specialist with experience in the interpretation of radiologic images of children.

A number of "artifacts" may be produced by therapeutic intervention, for example, bruising beneath the insertion of an intraventricular drain. The drain may unwittingly be removed prior to autopsy, leading to possible misinterpretation of this as an injury. This drain removal may well be obvious at the postmortem examination; however other "injuries" may be more subtle and lead to difficulties, for example, scalp edema with slight hemorrhage in the deep occipital tissues as a result of lying in the prone position.

Full skeletal survey is mandatory prior to any postmortem examination. In young infants this should not be a "baby gram," but multiple total body radiographs on radiographic plates. Any results should be transmitted to the presiding pathologist, and expert radiology interpretation of the skeletal survey is essential. Postmortem magnetic resonance scanning (MRI) may also be useful if available.[11,12]

If the child has survived for some time in the hospital, there will usually be hospital photographs taken. These may have been undertaken by the investigating or the hospital authorities. It is important to review these; however it should be recognized that during management/treatment in the hospital, detailed identification of injuries may be hindered by therapeutic procedures and items such as bandages. Movement involving a seriously ill child may also present problems for photography.

1.3.1 History Relating to the Events

At the time of the postmortem examination, the history may or may not be fully documented. In suspected cases of homicide, the evidence may change from initial presentation and subsequently prior to any trial or legal proceedings. However, usually a preliminary account is available.

If the alleged incident involves a scene, then visiting the scene by the investigating authority and forensic pathologist (when appropriate), together with video and photographic documentation, including for example measuring the heights of various items of furniture, may be essential.

The postmortem examination is only one part of what may be a prolonged legal process, and it is essential that the pathologist, with an open mind, be able to assess and reassess evidence as it comes to light.

Aside from the history given by the caregivers, it is essential that the history is obtained from witnesses and family/friends, together with the past medical history including birth history. This is particularly important in young infants where the issue of the "shaken baby syndrome" arises. It is becoming increasingly recognized that birth trauma, even in normal deliveries, may result in subdural hemorrhages and other physical findings. These may or may not have been identifiable clinically at birth.

Details of any resuscitation procedures should also be obtained, in particular in relation to pediatric head trauma, such as bruises to the face, injuries to the frenulum, and bruising to the mouth and scalp. The resuscitation history includes not only that of the caregiver who may or may not give an account, but also of the various medical personnel, including ambulance technicians, nurses, and any others involved. Varying resuscitation injuries including those seen in inflicted injury (such as liver lacerations and rib fractures) have been described.[13,14]

Not infrequently, initial documentation of injuries is limited due to the clinical urgency relating to the condition of the child.

After stabilization of the child or, if the child does not survive, death, detailed documentation of injuries is paramount. Other major injuries which may be found in association with fatal head injury include skull and rib fractures as well as abdominal trauma.

Abdominal injury is more common in the older infant or child and is the second major cause of mortality in inflicted injury.[15,16] Lesions include rupture and injury of the liver, mesentery, bowel, and spleen. Other blunt force injuries include injuries to the lung and major vasculature.

Skeletal injuries may give an indication of the mechanism of the head injury; for example, typical posterior rib fractures may indicate squeezing and gripping the child. Fractures of the long bones may occur when the child is grabbed around the wrists or ankles and flung against a wall or floor.

1.3.2 External Injuries

It is well recognized that external head injury, including skull fractures, with underlying severe brain injury may be absent or minimal in childhood head injury. This, of course, is also recognized in adult injury, where hair is known to conceal or diminish the effect of any blunt trauma, including patterned injury caused by weapons.[17]

Furthermore, bruising may develop over time after death. For example, immediately after death little or no injury may be evident externally, but after 24 hours or so, bruising becomes discernable.

The majority of cases of fatal child head injury relate to blunt trauma. The external findings include diffuse areas of bruising, smaller areas of bruising (which may indicate slapping or fingertip bruising), and rarely, impressions from an item such as a ring or a weapon (Figure 1.1). It is this author's experience that use of a weapon in inflicted pediatric head injury is unusual. With increasing mobility accidental bruises become more common, for example on the bony prominences of the head and face, and must be distinguished from abuse.[18]

Bruising must be differentiated from natural causes such as birth marks or various skin conditions.

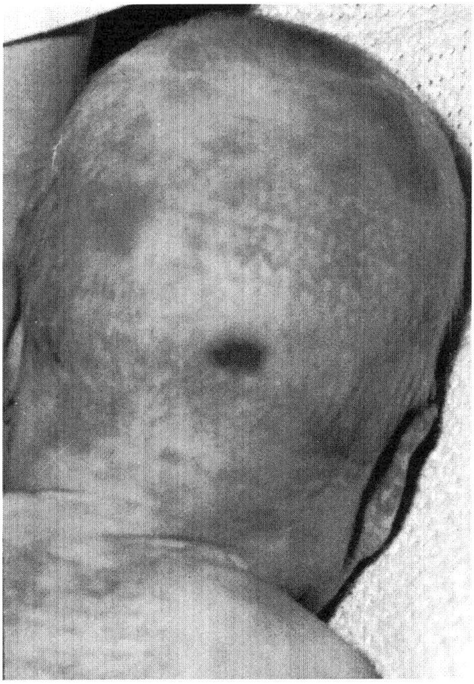

Figure 1.1 Abrasion and patchy bruising on the head of a 5-month-old infant. Note the pattern of the child's blanket on the skin.

Aging of bruises is notoriously difficult. The literature suggests that a minimum of 18 to 24 hours is required for yellow or green discoloration to occur in a bruise; thus a red-purple bruise may well imply recent origin. However the location of the bruise as well as the individual's susceptibility to bruising plays a role. The color of bruises may appear to age at different rates depending on location, further compounding the problem·

Histology may aid in dating of bruises.[19] The presence of hemosiderin is a debated topic in histological analysis of bruises, but would suggest a time of at least 36 to 48 hours following the injury. This matter may be further complicated by prolonged periods of hospitalization. Different criteria apply to aging of dural hemorrhages.

Other injuries that may be noted externally include abrasions and lacerations. These may be patterned if an object is used.

Photography is essential in recording external injuries. A ruler should be used in the photograph where appropriate.

1.3.3 Injuries to the Mouth

Injuries to the frenulum may occur as a result of direct blows or pressure from a baby bottle. Interpretation should however be done in the context of any resuscitation attempts. Frenulum injuries (albeit rare) may occur as a result of intubation procedures. In these cases however, injury is usually slight and would not normally be expected to involve both the upper and lower frenulum.[13]

Other injuries to the mouth include abrasions as well as bruising, and again care must be taken in any individual case in their interpretation.

1.4 Skull and Spinal Fractures

1.4.1 Skull Fractures

Skull fractures are a frequent finding in inflicted head injury. A skull fracture represents a focal impact. In the series of Geddes et al. (2001), 36% of pediatric head injury cases had one or more skull fractures.[15] This correlates well with other series.

Considerable work has been undertaken to attempt to differentiate inflicted skull fractures from those caused by accidental falls.[20] The majority of fractures seen in accidental situations tend to be linear, confined to a single bone, and the most common cause is a domestic accident (Figure 1.2). The majority of survivors of accidental head injuries have only minor residual symptoms, although a period of unconsciousness following the trauma is common. In inflicted head injury, fractures may be complex and may involve

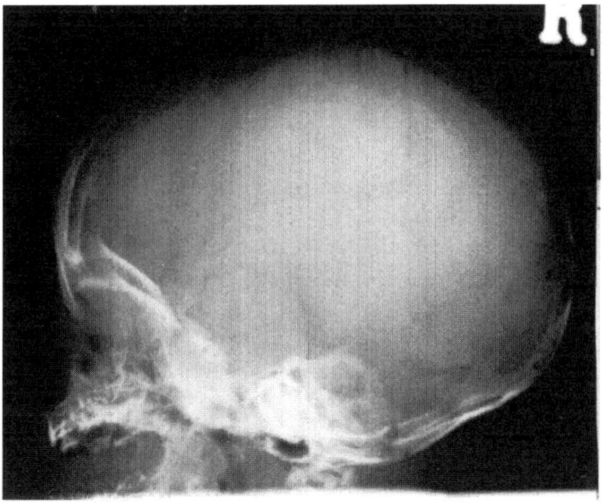

Figure 1.2 L-shaped fracture following a fall in a 6-month-old child.

more than one bone (Figure 1.3). Occipital fractures are more common, as are depressed fractures.[20,21] Diastatic fractures are also seen in inflicted head injury where fusion of the skull bones has not occurred. Growing fractures may also occur as a complication. It should be emphasized, however, that there are no specific features to positively differentiate between a fracture

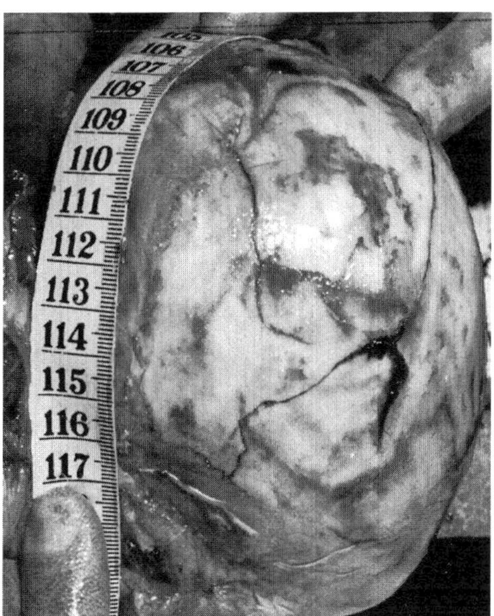

Figure 1.3 Complex skull fracture in a 2-year-old child hit against a wall.

caused by an accident and that caused by inflicted injury. The circumstances of the episode together with other findings should be taken into account.

It is essential also to exclude underlying bone abnormalities such as osteogenesis imperfecta, as well as metabolic conditions such as copper deficiency.[22]

Experimental work by Weber (1984) dropping infants onto various surfaces identified skull fractures in all cases dropped from a height of 82 cm.[23,24]

Fractures may occur in asymptomatic head-injured infants with occult intracranial findings in some cases.[25]

Histological examination should be undertaken, although the findings in infants and children are not well documented.

Radiological dating of skull fractures is difficult.

1.4.2 Spinal Fractures

Spinal fractures are recognized to occur in inflicted injury. The literature is scant on this topic. Much of it covers the accidental situation, including road traffic collisions. When spinal fractures occur, they are usually seen in the context of multiple other injuries. They may be demonstrated radiologically either by a plain radiograph, computed tomography (CT) scan, or magnetic resonance imaging (MRI). It is thought that some spinal fractures may go unidentified.[26,27] The mechanism in child abuse includes a direct impact, with fractures to the spinal processes, compression fractures as a result of compaction to the buttocks or head, and hyperextension–flexion injuries. It is difficult to identify the incidence of spinal fractures in child abuse. It is said to vary from 0% to 3%.[27]

Spinal cord injury and subdural and extradural (epidural) hematoma are described in cases of spinal fracture. In addition, spinal subdural hematoma is also recognized to occur in non-accidental head injury. This may be clinically occult. The origin of the spinal subdural hematoma is unclear. It may be related to anatomical continuity with posterior fossa subdural hematoma.[28] Epidural hemorrhage may occur artifactually with congestion in epidural vessels rather than as a result of trauma.[29,30]

Spinal neuropathological injury may occur and may help to determine the age of the injury along with histopathological examination of the bone.

1.5 Neuropathology of Inflicted Head Injury

This is a complex and ever-expanding area. The major findings include subdural hemorrhages, subarachnoid hemorrhages, cerebral swelling, hypoxic-ischemic damage, contusional tears, and axonal injury.

1.5.1 Subdural Hemorrhages

1.5.1.1 Acute Subdural Hemorrhages

Acute subdural hemorrhages occur frequently in inflicted head injury. The series of Geddes et al. (2001) records their presence in 84% of infants and 81% of the older child.[15] This concurs well with other series.[31]

There appears to be a difference between acute subdural hemorrhages seen in the younger infant in the so-called "shaken baby" situation as opposed to those in the older child. Neuroradiological examination shows subdural hematomas in infants are most common along the interhemispheric fissure and over the convexities of the brain.[32]

In the typical older child the mechanism of formation of the subdural hematoma is thought to be rupture of the bridging veins as a result of trauma. These are more likely to be space-occupying, sometimes requiring neurosurgical intervention. Bridging vein rupture has been identified in postmortem studies.[33] The location of the bleeding may be localized or remote from the impact site.

Where evidence of impact is minimal or absent in the so-called "shaken baby" situation, it is difficult radiologically, surgically, and pathologically to identify a precise bleeding point for the subdural hemorrhage. The bridging veins that penetrate the dural border are structurally weaker than those in the subarachnoid space, and it is postulated that bridging veins rupture more commonly as a result of traction at this site. However, proof that shaking can actually cause subdural hematomas is difficult to come by and still the subject of considerable debate. It is recognized biomechanically that impact produces much greater forces to the cranial cavity than that seen in pure shaking.[34] Biomechanical studies undertaken by Bandak (2005) have suggested that the intracranial components of the triad (subdural hemorrhage, cerebral swelling, and retinal hemorrhages) require forces that would cause significant structural neck injury in infants, although other studies have produced different findings suggesting that the forces necessary to cause shaking injury without impact may be lower.[35,36] This field is complex, and many studies highlight the limitations of using modeling (dolls, simulated skulls, and necks) in the human situation.

It is increasingly recognized that subdural hematomas may occur not only in complicated births, for example following ventouse extraction, but in normal births as well. This was first identified by Whitby et al. in 2003, and subsequent radiological studies have also indicated intracranial hemorrhage in 26% of normal births.[37,38] However those authors indicated that the pattern of hemorrhaging was different from that described in non-accidental injury, with absence of interhemispheric subdural hemorrhages. The birth subdural hemorrhages were identified in the posterior fossa and over the occipital region, although further work needs to be undertaken in this regard. Most studies indicate that these hemorrhages are relatively thin and patchy, resolving in a month or so.[39]

Symptomatic birth subdural hemorrhages are well recognized, with signs and symptoms including neurological symptoms from raised intracranial pressure. These not infrequently require treatment. Birth subdural hemorrhages may include both supratentorial subdural hemorrhage and infratentorial subdural hemorrhage.

Histological studies of the dura in cases of inflicted head trauma may show evidence of older bleeding.[15] This should not necessarily be taken as an indication that there has been previous inflicted trauma. The older bleeding may have occurred as a result of birth injury.

Histological studies relating to aging of dural hemorrhage can only be taken as an estimate. Organization with hemorrhage and membrane formation or hemosiderin deposition may occur. Hemosiderin deposition is said to occur at around 36 to 48 hours of hemorrhaging; however, this is variable. CD68, a marker for microglia cells, may be used to examine for early organization. It is said to occur within a few days (Figure 1.4, Figure 1.5).

It is important to look for underlying conditions that may predispose to subdural hematoma formation. These are numerous and include coagulation disorders, lymphoreticular disorders, infectious diseases including meningitis and encephalitis, metabolic disorders such as glutaric acidura type 1, and vascular malformations.[22] Shunted hydrocephalus and other conditions of increased extra axial space also appear to increase the risk of subdural hemorrhage.[40]

Of note is that extradural (epidural) hemorrhage, which represents a focal injury, is exceptionally rare in inflicted head injury and usually occurs in the accidental situation, typically a fall.[41]

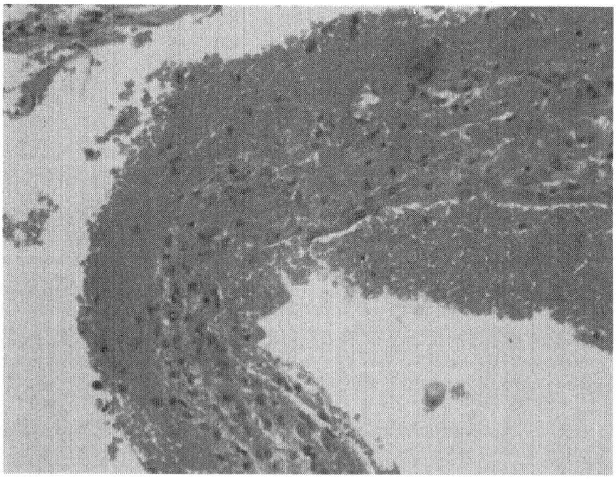

Figure 1.4 (see color insert following page 80) Histology of recent and older subdural hematoma with areas of membrane formation. (Courtesy of Dr. W. Squier.)

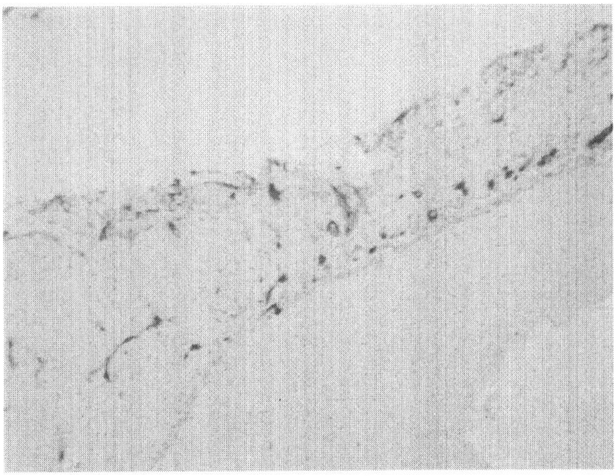

Figure 1.5 (see color insert following page 80) Histology of CD68 high-lighting macrophages in an area of older subdural hematoma. (Courtesy of Dr. W. Squier.)

1.5.1.2 Chronic Subdural Hematoma

This is a difficult area but is recognized to occur both in the accidental and inflicted situation. Clinical signs/symptoms, particularly in the young, may be minimal and nonspecific, including vomiting and other gastrointestinal symptoms. The presentation may also be rapid, with apnea or seizures. Underlying abnormalities should, again, be sought. Rupture of arachnoid cysts may predispose to both acute and chronic subdural hematomas.[42,43]

1.5.2 Subarachnoid Hemorrhage

Subarachnoid hemorrhage is seen in approximately half of the cases of pediatric head injury, usually in association with other intracranial findings. The subarachnoid hemorrhage is often patchy.[15] It is not an indicator of location of the site of impact. Radiological studies show it typically along the falx cerebri or within the sulci over the cerebral hemispheres.

1.5.3 Axonal Injury—Changing Concepts

In the 1950s pathological studies of adult head injury survivors showed widespread microscopic damage to neuronal axons within the brain. This was thought to be due to "shearing" damage to the nerve fibers at the time of injury.[44] These studies utilized what would now be considered as old-fashioned markers to identify damaged axons. This type of injury became known as "diffuse axonal injury" characterized by injury within the brain stem as well as injury within the cerebral hemispheres.

In the 1970s and 1980s, further work was undertaken neuropathologically which included the use of primates in biomechanical experimentation.[45,46]

As a result of these studies, diffuse axonal injury was identified as a result of angular or rotational acceleration of high magnitude, with the common scenarios being road traffic collisions and falls from significant heights. Diffuse axonal injury was clinically manifested by immediate unconsciousness after injury, prolonged coma, and death.

In the 1990s further neuropathological markers became available to identify histologically damaged axons, in particular beta amyloid precursor protein (APP), which identifies damaged axons by staining them brown or other colors, depending on the method used. APP identifies a protein which normally moves down axons in undetectable quantities, but in damaged axons this protein accumulates (Figure 1.6, Figure 1.7). It used to be thought that a period of survival post injury of around 1½ to 2 hours was required before

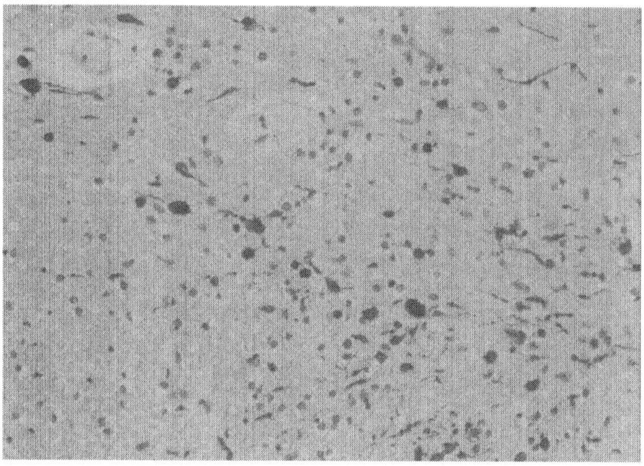

Figure 1.6 (see color insert following page 80) High power histology of APP staining in traumatic axonal injury.

Figure 1.7 High power histology of APP staining in the "vascular pattern" (hypoxic pattern).

detection of these accumulated proteins was possible; however it is now recognized that positivity in some circumstances may occur much earlier.

In 2000, new definitions of axonal injury were given by Geddes et al.[47] Axonal injury itself is nonspecific and refers to axonal injury from any cause, for example with brain swelling. Traumatic axonal injury occurs as a result of trauma, which is a spectrum ranging from small affected areas to widespread damage. At the most severe end of the spectrum, diffuse axonal injury occurs.

Subsequent publications regarding individuals who survived relatively minor head injury and then died later of an unrelated cause have shown axonal damage in small areas of the brain. Mild traumatic axonal injury is thought to be responsible for the recognized sequelae of head injury including neurological and behavioral features.[48]

Studies were carried out in the late 1990s involving a number of cases of inflicted head injury, with inclusion criteria designed at that time by Geddes (2001).[15] These criteria included confession, conviction plus extracranial injury, no conviction plus extracranial injury, conviction, and cases where there were major discrepancies between the findings and explanation. This study identified that the major neuropathology within the infant group was that of diffuse hypoxic brain damage with brain swelling rather than traumatic axonal injury, particularly diffuse traumatic axonal injury. This latter was identified only in infants showing significant evidence of impact (i.e., correlating a the road traffic collision or a significant fall scenario).[49]

This finding has been confirmed by others subsequently in pathological studies as well as neuroradiological studies. It is now recognized that the major neuropathological finding in non-accidental injury is that of hypoxic-ischemic damage with varying degrees of traumatic axonal injury.[50,51] In addition, in the infant group a number of cases showed evidence of craniocervical injury with damage to the corticospinal tracts raising the issue of "stretch" injury to the brain stem. Some cases also show focal cervical nerve root injury. This raised the question of how much injury to the cervical region was necessary to produce this type of focal injury, as opposed to diffuse axonal injury, which is widespread throughout the brain including the brain stem.[49]

Histologically, axonal injury follows the typical pattern of that seen in adults, apart from the cases that show localization in the craniocervical region. Axonal swellings are usually seen around 12 to 18 hours after injury. They vary from scattered areas within the white matter to much more extensive areas involving the brain stem. CD68 becomes positive a few days after injury and may be useful in terms of dating.

1.5.4 Contusional Tears

Contusional tears are a rare but well-recognized feature of infant head injury. They are particularly seen in the younger age group originally described by Lindenberg and Freytag (1969).[52] In addition, they can be identified radiologically and occur at the junction of the grey–white matter. They are believed to be a result of shearing forces, although they do not necessarily occur in the presence of significant traumatic axonal injury elsewhere. It may well be that the infant's brain, which is poorly or unmyelinated, reacts in a different manner than adults such that portions of the brain "slide" as a result of movement of the brain within the cranial cavity.

The tears comprise acute hemorrhage in the initial stages, which gradually resolve to leave slits with evidence of old hemorrhage and organization. They are usually, but not invariably, accompanied by subdural/subarachnoid hemorrhage.

1.5.5 Hypoxic-Ischemic Damage

Hypoxic-ischemic damage is acutely evident as brain edema/swelling (Figure 1.8). It is usually widespread, found throughout the brain. Histologically the classic time for its appearance in adults is 4 to 6 hours after injury; however in some cases it is possible to identify changes earlier. Histologically, it is important to differentiate hypoxic-ischemic cell change from postmortem artifacts such as the so-called "dark cell change" as well as

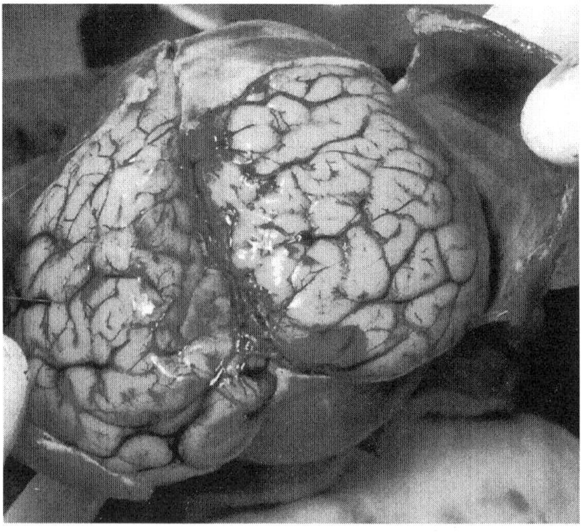

Figure 1.8 Brain edema in an infant.

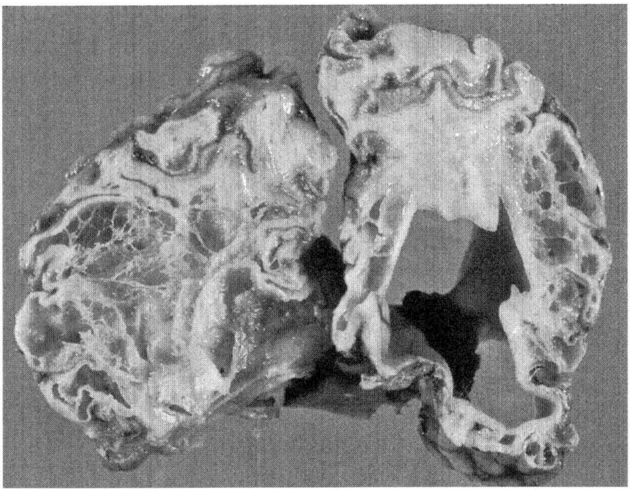

Figure 1.9 Coronal section of the brain in a 9 month old surviving several months after hypoxic-ischemic injury.

peri-neuronal vacuolation. Severe cerebral atrophy occurs in some cases in long-term survivors (Figure 1.9, Figure 1.10).

Identification of hypoxic-ischemic damage neuroradiologically is best shown on MRI, where it is either multifocal or widespread and not necessarily in arterial territories. CT scan shows loss of grey–white differentiation.[5]

Figure 1.10 (see color insert following page 80) Histology of hypoxic-ischemic injury with adjacent subarachnoid hemorrhage.

1.6 Problem Areas

1.6.1 "Shaken Baby Syndrome"

Shaken baby syndrome is a diagnosis associated with a triad of clinical signs. These include subdural hemorrhage, retinal hemorrhages, and encephalopathy (global brain swelling).

One of the earliest papers relating to shaken baby syndrome, or "SBS," was written in 1971 by Guthkelch, a British neurosurgeon, and is entitled "Infantile subdural haematoma and its relation to whiplash injury."[53] Much more widely quoted is the work of John Caffey. Since that time many papers have appeared in the literature covering the clinical, radiological, and other aspects of the syndrome.

Adding to the confusion is the considerable variety in the terminology used in these cases, including "shaken baby syndrome," "shaken impact syndrome," "battered baby," and "abusive head injury."[54,55] The labels are often applied in cases where there is limited evaluation of the history and circumstances. For example, if an infant presents with subdural hemorrhage and/or retinal hemorrhages, it is not infrequently labeled as a case of "SBS" in either the absence of a history of trauma or what may be regarded by many as a level of trauma incompatible with the findings of a simple fall or "whiplash" movement of the head. The term "shaken baby syndrome" has also been used extensively to include cases where there is evidence of significant impact, leading to even more confusion.[56] In this last scenario, it is not necessary to postulate shaking as an additional mechanism. It is known that variable degrees of neck hyperextension/flexion occur as part of an impact injury.

Because of the relatively large size of the infant head in proportion to the body, as well as its immature neck muscles that provide little support to the head, and with a relatively immature brain, the younger infant is thought to have increased vulnerability to the "triad."

In 1987 Duhaime published a paper on head injury using infant models.[34] This paper concluded that shaking alone produced considerably less force than did impact, raising the question as to whether shaking alone was sufficient to generate the forces required to produce subdural hematomas. Impact against a soft surface that would leave no evidence of a bruise or external impact injury was put forward as an explanation for brain injury with no external signs in impact cases.

However recent biomechanical work raises a wider debate in this controversial area. Cory and Jones (2003) concluded that it could not categorically be stated from the biomechanical perspective that pure shaking cannot cause fatal injuries in an infant.[57] Of note, in this study chin and occipital contacts were produced at the extremes of the shaking in the dummies.

In the dummy modeling by Prange et al. (2003), the study found that shaking and impact onto foam padding did not generate sufficient accelerational forces to produce subdural hemorrhage or axonal injury, but impact on to a firm surface did.[58]

The brain pathology in shaken baby syndrome was previously thought to be that of traumatic axonal injury, which is now known not to be the case. One of the clinical issues in an infant who has sustained a shaking injury with or without impact is that the infant would become immediately unconscious. This issue becomes less clear if it is appreciated that diffuse axonal injury or significant traumatic axonal injury only occurs where there is evidence of significant impact and is not a feature where so-called shaking alone occurs. This raises the issue of a possible lucid interval with delayed onset of cerebral swelling/hypoxic-ischemic damage.

The source of the subdural hematomas in the triad has been questioned. Pathologically it is recognized that these are extremely thin films which sometimes may not be identified neuroradiologically. Geddes proposed that the thin subdural hemorrhages may not be as a result of traumatic rupture of bridging veins but may occur where there is evidence of hypoxia in the presence of venous or systemic arterial hypertension or episodic surges in blood pressure with bleeding occurring intradurally and with subsequent extension in to the subdural space (Figure 1.11). This hypothesis has caused much debate in the literature.[59–61]

In 2007 Byard et al. published a retrospective study of 82 fetuses, infants, and toddlers that had hypoxic-ischemic damage from a variety of causes and had identifiable macroscopic subdural hematoma.[62] Whether or not there

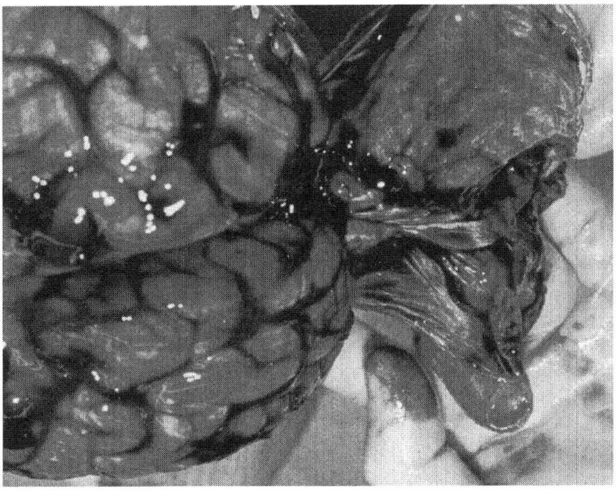

Figure 1.11 (see color insert following page 80) Brain and dura showing a thin film of subdural hemorrhage in a 2-month-old. (Courtesy of Dr. W. Squier.)

was microscopic intradural hematoma is unclear from this paper because the dura was not routinely examined.

The issue of retinal hemorrhages as part of the triad further compounds the problem. There are many causes of retinal hemorrhages, often relating to single poorly documented case reports. These include hematological disorders and infections as well as rarities such as tuberous sclerosis and malformations. There is considerable debate as to the significance of retinal hemorrhages together with other intraocular pathology, including macular folds and retinal detachment, in particular as to whether or not the extent of distribution can positively indicate inflicted injury from accidental injury. Vitreous bleeds and retinal folds are also identified in a significant proportion of head injury cases. The precise mechanism of causation of retinal hemorrhages is not fully understood, especially concerning the issue of the role of acceleration/deceleration forces. Mechanisms potentially include increased pressure as a result of intrathoracic or intracranial pressure.[63–65]

Retinal hemorrhages are also known to occur following birth delivery. These are said to normally resolve within a few weeks.

The presenting clinical history in the so-called triad cases appears to be relatively consistent with the infant presenting as a result of an apneic or a choking episode.[66] Whether or not the apnea or choking may play a role in the formation of intradural hemorrhage with potential leakage into the subdural space is unclear.

The accepted hypothesis that shaking causes the triad is based not only on literature but also confessions and convictions as well as witnessed episodes of shaking. The literature is extensive, however in many ways difficult to interpret, particularly with regard to inclusion criteria, which are limited in many studies.[67] The problem revolves around the definition of non-accidental head injury and its differentiation from accidental, as well as whether or not there is definite evidence of impact.

With regard to confession evidence, Leestma reviewed the medical literature from 1969 to 2001. In this paper, where shaking was admitted, only 11 of the cases did not show any evidence of impact.[68] Much of the other literature, including the series by Geddes et al., also supports the finding that pure shaking is uncommon. It is well recognized that confessions and convictions may be unreliable. Confessions may occur as part of the judicial process, particularly in civil cases. In 2005 the Court of Appeal in London overturned two cases of convicted individuals, with a further case being reduced from murder to manslaughter because of problems with the convictions.[69]

1.6.2 Re-Bleeding and Subdural Hematomas

Re-bleeding in subdural hematomas is well recognized to occur in the adult, and particularly in elderly individuals with chronic subdural hematomas. This may be clinically silent and occurs because neovasculature within the subdural membranes may rupture either with or without trauma.[70] Some authors suggest that it is not an explanation for the symptoms or presentation in the young; however it is recognized that subdural hematomas of varying ages are seen in infant head injury.[71]

Chronic subdural hematomas are seen in the field of inflicted head injury, and it is logical to assume that they have at some point been acute. It may be that the subdural hemorrhages were originally undetected because the injury at the time was not sufficient to be considered serious.[71] Some authors suggest, however, that the accumulation of blood by such a mechanism is likely to be slow and not cause acute collapse and neurological disturbance.

Birth injury is significantly higher than previously considered. These generally resolve. Further research is probably required to evaluate the incident and risk of re-bleeding into birth-related subdural hematomas, although it is suggested by some that it does not occur.

1.6.3 Timing of Injury

Timing of injury is often a major issue within the legal process. Each case needs to be evaluated individually, taking into account all the known circumstances as well as the clinical and radiological findings, together with other investigations.

Much of the work in this area has been done in the radiological literature with, in particular, CT dating of intracranial hemorrhages as acute, subacute, and chronic. With increased sophistication of MRI scanning, imaging can be divided into six stages: hyperacute, acute, early subacute, late subacute, early chronic, and late chronic. It is, however, important to realize that different patterns of density may occur at similar times.[70]

Timing of injury is predominantly within the realms of a clinical pediatrician; however, a pathologist is often asked to comment on the likely effects and symptomatology. The particular problematic area is the issue of immediate loss of consciousness as a result of severe primary traumatic brain injury. There are reported cases with delay in presentation, particularly related to delayed onset of complications such as cerebral swelling or intracranial hemorrhage.[72]

Delayed deterioration is a rare but recognized complication of head injury in infants/children, which may occur in nonfatal or fatal cases.[73] In cases with no other intracranial pathology, the pathology is that of diffuse generalized brain swelling. The precise mechanism is unclear. The syndrome may occur following trivial trauma. It is however accepted that in most cases of severe injury the infant would not appear normal to the caregiver.[74]

1.6.4 The Question of Low-Level Falls

This is another area that is gaining increasing significance in the field of pediatric head injury. The generally accepted view was that an infant or child could not sustain a fatal head injury with a low-level fall, usually taken to be less than 3 feet, although series vary. Accurate witness description in a number of surveys is lacking. There are many reported series indicating that fatalities/significant injuries are exceptionally rare in injuries due to falls.[75] There are, however, both case reports and series of documented falls where fatalities have occurred.[76] In any given case, it may not be possible to be dogmatic as to what may or may not have happened, however rare the literature may suggest, in terms of serious injury/death. Again, other evidence is often crucial.

Biomechanical reconstruction of individual cases is becoming more prevalent, although this clearly has limits in terms of applicability to humans.[77,78]

1.7 Conclusion

Inflicted head injury and head injury in infants and children in the broader sense is one of the most complex areas of pediatric forensic pathology and forensic neuropathology. Our understanding of both the pathology and the mechanisms of injury have developed, particularly over the last decade.

As a result, the most difficult cases, which include the so-called "shaken baby syndrome" cases—or triad cases—and those involving the question of a low-level fall, have to some extent become more difficult to interpret. There is a general lack of evidence-based medicine in this field, and critical appraisal of the available evidence is essential.

References

1. Hargrave DR, Earner DP. 1992. A study of child homicide over two decades. *Med Sci Law* 32:247–50.
2. Barlow KM, Milne S, Minns RA. 1998. A retrospective epidemiological analysis of non-accidental head injury in children in Scotland over the last 15 years. *Scott Med J* 43:112–14.
3. Ellis PSJ. 1997. The pathology of fatal child abuse. *Pathology* 29:113–21.
4. Barlow KM, Minns RA. 2000. Annual incidence of shaken impact syndrome in young children. *Lancet* 356:1571–72.
5. Gerber P, Coffman K. 2007. Non-accidental head trauma in infants. *Childs Nerv Syst* 23:499–507.
6. Pierce MC, Bertocci G. 2008. Injury biomechanics and child abuse. *Annu Rev Biomed Eng* 10:85–106.

7. Kesler H, Dias MS, Shaffer M, Rottmund C, Cappos K, Thomas NJ. 2008. Demographics of abusive head trauma in the Commonwealth of Pennsylvania. *J Neurosurg Pediatrics* 1:351–56.
8. Duhaime AC. 2008. Editorial demographics of abusive head trauma. *J Neurosurg Pediatrics* 1:349–50.
9. Whitwell HL. 2001. Non-accidental injury in children. In *Recent Advances in Histopathology,* eds. DG Lowe and JCE Underwood, 67–82. Edinburgh:Churchill Livingstone.
10. Royal College of Pathologists and Royal College of Paediatrics and Child Health. 2004. *Sudden Unexpected Death in Infancy.* London:RCPath and RCPCH.
11. Hart BL, Dudley MH, Zumwalt RE. 1996. Postmortem cranial MRI and postmortem examination correlation in suspected child abuse. *Am J Forensic Med Pathol* 17:217–24.
12. Kahana T, Hiss J. 1999. Forensic radiology. Review article. *Br J Radiol* 72:129–33.
13. Leadbeatter S. 2001. Resuscitation injury. In *Essentials of Post Mortem Examination Practice,* ed. GN Rutty. London:Springer-Verlang.
14. Plunkett J. 2006. Resuscitation injuries complicating the interpretation of premortem trauma and natrual disease in children. *J Forensic Sci* 51:127–29.
15. Geddes J, Hackshaw AK, Vowles GH, Nickols CD, Whitwell HL. 2001. Neuropathology of inflicted head injury in children. 1. Patterns of brain damage. *Brain* 124:1290–98.
16. Fatal child abuse. 2004. In *Knight's Forensic Pathology,* eds. P Saukko and B Knight, 461–79. London:Arnold.
17. Atwal GS, Rutty GN, Carter N, et al. 1998. Bruising in non-accidental head injured children: a retrospective study of the prevalence, distribution and pathological associations in 24 cases. *Forensic Sci Int* 96:215–30.
18. Carpenter RF. 1999. The prevalence and distribution of bruising in babies. *Arch Dis Child* 80:363–66.
19. Perper JA, Wecht CH. 1980. In *Microscopic Diagnosis in Forensic Pathology,* eds. JA Perper and CH Wecht. Springfield, IL:Thomas.
20. Hobbs CJ. 1984. Skull fracture and the diagnosis of abuse. *Arch Dis Child* 59:246–52.
21. Rao P, Carty H. 1999. Non-accidental injury: review of the radiology. *Clin Radiol* 54:11–24.
22. Whitwell HL. 2005. Head injury in the child. In *Forensic Neuropathology,* ed. HL Whitwell, 135–51. England:Hodder Arnold Publication.
23. Weber W. 1984. Experimental studies of skull fractures in infants. *Z Rechtsmed* 92:87–94.
24. Weber W. 1985. Biomechanical fragility of the infant skull. *Z Rechtsmed,* 94:93–101.
25. Greenes D, Schutzman S. 1998. Occult intracranial injury in infants. *Ann Emerg Med* 32:680–86.
26. Akbarnia BA. 1999. Pediatric spine fractures. *Orthop Clin N Am* 30:521–36.
27. Cramer KE. 1996. Orthopedic aspects of child abuse. *Pediatr Clin N Am* 43:1035–51.
28. Koumellis P, McConachie NS, Jaspan T. 2009. Spinal subdural haematomas in children with non-accidental head injury. *Arch Dis Child* 94:216–19.

29. Valdes-Dapena M. 1975. Sudden death in infancy: a report for pathologists. *Perspect Pediatr Pathol* 2:1–14.
30. Rutty GN, Squier WM, Padfield CJ. 2005. Epidural hemorrhage of the cervical spinal cord: A post-mortem artifact? *Neuropath Appl Neurobiol* 31:247–57.
31. Jayawant S, Rawlinson A, Gibbon F, et al. 1998. Subdural haemorrhages in infants: population based study. *BMJ* 317:1558–61.
32. Poussaint TY, Moeller KK. 2002. Imaging of pediatric head trauma. *Neuroimaging Clin N Am* 12:271–94, ix.
33. Maxeiner H. 2001. Demonstration and interpretation of bridging vein ruptures in cases of infantile subdural bleedings. *J Forensic Sci* 46:85–93.
34. Duhaime AC, Gennarelli TA, Thibault LE, et al. 1987. The shaken baby syndrome. A clinical, pathological, and biochemical study. *J Neurosurg* 66:409–15.
35. Bandak, Faris A. 2005. Shaken baby syndrome: a biomechanics analysis of injury mechanisms. *Forensic Sci Int* 151:71–77.
36. Margulies S, Prange M, Myers BS, et al. 2006. Shaken baby syndrome: a flawed biomechanical analysis. *Forensic Sci Int* 164:278–79.
37. Whitby EH, Griffiths PD, Rutter S, et al. 2003. Frequency and natural history of subdural haemorrhages in babies and relation to obstetric factors. *The Lancet* 362:846–51.
38. Looney CB, Smith JK, Merck LH, Wolfe HM, et al. 2007. Intracranial haemorrhage in asymptomatic neonates: prevalence on MR images and relationship to obstetric and neonatal risk factors. *Radiology* 242:535–41.
39. RooksVJ, Eaton JP, Ruess L, Petermann GW, et al. 2008. Prevalence and evolution of intracranial haemorrhage in asymptomatic term. *AJNR Am J Neuroradiol* 29:1082–89.
40. Duhaime AC, Christian CW, Rorke LB. Zimmerman RA. 1998. Nonaccidental head injury in infants—the "shaken-baby syndrome." *N Engl J Med* 338:1822–29.
41. Myhre MC, Groggard JB, Dyb GA, Nordhov M. 2007. Traumatic head injury in infants and toddlers. *Acta Paediatrica* 96:1159–63.
42. Page A, Paxton RM, Mohan D. 1987. A reappraisal of the relationship between arachnoid cysts of the middle fossa and chronic subdural haematoma. *J Neurol Neurosurg Psychiatry* 50:1001–07.
43. Demetriades AK, McEvoy AW, Kitchen ND. 2004. Subdural haematoma associated with an arachnoid cyst after repetitive minor heading injury in ball games. *Br J Sports Med* 38.1–3.
44. Strich SJ. 1956. Diffuse degeneration of the cerebral white matter in severe dementia following head injury. *J Neurol Neurosurg Psychiatry* 19:163–85.
45. Adams JH, Doyle D, Ford I, Gennarelli TA, et al. 1989. Diffuse axonal injury in head injury: definition, diagnosis and grading. *Histopathology* 15:49–59.
46. Adams JH, Graham DI, Gennarelli TA, Maxwell WL. 1991. Diffuse axonal injury in non-missile head injury. *J Neurol Neurosurg Psychiatry* 54:481–83.
47. Geddes JF, Whitwell HL, Graham DI. 2000. Traumatic axonal injury: practical issues for diagnosis in medicolegal cases. *Neuropathol Appl Neurobiol* 26:105–16.
48. Blumbergs P., Scott G, Manavis J, Wainwright H, et al. 1994. Staining of amyloid precursor protein to study axonal damage in mild head injury. *Lancet* 344:1055–56.

49. Geddes JF, Vowles GH, Hackshaw AK, et al. 2001. Neuropathology of inflicted head injury in children. 2. Microscopic brain injury in infants. *Brain* 124:1299–1306.
50. Reichard RR, White CL, Hladik CL, Dolinak D. 2003. Beta-amyloid precursor protein staining of non-accidental central nervous system injury in paediatric autopsies. *J Neurotrauma* 20:347–55.
51. Stoodley N. 2002. Non-accidental head injury in children: gathering the evidence. *Lancet* 360:271–72.
52. Lindenberg R, Freytag E. 1969. Morphology of brain lesions from blunt trauma in early infancy. *Arch Pathol* 87:298–305.
53. Guthkelch AN. 1971. Infantile subdural haematoma and its relationship to whiplash injuries. *BMJ* 11:430–31.
54. Caffey J. 1972. On the theory and practice of shaking infants. Its potential residual effects of permanent brain damage and mental retardation. *Am J Dis Child* 124:161–63.
55. Caffey J. 1974. The whiplash shaken infant syndrome: manual shaking by the whiplash-induced intracranial and intraocular bleedings, linked with residual damage and mental retardation. *Pediatrics* 54:396–403.
56. Savageau A, Bourgault A, Racette S. 2008. Cerebral traumatism with a playground rocking toy mimicking shaken baby syndrome. *J Forensic Sci* 53:479–82.
57. Corey CZ, Jones BM. 2003. Can shaking alone cause fatal brain injury? A biomechanical assessment of the Duhaime shaken baby syndrome model. *Med Sci Law* 43:317–33.
58. Prange M, Myers B. 2003. Pathobiology and biomechanics of inflicted child neurotrauma-response. In *Inflicted Childhood Neurotrauma,* eds. R Reece and C Nicholson. AAP Monograph.
59. Geddes JF, Tasker RC, Hacksha CD, et al. 2003. Dural haemorrhage in non-traumatic infant deaths: does it explain the bleeding in "shaken baby syndrome"? *Neuropathol Appl Neurobiol* 29:14–22.
60. Punt J, Bonshek RE, Jaspan T, et al. 2004. The 'unified hypothesis' of Geddes et al. is not supported by the data. *Pediatric Rehabil* 7:173–84.
61. Geddes JF, Talbert DG. 2006. Paroxysmal coughing, subdural and retinal bleeding: a computer modelling approach. *Neuropath Applied Neuropath* 32:625–34.
62. Byard RW, Blumbergs P, Rutty G, Sperhake J, et al. 2007. Lack of evidence for a casual relationship between hypoxic-ischaemic encephalopathy and subdural haemorrhage in fetal life, infancy and early childhood. *Pediatric Devel Pathology* 10:348–50.
63. Gilliland MGF, Luthert P. 2003. Why do histology on retinal haemorrhages in suspected non-accidental injury? *Histopathology* 43:592–602.
64. Lantz PE, Sinal SH, Stanton CA, et al. 2004. Perimacular retinal folds from childhood head trauma. *BMJ* 328:754–56.
65. Ommaya AK, Goldsmith W, Thiabult L. 2002. Biomechanics and neuropathology of adult and paediatric head injury. *Br J Neurosurg* 16:220–42.
66. Squier W. 2008. Shaken baby syndrome: the quest for evidence. *Dev Med Child Neurol* 50:10–14.
67. Donohoe M. 2003. Evidence-based medicine and shaken baby syndrome, Part 1: Literature review, 1966–98. *Am J Forensic Med Pathol* 24:239–42.

68. Leestma JE. 2005. Case analysis of brain injured admittedly shaken infants: 54 cases, 1969–2001. *Am J Forensic Med Pathol* 26:199–212.
69. Harris RV, Rock, Cherry, and Faulder. 2005. This is how our legal judgments are published. *EWCA Crim 1980.*
70. Jaspan T. 2008. Current controversies in the interpretation of non-accidental head injury. *Paediatr Radiol* 38:378–87.
71. Uscinski R. 2002. Shaken baby syndrome: fundamental questions. *Br J Neurosurg* 16:217–219.
72. Denton S, Mileusnic D. 2003. Delayed sudden death in an infant following an accidental fall. *Am J Forensic Med Pathol* 24:371–76.
73. Bruce DA, Alavi A, Bilaniuk B, et al. 1981. Diffuse cerebral swelling following head injuries in children: the syndrome of "malignant brain edema." *J Neurosurg* 54:170–78.
74. Case ME. 2008. Abusive head injuries in infants and young children. *Brain Pathology* 18:583–89.
75. Case ME. 2008. Accidental traumatic head injury in infants and young children. *Brain Pathology* 18:583–89.
76. Plunkett J. 2001. Fatal pediatric head injuries caused by short-distance falls. *Am J Forensic Med Pathology* 22:1–12.
77. Coats B, Margulies S. 2008. Potential for head injuries in infants from low height falls. *J Neurosurg Pediatrics* 2:321–30.
78. Duhaime A, Dodge C. 2008. Closer but not there yet: models in child injury research. *J Neurosurg Pediatrics* 2:320.

Neonaticide

2

KIM A. COLLINS

Contents

2.1 Definitions

Neonaticide is the deliberate killing, or homicide, of a child within 24 hours of its birth. Previously, researchers used less than 30 days as the timeframe for neonaticide, but currently the studies of this entity refer to the definition of within 24 hours. Infanticide is the killing of a child under the age of one year. Filicide is the killing of one's son or daughter (Table 2.1).

2.2 Victim and Perpetrator

The victim of neonaticide is often the product of an unwanted pregnancy. No gender or racial bias has been determined for the victim.[1,2] The perpetrator is usually the mother, young, described as immature, and unmarried.[1–25] Often the mother will still be living at home with her parents (Table 2.2). In virtually every case, the mother is the lone perpetrator, the birth and the killing

Table 2.1 Definitions in Neonaticide

Neonaticide	The deliberate killing of a child within 24 hours of birth
Infanticide	Killing of a child under the age of 1 year
Filicide	Killing of one's son or daughter

Table 2.2 Characteristics of the Perpetrator in Neonaticide

Mother
Young
Immature
Unmarried
Living with her parents

are unwitnessed, and the killing occurs immediately after the birth.[1–29] Most cases of neonaticide occur outside of the hospital setting.[10] Often both the pregnancy and the fact that there was even a birth are concealed.[26–29] The exact prevalence of neonaticide is difficult to determine because of these factors (Table 2.3).

2.3 Cause of Death

The cause of death in neonaticide is most often asphyxia (by smothering, suffocation, or drowning) or abandonment (Figure 2.1). Abandonment includes elements of hypothermia, hyperthermia, lack of food and water, and exposure to the elements. Other less common causes of death include blunt force trauma (usually head) and sharp force injury (Table 2.4).

2.4 Scene Investigation

The scene investigation is very important in cases of neonaticide, because the usual causes of death, asphyxia and abandonment, leave no pathognomonic gross or microscopic findings (Table 2.5). The child is usually found in the location of the delivery but hidden, as in plastic bags, a bathroom

Table 2.3 Characteristics of the Circumstances in Neonaticide

Unwitnessed
Occurs immediately after birth
Occurs outside of the hospital setting
Pregnancy and delivery are often concealed

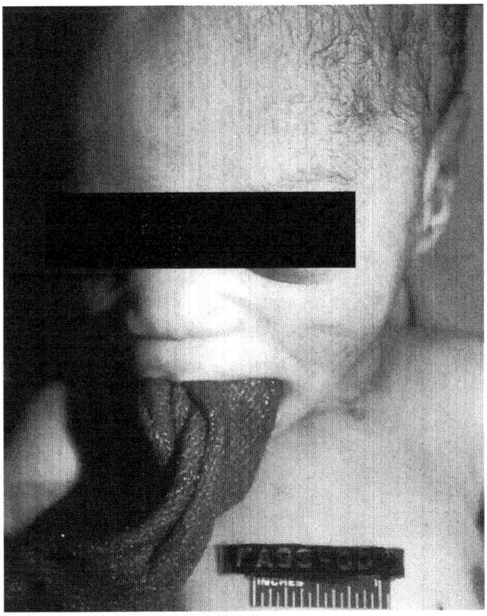

Figure 2.1 Neonatal asphyxia by occlusion of the mouth with a sock.

Table 2.4 Causes of Death in Neonaticide

Asphyxia	Smothering, suffocation, drowning
Abandonment	Hypothermia, hyperthermia, lack of food/water, exposure to the elements
Blunt force trauma	
Sharp force trauma	

Table 2.5 Characteristics of the Scene in Neonaticide

Body usually found at delivery location or immediate vicinity
Body hidden (in plastic bags, cabinets, public restrooms, etc.)
Airway may be occluded by a foreign object (e.g., tissues, towel)
Body may be found in toilet
If drowning, foreign material may be in airway
No external signs of trauma
No witnesses

cabinet, public restroom, or under a bed (Figure 2.2 A and B). In other cases, the child is found in a nearby trashcan, dumpster, or outdoor area. In cases of asphyxia, the airway may be occluded by a foreign object (tissues, sock, towel), or the body may be in the toilet. If the asphyxia is due to drowning, foreign material may be identified in the airways. Otherwise, no signs will be on the body indicating asphyxia. Since the mother was alone

(A)

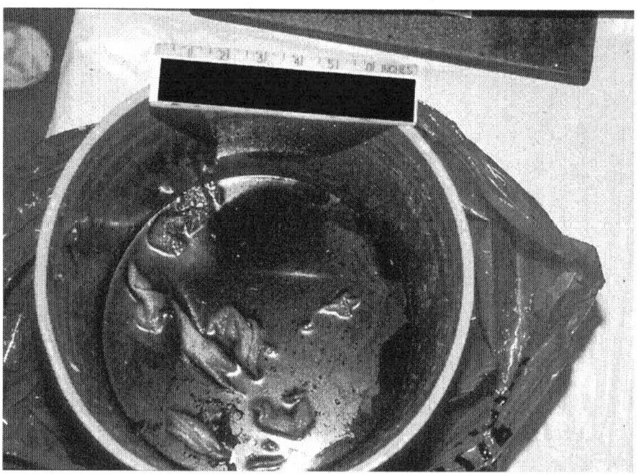

(B)

Figure 2.2 (A) A bucket found under a young mother's bed after it was determined that she had recently delivered. (B) Inside the bucket was a dead fetus versus infant.

at the time of the birth, there are no witnesses. Even family members in adjacent rooms will report hearing no screams or cries from the mother during the delivery. Amazingly, in some reports the mother will deliver the newborn and then continue to resume her previous activity, leaving the dead neonate behind.

2.5 Concealment and Denial of Pregnancy and Birth

Often when presented with a suspected neonaticide, investigators will note whether or not the mother attempted to conceal or deny the pregnancy and/or the delivery of the child. Does concealment of a pregnancy support neonaticide versus intrauterine or intrapartum death? Such concealment is definitely a suspicious factor, but studies have shown that there are many social, cultural, and religious reasons for concealing or denying a pregnancy (Figure 2.3).[26–29] Although this action is not in the best interests of the unborn child, the concealment of a pregnancy in and of itself is not a strong indicator of neonaticide. On the other hand, concealment or denial of a birth is a much stronger piece of evidence supporting neonaticide. Concealment and denial of a birth with disposal of the body raises the strong probability of neonaticide.

Figure 2.3 An autopsy determined that the child was a stillborn fetus and the cause of death was chorioamnionitis. No signs of trauma were identified.

2.6 Stillborn versus Liveborn

Before a death can be certified as neonaticide, it must first be determined that a child was born alive (Table 2.6).[30–33] Was the neonate viable? This determination can be very difficult because most neonaticides take place immediately after delivery. Viability of a newborn, defined as the time at which a neonate is able to exist separately from its mother, varies from state to state, and around the world. Most jurisdictions define the time of viability as greater than 24 weeks gestation or greater than 28 weeks gestation. Morphological measurements to assess the gestational age must include weight, crown-heel (body) length, crown-rump length, head circumference, and foot length. If born alive, viability based on gestational age is not an issue. From a forensic pathology standpoint, one approaches these cases by looking for signs that the child was born alive, findings consistent with intrauterine death, maceration, reasons for intrapartum death, and autopsy findings supporting a natural cause of death (Figure 2.4, Figure 2.5, and Figure 2.6 A and B).

2.6.1 Autopsy Findings: Stillborn versus Liveborn

Several nonspecific but important areas that should be examined postpartum when questioning a live birth are radiographic evidence of air in the lungs, middle ear, stomach; food in the stomach; and inflation of the lungs grossly or microscopically.[30,31] Radiographs can show air in the lungs or stomach supporting breathing or swallowing, respectively. Putrefactive gases of decomposition or air introduced during cardiopulmonary resuscitation (CPR) will show on radiographs and should not be misinterpreted. Radiographs can also be helpful in identifying inflicted trauma. Food in the stomach is a definite indicator of live birth. However, fetuses do swallow *in utero*, so there may be some white mucoid material within the stomach of fetuses or newborns that have not ingested food after birth. The lungs should be examined *in situ* for crepitance and expansion in the chest cavity as compared to the dark, rubbery, airless lungs of a stillborn.

Table 2.6 Possible Determinants of Live Birth

Gestational age compatible with life (viability)
No signs of maceration
No determinable reason for intrapartum death
Radiologic air in lungs, middle ear, stomach/GI
Food in the stomach
Inflation of the lungs, grossly or microscopically
Positive "flotation test" with no signs of putrefaction/CPR
Hyaline membranes in the lung

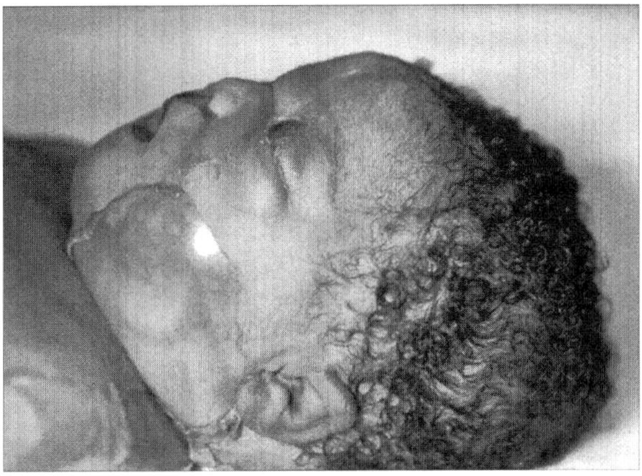

Figure 2.4 Early maceration of a fetus with sloughing of the epidermis and reddening of the underlying dermis.

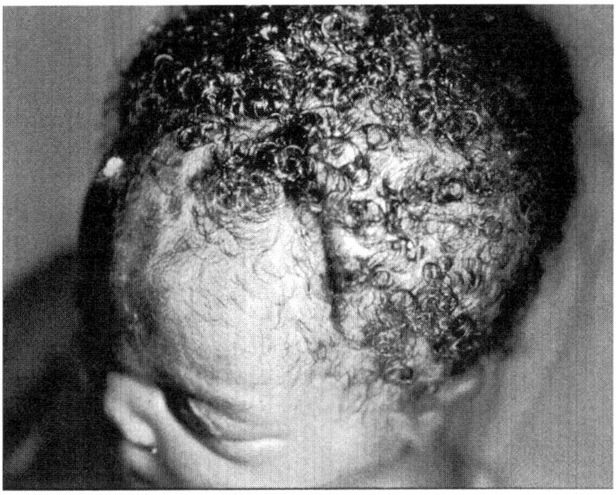

Figure 2.5 Overriding skull plates are evident as the macerated fetus' brain liquefies.

Microscopic analysis of the lungs is more difficult, but findings of well-expanded air spaces or atelectatic airspaces can support the gross findings, respectively.[30–32] However, the pathologist must be aware that children who are born alive and take a few breaths or shallow breaths will have poorly inflated/expanded lungs grossly and microscopically. Therefore the distinction can be difficult.

The hydrostatic test, better known as the "flotation test," is a gross and inaccurate test that is performed at the autopsy table. The underlying premise is that if the child was born alive and was breathing, then the aerated lungs

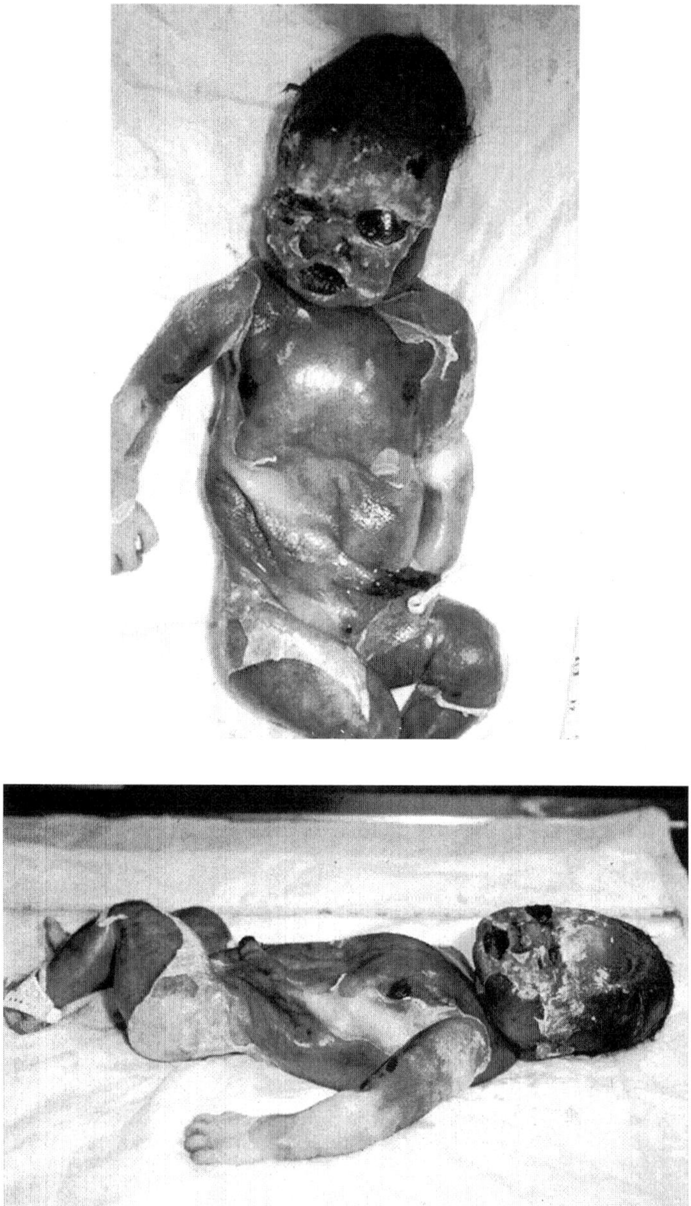

Figure 2.6 A macerated and decomposed fetus delivered at full term gestation.

will float in water or formalin. Many pathologists will first float the lungs *in toto* and then repeat the test with lung sections.[32] If the lungs sink, presumably the child had not taken a breath and was a stillborn. However, any air or gas can cause the lungs to float, so cardiopulmonary resuscitation and decomposition must be ruled out. To address whether decomposition caused

Table 2.7 Placenta Examination in Neonaticide

Placenta	Placental weight and measurements
	Signs of abruption, placental abnormality
	Signs of infection, grossly or microscopically
	Signs of circulatory disturbances
Umbilical Cord	Umbilical cord dimensions
	Number of cord vessels
	Signs of umbilical cord abnormality
	Umbilical stump/severed end—torn, cut, maceration
	Microscopic examination, vital reaction

floatation, a piece of liver can be used as a control; if the liver floats along with the lungs, then the test is void.

Of note, hyaline membranes within the lungs are indicative of a live birth.[31]

2.7 Placenta and Umbilical Cord

The placenta and umbilical cord should be examined in every case of neonatal death, including the placental weight and measurements and the umbilical cord dimensions. Grossly, either may be disrupted or abnormal as exemplified in the case of abruption with sudden onset of labor. They can show disease supporting intrauterine death such as infection or circulatory disturbances. In many cases, the placenta and cord determine the cause of fetal or neonatal death (Table 2.7).

2.7.1 Umbilical Cord

In cases of suspected neonaticide, the placenta may be found detached from the child. The cord is severed so that there is a fetal end and a placental end. The severed area can be examined for signs of tearing, softening, or maceration as well as for clean margins if it was cut with an instrument, knife or scissors. The umbilical stump on the fetal end can also be examined microscopically for vital reaction supporting a live birth. The vital reaction consists of inflammation, hemorrhage, and necrosis. However, this reaction takes 24 to 48 hours to occur and is usually not evident in the immediate postpartum period when most neonaticides occur.

2.8 Ancillary Studies

As discussed above, radiographs and procedures such as the hydrostatic "flotation" test can supplement the postmortem examination. Other

Table 2.8 Ancillary Studies in Neonaticide

Radiology, skeletal survey
Toxicology (blood, meconium, brain)
Genetic and chromosomal
DNA—identity, maternity, paternity
Microbiology/virology

important ancillary studies are toxicology (especially on blood, meconium, and brain), genetic and chromosomal studies (blood and tissue such as Achilles tendon), and microbiology/virology (Table 2.8). The intrauterine fetus is sterile. Therefore, microbiology/virology studies are very useful when ruling out infection as a cause of death and/or premature labor and delivery. Such studies can be performed on blood, spleen, lung, and liver.

2.8.1 Identity

In some cases, the identity of the neonate is not known (i.e., no connection is made to the mother). Blood for DNA analysis should be procured either in a Vacutainer™ (lavender tube with EDTA is preferred) or as a blood spot on filter paper.

2.9 Blunt Force Trauma

Although not as common as asphyxia and abandonment, neonaticide can be by blunt force trauma. To classify the trauma as inflicted, birth trauma must be ruled out (Table 2.9). Severe blunt force trauma is rare during delivery and is usually due to dystocia, prolonged difficult labor, and/or instrumentation and is more often to the skin and soft tissue (such as cephalohematoma) or peripheral nervous system (as in the brachial plexus). Bony fractures (the clavicle is number one) can occur, but are usually secondary to malpresentation, maternal–fetal disproportion, or dystocia and are not associated with

Table 2.9 Blunt Force Trauma in Neonaticide

Inflicted, especially head
Birth trauma—Dystocias, difficult labor
Soft tissue injury
Scalp, galeal, and periosteal injury
Peripheral nerve damage
Fractures
Retinal hemorrhage

Table 2.10 Investigation of Toilet Deliveries

Event history
Prenatal history
Delivery/labor history—precipitous vs. prolonged
Scene investigation
Gynecologic examination of mother
Parosity of mother
Gestational age
Signs of live birth
Cause of death

visceral injury. Of note, retinal hemorrhage(s) can occur as a result of birth and are not necessarily the result of inflicted trauma.

2.9.1 Toilet Deliveries

Births into toilets have been investigated in the realm of neonaticide.[34] Case history, prenatal history, scene investigation, and obstetrical/gynecologic examination of the postpartum mother are very important (Table 2.10). In cases of neonaticide, the cause of death of a liveborn infant delivered into the toilet is asphyxia with or without aspiration of definitive excreta and/or fragments of toilet paper (Figure 2.7 and Figure 2.8). The neonate is delivered and then disposed of, or is neglected and left in the toilet. Usually, these neonates are of term gestation. They may show signs of prolonged (nonprecipitous)

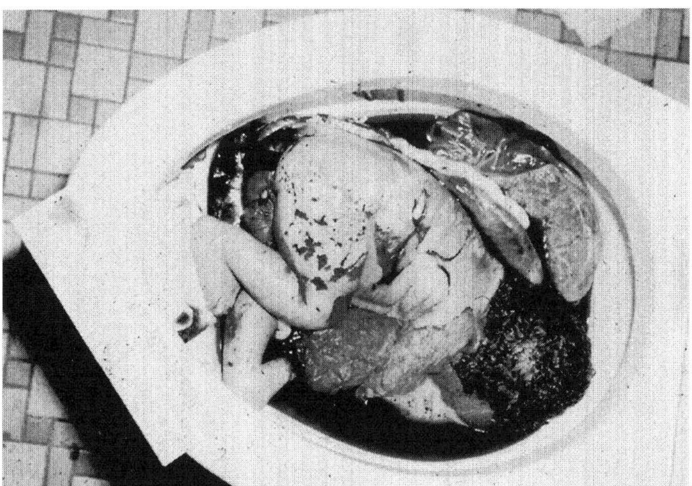

Figure 2.7 A full term neonate with attached placenta found in the toilet of a public restroom.

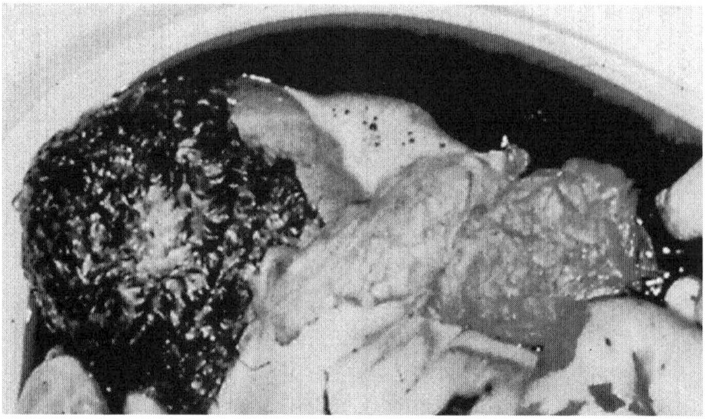

Figure 2.8 Note the froth within the water over the newborn's mouth indicating live birth and asphyxia by drowning.

labor such as hematomas of the presenting part.[35] Perpetrators of neonaticide toilet deliveries often conceal both the pregnancy and the delivery.

A precipitous delivery is a rapid delivery with less than 3 hours of active labor. Spontaneous, precipitous deliveries into toilets can indeed happen. Often precipitous deliveries are preterm, stillborn, and there is no denial of the pregnancy or concealment of the delivery. Precipitous deliveries can also occur in multiparous women at term gestation. Even if they occur at term gestation, the aforementioned findings of a difficult or prolonged labor will not be seen and, again, there is no concealment.

By examining both term and preterm newborns delivered into toilets, the act of delivery itself into the bowl is not known to cause any appreciable blunt force trauma. Skull fractures have not been reported to result from the short distance falls from mother (vulva) to the toilet bowl (with or without water).

2.10 Conclusion

Neonaticide, the killing of a liveborn infant within 24 hours of birth, is usually by asphyxia or abandonment. The perpetrator is most often a single, young mother who gives birth alone and outside of the hospital. The child is unwanted, and often the birth and pregnancy are concealed. The pathologist must determine if the child was born alive and rule out natural causes of death. The placenta and cord must be examined and ancillary studies utilized. If blunt force injury to the body is identified, birth trauma must be addressed. Toilet delivery is not reported to cause blunt force trauma.

References

1. Laporte L, Tzoumakis S, Marieau JD, Allaire JF. 2005. Sex of victims in maternal filicide. *Psychol Rep* 96:637–43.
2. Marleau JD, Dube' M, Leveillee S. 2004. Neonaticidal mothers: are more boys killed? *Med Sci Law* 44:311–16.
3. Yamauchi M, Usami S, Ikeda R, Echizen N, Yoshioka N. 2000. Medico-legal studies on infanticide: statistics and a case of repeated neonaticide. *Forensic Sci Int* 113:205–8.
4. Trautmann-Villalba P, Hornstein C. 2007. Children murdered by their mothers in the postpartum period. *Nervenarzt* 78:1290–95.
5. Rouge-Maillart C, Jousset N, Gaudin A, Bouju B, Penneau M. 2005. Women who kill their children. *Am J Forensic Med Pathol* 26:320–26.
6. Dube' M, Leveillee S, Marleau JD. 2003. Five cases of neonaticide in Quebec. *Sante Ment Que* 28:183–94.
7. Marcikic M, Dumencic B, Matuzalem E, Marjanovic K, Pozgain I, Ugljarevic M. 2006. Infanticide in Eastern Croatia. *Coll Antropol* 30:437–42.
8. Craig M. 2004. Perinatal risk factors for neonaticide and infant homicide: can we identify those at risk? *J R Soc Med* 97:57–61.
9. Greenland C. 2004. Risk factors for neonaticide and infant homicide. *J R Soc Med* 97:258.
10. Overpeck MD, Brenner RA, Trumble AC, Trifiletti LB, Berendes HW. 1998. Risk factors for infant homicide in the United States. *N Engl J Med* 339:1211–16.
11. Shiono H et al. 1986. Medicolegal aspects of infanticide in Hokkaido District, Japan. *Am J Forensic Med Pathol* 7:104–6.
12. Funayama M, Sagisaka K. 1988. Consecutive infanticides in Japan. *Am J Forensic Med Pathol* 9:9–11.
13. Bourget D, Grace J, Whitehurst L. 2007. A review of maternal and paternal filicide. *J Am Acad Psychiatry Law* 35:74–82.
14. Stone MH, Steinmeyer E, Dreher J, Krischer M. 2005. Infanticide in female forensic patients: the view from the evolutionary standpoint. *J Psychiatr Pract* 11(1):35–45.
15. Herman-Giddens ME, Smith JB, Mittal M, Carlson M, Butts JD. 2003. Newborns killed or left to die by a parent: a population-based study. *JAMA* 289:1425–29.
16. Spinelli MG. 2001. A systematic investigation of 16 cases of neonaticide. *Am J Psychiatry* 158:811–13.
17. Vallone DC, Hoffman LM. 2003. Preventing the tragedy of neonaticide. *Holist Nurs Pract.* 17:223–28.
18. Kaye NS, Borenstein NM, Donnelly SM. 1990. Families, murder, and insanity: a psychiatric review of paternal neonaticide. *J Forensic Sci* 35:133–39.
19. Friedman SH, Resnick PJ. 2007. Child murder by mothers: patterns and prevention. *World Psychiatry* 6:137–41.
20. Krouse HF, Nadeau JM, Silva PD, Byard RW. 2002. Infanticide: is its incidence among postneonatal infant deaths increasing? An 18-year population-based analysis in California. *Am J Forensic Med Pathol* 23:127–31.
21. Stone MH, Steinmeyer E, Dreher J, Krischer M. 2005. Infanticide in female forensic patients: the view from the evolutionary standpoint. *J Psychiatr Pract* 11:35–45.

22. Putkonen H, Weizmann-Henelius G, Collander J, Santtila P, Eronen M. 2007. Neonatacides may be more preventable and heterogeneous than previously thought—neonaticides in Finland 1989–2000. *Arch Womens Ment Health* 10:15–23.
23. Kaye NS. Infanticide (Letter to the Editor). 2005. *Am J Psychiatry* 162:1228–29.
24. Friedman SH, Horwitz SM, Resnick PJ. 2005. Child murder by mothers: a critical analysis of the current state of knowledge and a research agenda. *Am J Psychiatry* 162:1578–87.
25. Bennett MD, Hall J, Frazier L, Patel N, Barker L, Shaw K. 2006. Homicide of children aged 0–4 years, 2003–4: results from the national violent death reporting system. *Inj Prev* 12:ii39-ii43.
26. Del Giudice M. 2007. The evolutionary biology of cryptic pregnancy: a re-appraisal of the "denied pregnancy" phenomenon. *Med Hypotheses* 68:250–58.
27. Lee ACW, Li CH, Kwong NS, So KT. 2006. Neonaticide, newborn abandonment, and denial of pregnancy—newborn victimisation associated with unwanted motherhood. *Hong Kong Med J* 12:61–64.
28. Wessel J. 2007. Additional information on German study about denial and concealment of pregnancy. *Psychosomatics* 48:548.
29. Friedman SH, Heneghan A, Rosenthal M. 2007. Characteristics of women who deny or conceal pregnancy. *Psychosomatics* 48:117–22.
30. Spitz WU. 2006. Feticide and Neonaticide. In *Spitz and Fisher's Medicolegal Investigation of Death,* eds. WU Spitz and RS Fisher, 343–354. Springfield:Charles C Thomas.
31. Saukko P, Knight B. 2004. Infanticide and Stillbirth. In *Knight's Forensic Pathology,* eds. P Saukko and B Knight, 439–450. New York:Oxford University Press.
32. DiMaio VJ, DiMaio D. 2001. Neonaticide, infanticide, and child homicide. In *Forensic Pathology,* eds. VJ DiMaio and D DiMaio, 336–339. Boca Raton:CRC Press.
33. Sims MA, Collins KA. 2001. Fetal death: a 10-year retrospective study. *Am J Forensic Med Pathol* 22:261–65.
34. Mitchell EK, Davis JH. 1984. Spontaneous births into toilets. *J Forensic Sci* 29:591–96.
35. Sauvageau A, Belley-Cote EP, Racette S. 2007. Utility of caput succedaneum in the forensic investigation of neonaticide: a case report. *Med Sci Law* 47:262–64.

Intentional Suffocation in Infants and Young Children

3

KAREN J. GRIEST

Contents

3.1 Definitions

Asphyxia can be defined as the injuries to the body caused by oxygen deficiency (hypoxia) due to impairment or interruption of the oxygen supply or utilization in the tissues. The term suffocation in forensic medicine applies to cases in which environmental suffocation (inadequate oxygen in the atmosphere due to environmental conditions), smothering (due to mechanical obstruction of the nose and mouth), choking (due to blockage of the internal airways), or mechanical factors (due to strangulation or pressure on the chest) lead to asphyxia (Table 3.1).[1]

3.2 Intentional Strangulation in Infants and Young Children

3.2.1 Physical Findings in Manual and Ligature Strangulation

In infants and young children, the signs of strangulation, both manual and by ligature, may be absent or very subtle. However, external physical findings that may be present include abundant yellow froth at the nostrils, abrasions and/or bruises of the skin on the anterior and/or posterior neck (Figure 3.1). The bruises or abrasions may be very faint and subtle.[2] Abrasions may become more distinct with drying over the subsequent 24 hours. Bruises also may become more evident in the days after injury or death. Additional findings may be a swollen face, petechial hemorrhages in the face or buccal mucosa, subconjuctival hemorrhages, and ligature marks that may be patterned (Figure 3.2A and B, Figure 3.3A, B, and C).[3] Fingernail imprints may occur in manual strangulation.[4]

Internally, at autopsy, one may find petechiae over the visceral pleura, epicardium, and/or thymus. There may be hemorrhages in the internal soft tissues in the anterior and/or posterior neck.[2] There may be bilateral cerebral hemorrhages and congested leptomeninges.[3] Strangulation can lead to hyoid bone fracture.[5] Laryngeal edema may subsequently develop due to the neck compression (Table 3.2).[3]

Clinically, nearly one-third of cases present with seizures due to hypoxic brain injury. Elevated intracranial pressure is rare at admission; however 60%

Table 3.1 Types and Definitions of Suffocation

Type of Suffocation	Definition
Environmental	Inadequate atmospheric oxygen
Smothering	Obstruction of nose and mouth
Choking	Blockage of internal airways
Mechanical	Strangulation or pressure on chest

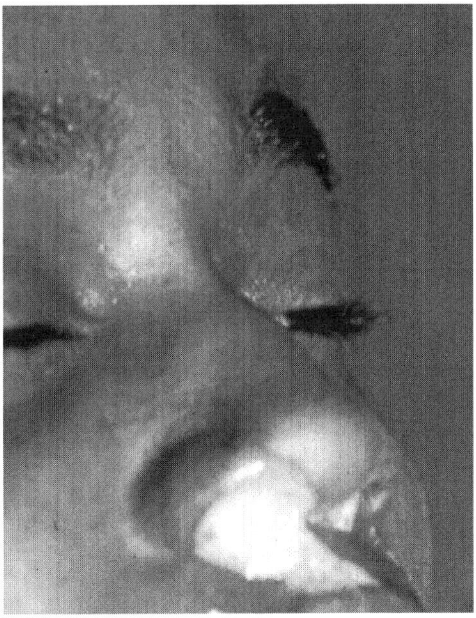

Figure 3.1 Abundant froth at nostrils in asphyxia case.

of children may develop signs of "late herniations" after 24 hours, with subsequent brain death. Neuroradiological imaging (CT and MRI) at admission is usually normal; however MRI may show evidence of white matter edema in survivors. Bone fractures and laryngeal edema associated with direct injury may compromise the airway, leading to brain asphyxia. Survivors of strangulation injury demonstrate a variety of cognitive disabilities indicating the vulnerability of the hippocampus to global hypoxic-ischemic injury.[3]

Manual strangulation may be achieved by a fixed gripping of the neck with the fingers adducted and placed anteriorly, the thumb placed posteriorly, the child facing away from the assailant.[2] The reverse may also be true, with the thumb placed on the anterior neck, the fingers placed posteriorly, the child facing the assailant (Figure 3.4).

3.2.2 Resuscitation and Signs of Strangulation

Although the presence of bruising and abrasions on the neck arouses suspicion of homicide, such injuries may also result from attempted resuscitation. Crescentric fingernail abrasions around the lower jaw, mouth, and cheeks, and injuries to the buccal mucosa are typically described as artifacts of resuscitation.[2] Fingertip-sized bruising may also be found along the jaw line or on the cheeks.

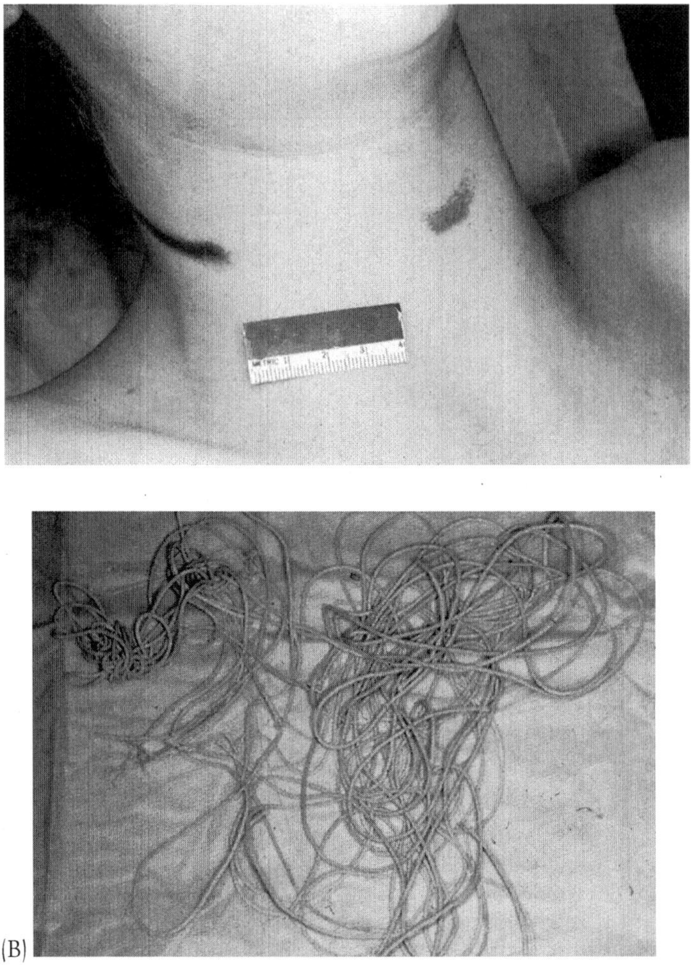

(A) (B)

Figure 3.2 (A) Patterned injury on the neck due to ligature strangulation. (B) Rope that caused patterned injury in (A).

3.2.3 The Thyroid Gland in Strangulation

Because of its anatomic location, the thyroid gland is exposed to trauma from the mechanical forces of manual and ligature strangulation as well as hanging. Studies of the blood levels of thyroid hormones after death from mechanical compression of the neck demonstrate that these hormones are higher compared to cases with other causes of death. Therefore, postmortem elevated levels of thyroglobulin may be used as an indicator of vital reaction in cases of mechanical asphyxiation.[6–11] In addition, there are significant differences observed between cases of strangulation-choking and cases of strangulation by ligature, and cases of strangulation-choking and cases of manual strangulation. All studies on thyroid hormone levels in mechanical asphyxia to date have involved adults. Further detailed studies of thyroglobulin and free triiodothyronine (fT3) are recommended in adults and children.[12]

Although diseases of the thyroid gland such as thyroid cancer, Graves' disease, and Hashimoto thyroiditis are uncommon in the general population, they may cause false positive results in the study of thyroglobulin levels in strangulation; therefore examination for thyroid pathologies by microscopic examination and by determining the levels of free thyroxine (fT4) and thyroid-stimulating hormone (TSH) is of crucial importance.[12] Postmortem serum TSH levels remain unchanged in adults and children for more than 24 hours.[11]

3.2.4 The Brain and Strangulation

In addition to brain edema, delayed postanoxic encephalopathy after strangulation has been reported. Clinical signs of choreoathetosis, dystonia, and marked pseudobulbar paralysis may develop in the weeks after injury. The computed tomography scans and T_2-weighted magnetic resonance images obtained at that time may reveal low density and high signal intensities in the region of the putamen and caudate nucleus bilaterally. These symptoms and the changes in the computed tomography (CT) scans and magnetic resonance images subside during the ensuing months. Sequential analysis of the cerebrospinal fluid for gamma-aminobutyric acid and dopamine concentrations during the illness reveal reciprocal changes with normal recovery. Because of the delayed onset of neurological changes and the cerebrospinal fluid showing reversible symptoms, delayed encephalopathy after strangulation has been related to the biochemical alterations that follow anoxia.[13] The symptoms and studies of delayed encephalopathy should help in the diagnosis of strangulation cases that lack a history.

Bird et al. (1987) presented three cases, all 7 months old, of strangulation in child abuse in which CT demonstrated a large cerebral infarction confined to vascular territories, associated with small subdural hematomas. There was no history or a history of a minor fall, and there was no visible evidence of significant head trauma. Autopsy of one infant confirmed the presence of a hemispheric infarct, thin subdural hematoma, and an area of subintimal hemorrhage in the carotid artery ipsilateral to the infarct. Strangulation was diagnosed in all three cases. CT findings of a large cerebral infarction with an associated subdural hematoma in an infant without a history of significant trauma should suggest the possibility of child abuse. The mechanism producing hemispheric infarcts in these patients appears to be compression of the common carotid artery in the neck. Above the level of the cricoid cartilage, the common carotid artery is trapped between the sternocleidomastoid muscle superficially and the transverse processes of the C-4, C-5, and C-6 vertebral bodies posteriorly. The carotid artery is easily subjected

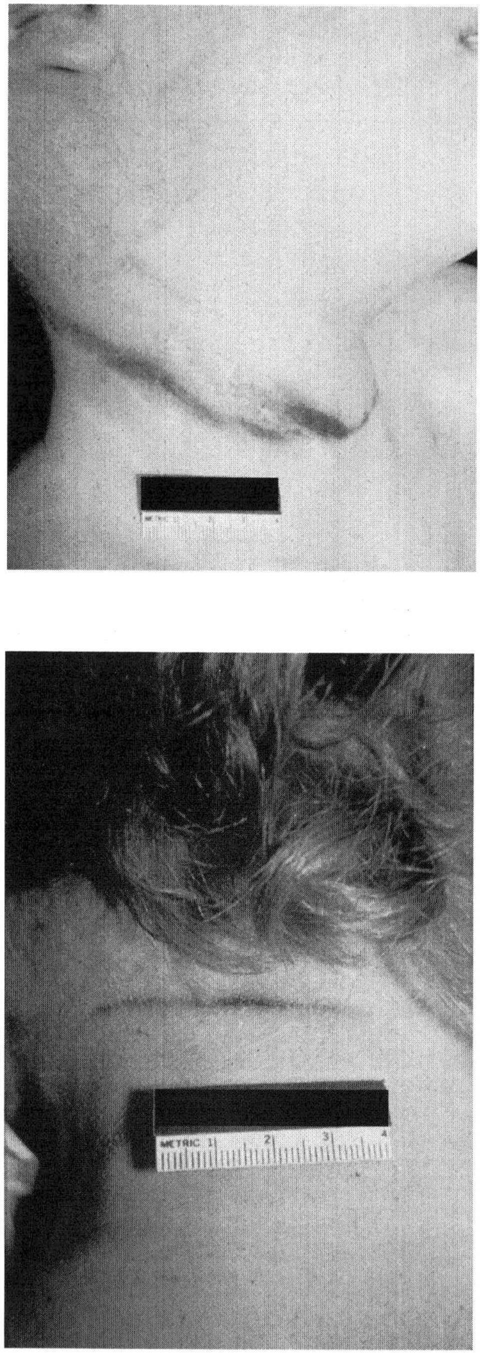

(A)

(B)

Figure 3.3 (A) Patterned injury on anterior and lateral aspects of neck due to ligature strangulation. (B) Patterned injury on posterior aspect of neck due to same ligature strangulation as in (A).

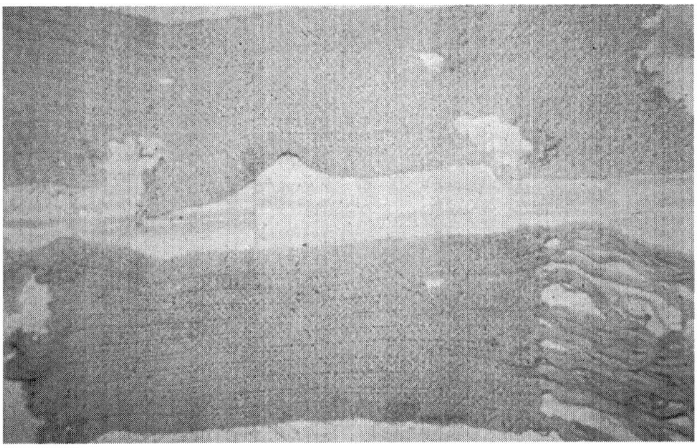

(C)

Figure 3.3 (Continued.) (C) Scarf that caused patterned injuries in (A) and (B).

Table 3.2 Physical Findings in Intentional Strangulation

None
External Physical Findings
Yellow froth at nostrils and in airways
Abrasions and/or bruises of the neck
Fingernail marks on the skin of the neck
Ligature marks
Petechial hemorrhages of the face and/or buccal mucosa
Subconjuctival hemorrhages
Swollen face
Internal Physical Findings
Hemorrhage in soft tissues of neck
Petechial hemorrhages on thoracic organs or in thymus
Laryngeal edema
Hyoid bone fracture
Cerebral hemorrhage
Congested leptomeninges
Brain edema
Delayed encephalopathy

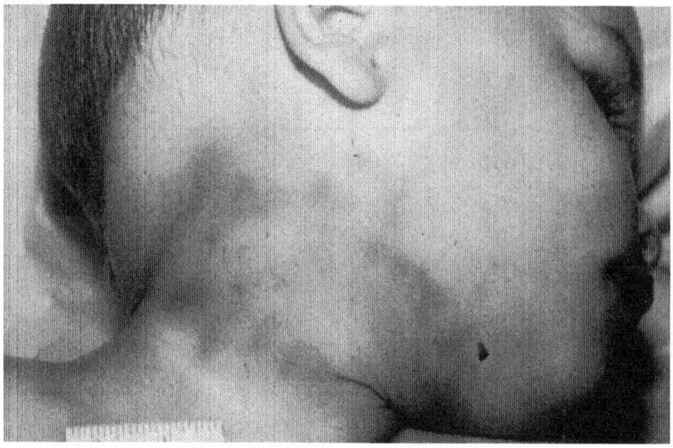

Figure 3.4 Example of bruising to neck in case of manual strangulation.

to compression in this location and may be occluded by as little as 2.3 kg of weight. In contrast, the vertebral arteries are relatively immune from direct manual compression because they are protected in the foramen transversarium. As a result, the posterior brain is usually spared in cases of manual strangulation. The size and distribution of the infarcts in these children suggest the cause. Since there is extensive involvement of multiple vascular territories, the level of obstruction should be at the level of the internal carotid or common carotid artery. These infarcts may be unilateral, probably due to the way the force is applied to the neck. If one hand is used, there is more local force transmitted from the thumb side, occluding the carotid artery, while on the fingers side the force is more diffuse, and therefore the carotid artery may remain patent. This association has been used to determine the handedness of the perpetrator. The reason that the collateral circulation from the opposite hemisphere was not sufficient to prevent infarction in these cases is probably related to the contralateral carotid artery being partially compressed and the systemic drop in blood pressure at the time of injury. Size and patency of the various anastomoses at the circle of Willis will also have a major influence on the efficacy of collateral circulation. When strangulation is bimanual or when both carotid arteries are occluded by strangulation, bilateral hemispheric infarcts may occur, producing an image on CT similar to that seen with a diffuse hypoxic/ischemic injury (Table 3.3).[14]

3.2.5 Measurement of External Pressure and Airway Occlusion in Children

Stevens et al. (2000) performed a study to determine the amount of external pressure that occludes the airway in children. A force gauge was applied to the suprahyoid region in 90 children under standardized anesthesia. Age was

Table 3.3 Neurologic Presentation in Intentional Strangulation in Infants and Young Children

Seizures
Brain edema in survivors
Global hypoxic-ischemic brain injury in survivors
Delayed postanoxic encephalopathy choreoathetosis, dystonia, pseudobulbar paralysis
Cerebral infarction with associated small subdural hematomas
Death

the most significant variable in the occlusion of the airway. The younger the age, the less the force needed to occlude the airway. Obstruction appears to occur at the level of the larynx.[15]

3.2.6 Laryngothyroid Fractures and Injuries in Strangulation

Maxeiner et al. (2003) compared the findings of 19 cases of suicidal hangings versus 47 cases of homicidal ligature strangulations. In the homicidal series, the laryngothyroid structures were unaffected in 26 cases (12 of these victims were children or adolescents), single horn fractures were present in three cases, and more significant injuries in 18 cases. Macroscopic bleeding in the laryngeal muscles was found in 12 victims of the homicidal group and in none of the suicides. Two of the 19 suicidal victims had single fractures of the upper thyroid horns, and one victim had a fracture of a lower thyroid horn; other types of laryngohyoid injuries were not observed.[16]

Brockholdt et al. (2003) studied the force needed to fracture the upper thyroid horns. Fractures of the upper thyroid horns are a frequent finding after a variety of neck injuries resulting from direct mechanical trauma (e.g., compression of the neck in manual strangulation or ligature strangulation), from blunt injuries (falls or blows against the neck), and sometimes from indirect trauma (whiplash injuries). Although it is well known that thyroid horns can be broken with relatively little pressure, no quantitative data was available in the literature. Ages of the study subjects ranged from 16 to 95 years. The location of the fractures in nearly all cases was at the base of the horns. The mean weight resulting in an injury of the horn was 3 kg (men: 3.3 kg, women: 2.6 kg). The required weight was dependent on the degree of ossification of the thyroid horns. The highest rate of fractures was found in cases with incomplete ossification; in cases without ossification, specimens often remained macroscopically uninjured.[17]

The most widely used methods for medicolegal examination of the hyoid bone and laryngeal cartilages (i.e., palpation, radiography, and gross inspection) reveal less than 60% of injuries present (fractures, infractions, fissures, etc.). Stereomicroscopic investigation of the skeletized hyoid bone and laryngeal cartilage found injuries in 76.6% of suicidal hangings as well as in other methods of injury in a study by Khokhlov (1997).[5]

Maxeiner (1998) presented a study that was designed to demonstrate that the usual method of laryngeal dissection could miss important laryngeal injuries. The basic steps of Maxeiner's method included complete resection of the thyroid cartilage, a horizontal incision through the cricoid cartilage before opening the larynx dorsally, inspection of the laryngeal joints, and incisions of the laryngeal muscles. Using this procedure allowed detection of the following injuries, which otherwise would have been destroyed or overlooked:

1. Incomplete fractures restricted to the dorsal surfaces of the thyroid laminae and incomplete or nondislocated fractures of the cricoid cartilage. A "hidden" fracture was the only laryngeal injury resulting from neck compression in some cases.
2. Extensive laryngeal muscle hemorrhages, especially of the vocal folds, were found in almost half of all cases, more rarely in strangulation by ligature and more frequently in manual strangulation. Gross hemorrhages were the decisive local laryngeal finding in some cases.
3. Laryngeal joint injuries (bleeding) were found in 18% to 52% of the different strangulation types.
4. Hemorrhages of the laryngeal mucosa was a common finding that occurred in about 60% of all cases; only in rare cases does such bleeding indicate a specific diagnosis (Figure 3.5).[18]

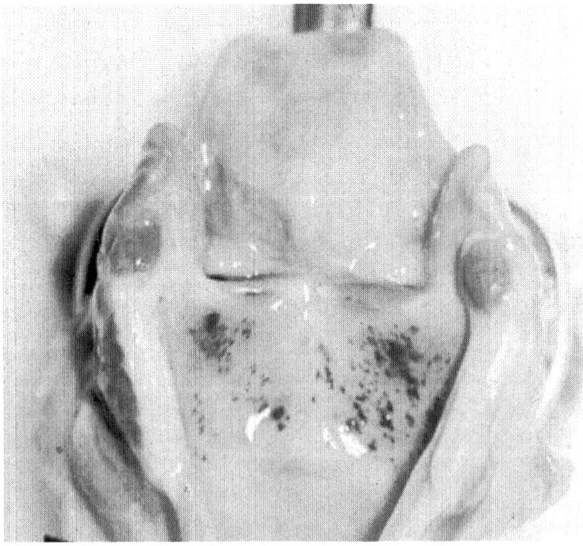

Figure 3.5 Laryngeal mucosa hemorrhages.

3.2.7 Tongue Hemorrhages and Neck Compression

Hemorrhage of the tongue can be useful in diagnosing lethal neck compression. The reported frequencies of tongue hemorrhages in the literature in cases of suicidal hanging range from 0% to 14%, and in homicidal strangulation from 5% to 37%. In 25% of all homicides, significant or massive hemorrhages of the tongue were detected. In contrast, in suicidal hanging the tongue was unaffected in 95% of cases. The causes of massive hemorrhages in suicidal hanging (2%) could be explained by an "abnormal" position of the loop.[19]

Quan et al. (2003) examined hemorrhages in the root of the tongue. These hemorrhages have been associated with asphyxiation. They examined the incidence and diagnostic value of central, lingual hemorrhages in fire fatalities, asphyxiation, and drowning cases. In fire fatalities, small to marked hemorrhages were observed in 28.9% of cases. In fire fatalities, the hemorrhages were closely associated with a lower blood carboxyhemoglogin (COHb) level. These findings suggested possible acute hemodynamic disturbance in the head including brain (cranial congestion) in the dying process due to fire. The hemorrhages were frequently observed in manual and ligature strangulation and traumatic asphyxia, whereas they were infrequent in hanging, aspiration/choking, and drowning. The sporadic or streaking patterns of the hemorrhages suggest the influence of cranial congestion similar to that seen in fatal pressure on the neck or chest. Deep lingual hemorrhages adjacent to the hyoid bone may be important for diagnosing death from pressure on the neck.[20]

3.2.8 Skeletal Muscle of the Neck and Neck Compression

Tabata (1998) studied the morphological changes in traumatized skeletal muscle of the neck. Cervical muscles of 15 cases of compression of the neck and other traumatized skeletal muscles from 54 autopsy cases (aged 14 to 83 years) were examined histologically and immunohistochemically. Round and thick fibers with a loss of cross striations, that is, opaque fibers, were observed in the muscles beneath compression marks on the neck, whereas in areas where no force had been applied, such fibers did not exist. The opaque fibers stained deep pink with H&E, blue-green and sometimes red in modified Gomori trichrome. Furthermore, opaque changes appeared around cavities which formed within severely compressed injured muscle tissue. This cavity formation was observed in cases with severe injury caused by hanging. The intensity of the compression mark did not necessarily correspond to that of the force. In this study, opaque fibers were observed in the cervical muscles beneath not only the most pronounced mark, such as a groove, but also under vague marks on the neck. Opaque fibers are probably produced by damage to muscles from directly applied extreme forces. The high incidence of opaque fibers beneath compression marks on the neck should be regarded as an indication of strangulation and/or hanging. Furthermore, the distribution and direction of the force on the neck might be indicated, to a certain extent, by the pattern of opaque fibers in cervical muscles.[21]

In cases of blunt force, opaque fibers were observed in muscle tissue where there was bleeding. In cases where death occurred immediately after injury, rounded and large opaque fibers were aggregated in the injured muscle. In cases where the patient survived for several hours after injury, opaque fibers, disintegrated fibers, and infiltration of leukocytes were observed. In bodies with putrefactive changes, opaque fibers were still seen in traumatized muscle tissues.[21]

Skeletal muscle opaque fibers are not specific to trauma of skeletal muscle. It is known that opaque fibers are caused by myopathies, by local intramuscular injection of myotoxic agents, and by focal lysis of the muscle fiber plasma membrane by detergents.[21]

Opaque fibers are caused by traumatic damage to the plasma membrane, with ingress of calcium-rich extracellular fluid into muscle fibers. Individual cells remain alive for a while after the individual dies. Thus morphological changes of skeletal muscle could be produced by trauma in the supravital period, which is defined as the period when vital reaction of tissues is obtainable due to excitation of the tissues after a person's death. In deaths due to reflex cardiac arrest (vagal inhibition) and prolonged asphyxia such as gradual and slow compression of the neck, bleeding and/or opaque fibers may not occur in the cervical muscles.[21]

Besides the observation of opaque fibers and hemorrhages, FN (fibronectin) was detected after cervical muscle injuries. FN is a cell adhesive protein with a relative molecular mass of about 250 kDa existing in two forms, soluble (plasma) and insoluble (cellular). FN appears immediately (approximately 30 minutes) after injury and continues to be seen for a long period (1 month). It has been thought that FN is a useful marker for vital wounds of skin and muscle. A positive reaction for FN was clearly seen not only in the muscles of the cases where death occurred immediately after injury, but also in the muscles of those who died 1 or 2 hours after injury. Furthermore, in cases with decompositional changes but in good preservation, FN was detectable in the marginal areas of the injured skeletal muscles. Nonspecific reactions are avoided by using the monoclonal antibody to FN (Table 3.4).[21]

Table 3.4 Autopsy Studies in Strangulation in Children

Thyroglobulin (in older children)
CT and MRI studies of the brain
Detailed laryngothyroid dissection
Tongue dissection
Microscopic examination of skeletal muscle under suspected neck injury
Monoclonal antibody to fibronectin studies

3.3 Intentional Smothering, Choking, and Compression Asphyxia in Infants and Young Children

3.3.1 Characteristics of Smothering and Compression Asphyxia in Young Children

Smothering happens to young children under the age of 3 years, most being infants under the age of 1 year. They may present to the emergency department or rescue personnel as either sudden unexplained deaths in infancy, sudden infant death syndrome, moribund near-miss sudden infant deaths, or repeatedly as cyanotic or floppy children who are presumed to have had an apneic episode or a seizure.[22]

Admitted means of smothering include placing a hand over the infant's mouth and nose, pressing the child's face into a cushion or pillow, putting a plastic film over the mouth and nostrils, and completely covering the child with clothing or bedding for prolonged periods of time.[23,24]

Signs of smothering may be few or absent. In general, someone who is asphyxiated tends to develop multiple petechiae on the face, particularly on the eyelids, as a result of the raised blood pressure, lack of oxygen, and retention of carbon dioxide.[25] Petechiae of the face and eyelids are nonspecific signs of asphyxia and as a rule are not necessarily produced by smothering an infant.[26] The occasional occurrence of conjunctival and facial petechiae in homicidal smothering of older children (versus infants) might be attributed to the increased cephalic venous pressure of the Valsalva effect caused by more violent struggling and screaming against obstruction of the airways.[27] Petechiae of the skin extending over the entire drainage area of the superior vena cava are not usually found in smothering cases.[25,27,28] This may be due to the fact that besides smothering no additional compression of the chest has occurred (Figure 3.6).[25]

Other signs of suffocation may be congestive changes in the face or general cyanosis. Hand pressure on the face may leave thumbprint bruises, fingerprint bruises, abrasions around the nose or mouth, abrasions inside the mouth, or bruising of the gums, but more often, smothering is done with a pillow or with bedding, and no external pressure marks are visible unless the victim puts up rigorous resistance. Quite often neither petechiae nor swelling of the face are apparent.[22,25,29,31] Foreign material may be found in the mouth or nose from objects placed on the face or in the mouth.[30] Blood-tinged fluid leaking from the nose may also be a sign of suffocation, although this is seen only in 39% of cases.[32]

Bleeding from the nose and mouth is reported to be common in nonfatal imposed suffocation and is a frequent finding in infants who have died of sudden infant death (SIDS), but it is not mentioned in standard accounts of acute life-threatening episodes (ALTE) of presumed natural causes.[33–35]

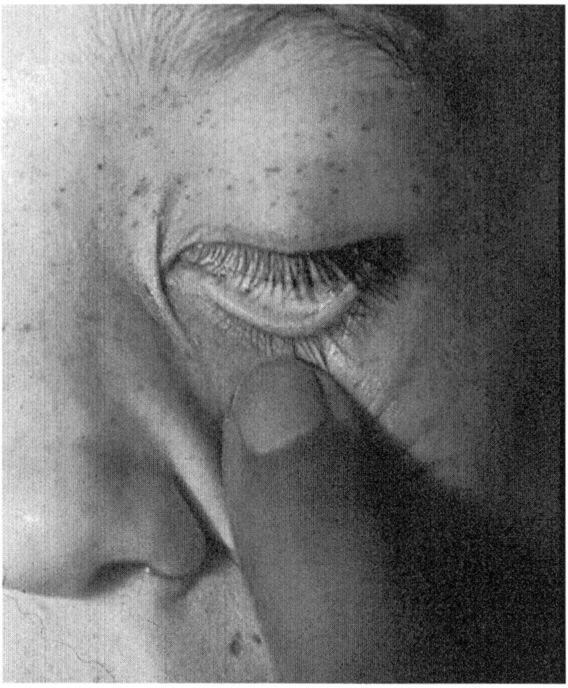

Figure 3.6 Petechiae of the face and conjunctivae due to asphyxia caused by compression of the chest.

Signs of compression asphyxia include pressure marks on the back of the neck and the upper chest or extremities as well as unilateral or bilateral anterolateral rib fractures (Figure 3.7).[30,36] Infants have been shown to respond differently to hypoxia than adults. Term and preterm infants have a biphasic response to mild hypoxia. An initial increase in ventilation is followed by ventilatory depression, which leads to further hypoxia. The biphasic response has been demonstrated in some term infants up to 8 weeks of age. A reiterative cycle of hypoxia and hypoventilatory response may continue after inflicted thoracic constriction is released, ultimately resulting in fatal apnea. The case of a young infant who dies with rib fractures and no other cause of death needs to be scrutinized for a history of chest constriction and cessation of crying preceding the child's death.[37]

At autopsy, internal signs of suffocation include petechiae of the pleural surfaces, the epicardium and thymus, visceral congestion, fluidity of the blood, acute emphysema, and anemia of the spleen.[23,30,38,39] The cause for the frequent absence of petechial thymus hemorrhages in extrinsic suffocation, compared to SIDS cases, might be the rapid onset of death and the acute asphyxia.[40]

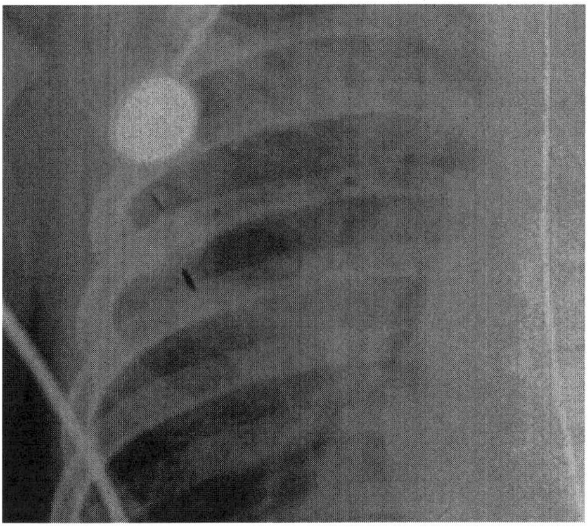

Figure 3.7 Radiograph of healing anterolateral rib fracture.

With both SIDS and suffocation, petechial hemorrhages of the serous membranes as well as pulmonary and cerebral edema may be found (Table 3.5).[28]

The simultaneous appearance of conjunctival petechiae and of acute pulmonary emphysema strongly indicates death by asphyxiation. Petechial hemorrhages of the conjunctivae and of the eyelids strongly indicate asphyxiation, but can also be observed in other conditions, in particular following cardiopulmonary resuscitation.[28] The evidence of conjunctival petechiae in nonresuscitated children must be regarded as a very strong sign of asphyxiation. Acute pulmonary emphysema is a frequent but not a specific finding in asphyxiation. Even though the lungs of children dying of SIDS may fill the pleural cavities, dystelectasis of the lungs is a more common finding.[28] The absence of pulmonary emphysema in asphyxia cases may be the result of putrefaction leading to a reduction of possible initial overinflation of the lungs.[28]

Although generally smothering has to persist for a minute to cause seizures—longer to cause brain damage and perhaps two minutes (depending upon other circumstances) to cause death—damage may be more sudden and catastrophic if the child, as a result of the sudden assault, has a cardiac arrest or vomits and chokes.[22] There are no more than 30 seconds until bradycardia starts, and 90 seconds until the EEG is flattened (Table 3.6).[41]

Evidence in siblings suggests that in 50% of families with a suffocated child from Münchausen syndrome by proxy and 40% with non-accidental poisoning, there will be further abuse, some fatal.[42]

Table 3.5 Characteristics of Smothering and Compression Asphyxia in Children

Presentation
Sudden infant death
ALTS
Cyanotic or floppy baby
Seizure
Apneic episode
External Physical Signs
Less than 3 years old
Few or absent physical signs
Petechiae on eyelids
Petechiae on conjunctiva and face
Congestion face
General cyanosis
Thumb or fingerprint bruises around nose or mouth
Abrasions around nose and mouth
Foreign material in the mouth or nose
Blood-tinged fluid from the nose or mouth
Pressure marks on the neck, upper chest, or extremities
Anterolateral rib fractures
Internal Physical Signs
Petechiae of pleural surfaces, epicardium, and thymus
Visceral congestion
Fluidity of the blood
Acute pulmonary emphysema
Anemia of the spleen
Epidural cervical hemorrhage

Table 3.6 Timing of Symptoms in Smothering of Infants and Young Children

Symptom	Time from Onset of Smothering
Bradycardia	30 seconds
Seizures	Approximately 1 minute
Brain damage	Greater than 1 minute
EEG flatline	90 seconds
Death	Approximately 2 minutes

3.3.2 The Investigation in Smothering Cases

Warning features that the sudden infant death syndrome case may have been caused by a mother smothering her child are:

- Previous episodes of unexplained apnea, seizures, or near-miss sudden infant death
- An infant aged over 6 months
- Previous unexplained disorders affecting that child or a sibling
- Other unexplained deaths of children in the same family[22]

For some children the smothering is associated with other forms of child abuse, particularly physical abuse and Münchausen syndrome by proxy.[22,43]

There may be diagnosable psychiatric disorder in the mother, father, or other caregiver.[23] The chance of death is high in those families in which the father had Münchausen syndrome or marked somatic disorders.[43] There are reports that a child smothered by the mother died in the afternoon or evening after being discharged back to the parents following a period of hospital observation for unexplained acute onset, repeat illnesses. Unusual illnesses and deaths of pets have also been observed in families in which the mother is the perpetrator of factitious illness abuse. Similarly, an unusual frequency of home fires has been noticed with female perpetrators. Complaints about the health service and instigation of litigation are also features of cases involving female perpetrators.[43]

There may be inconsistent and untruthful accounts of the events from the perpetrator, evidence of smothering or other abuse of a subsequent child, and sometimes admissions by the perpetrator.[43]

Male caretakers are a significant risk factor in a variety of child abuse situations, especially inflicted head trauma.[44] Prior research has shown that men have a lower threshold of frustration for a crying infant.[45]

Other possible signs of abuse are multiple hospital admissions, poor weight gain and failure to thrive (cachectic), failure to thrive with subsequent weight gain in hospital or in foster care, withdrawn affect, not keeping scheduled medical appointments, and positive signs at the scene investigation (blue, face down in pillow) (Table 3.7).[39]

The differentiation between the sudden infant death syndrome and smothering, by an autopsy alone, may be impossible.[29] A homicide by smothering may leave unobtrusive or even no injuries if the victim is not able to struggle. This is especially true for infants up to 12 months of age. As demonstrated by video surveillance, even infants react to the attempt at smothering by struggling violently.[46] But the sequence of physiological events shows that their ability to defend themselves is limited. Thus the amount of force necessary to overcome an infant's resistance is so small that in this age group as a

Table 3.7 Investigation of Smothering in Infants and Young Children

Previous episodes of unexplained apnea, seizures, or near-miss SIDS
Infant older than 6 months old
Previous unexplained disorders of the child or a sibling
Evidence of abuse in a subsequent child
Other unexplained child deaths in the same family
Death soon after child returned to parent following hospitalization or CPS removal
Unusual illnesses and deaths of pets
Frequent home fires
Complaints and litigation against the health service by the parent
Inconsistent and untruthful accounts of the event from the parent
Parental psychiatric disorders
Parent with Münchausen syndrome
Father with somatic disorder
Multiple hospital admissions
Poor weight gain
Failure to thrive
Weight gain in hospital or foster care following poor weight gain at home
Missed medical appointments
Withdrawn affect of the child
Found face down in pillow
When found, blue coloration

rule, no or minimal external evidence of trauma results. On the other hand, the older the children are, the more injuries they will have.[29]

3.3.3 Apnea and Smothering

True apnea, in which the breathing stops for 20 seconds or more and is followed by bradycardia, cyanosis, or pallor, is frightening and often unexplained. It is more likely in small preterm babies and usually starts in the neonatal period. In early life both respiratory syncytial virus infection and whooping cough can be associated with spells of apnea in previously well infants; the apnea may precede the cough or other respiratory signs by a few days. Whenever apnea starts unexpectedly in a previously well baby it must be investigated thoroughly. The investigations should include careful checks for cardiac or respiratory disorder, esophageal reflux, and a biochemical or seizure disorder. When these investigations give normal results, consideration should be given to whether the episodes are being caused by the mother or other caregiver. If the episodes are frequent, a period in the hospital without the mother might be an appropriate diagnostic test (Table 3.8).[22]

Table 3.8 Medical Tests in Suspected Suffocation in Infants and Young Children

Skeletal survey
Respiratory syncytial virus infection
Whooping cough
Cardiac disorders
Respiratory disorders
Esophageal reflux
Biochemical disorders
Seizure disorder

3.3.4 Sudden Infant Death Syndrome or Smothering?

Victims of intentional suffocation by a parent or caregiver are difficult to identify at autopsies on infants dying suddenly because, apart from the rare occurrence of pressure marks, the findings are usually indistinguishable from those of the sudden infant death syndrome (SIDS).[47] Between 2% and 10% of babies currently labeled as dying from SIDS have probably been smothered by their mothers. Many of these have had previous recurrent episodes of apnea or seizures that may have been thoroughly investigated with conventional radiology, biochemical, and other laboratory testing.[22]

In a retrospective study of 57 infant deaths in 27 families (24 families with two deaths, three families with three deaths) it was found that death was caused by suffocation in 55% of the cases and that SIDS could be assumed only in 9% of the cases.[48]

Becroft et al. (2001) studied nasal hemorrhage in SIDS deaths and found that nasal hemorrhage was reported by the parents in 15% of cases. Pathologically significant intra-alveolar pulmonary hemorrhage was found in 47% of cases and was severe in 7% of cases. In multivariate analysis, nasal hemorrhage was associated with younger infant age, bed sharing, and the infant being placed non-prone to sleep. There was no significant association between nasal or intra-alveolar hemorrhages and intrathoracic petechiae. Nasal and intrapulmonary hemorrhages have common associations not shared with intrathoracic petechiae. Smothering is a possible common factor, although unlikely to be the cause in most cases presenting as SIDS.[32]

Conjunctival petechiae are usually not reported in SIDS except in cases showing vomit aspiration. Kleemann et al. (1995) reported an incidence of conjunctival petechiae in 2.4% of SIDS cases, compared with 8.1% found in a control group of natural deaths, and with 21.9% in a group of lethal trauma including cases of strangulation. In this study, no differentiation between children with and without cardiopulmonary resuscitation was made.[49] Pulmonary overinflation in SIDS cases may be a result of artificial respiration and/or vomit aspiration.[28] Both petechiae and pulmonary emphysema have been found in asphyxiated individuals but not in (resuscitated or nonresuscitated) control cases.[28] Since vomit aspiration can occur in SIDS, aspiration should be considered when there are both conjunctival petechiae and acute pulmonary emphysema.[28]

Petechial thymus hemorrhages are found most frequently in SIDS (87%) and more rarely in fetuses after abortion and stillbirths (55%) as well as perinatal deaths (40%). In these groups, there is a uniform histological bleeding pattern with emphasis on the cortical zone. In non-SIDS deaths of natural causes or extrinsic suffocation in babies and infants, thymus petechiae are present in 39% of cases. In extrinsic suffocation, the thymus hemorrhages are fewer than in SIDS. However, there are indications that both a typical distribution pattern as in SIDS and a bleeding pattern deviating from this may occur in extrinsic suffocation. In non-SIDS (without extrinsic suffocation), a hemorrhage pattern different from SIDS could be detected with hemorrhages of different sizes and irregularly distributed over the cortex and medulla (Table 3.9).[40]

3.3.5 Microscopic Examination of the Lung and Asphyxiation

Significant lung findings in deaths from asphyxia due to obstruction of the respiratory passages are acute pulmonary emphysema in combination with intra-alveolar hemorrhages involving greater than 5% of the pulmonary tissue (hemorrhagic-dysoric syndrome), and occasionally microembolism syndrome with migration of bone marrow cells into the pulmonary circulation.[23,32,38,48] In cases of previous episodes with survival, intra-alveolar siderosis can be found.[50] The hemorrhage-dysoric syndrome as originally described by Brinkmann et al. (1984) does not refer to infants, but to older victims (Table 3.10).[38]

Table 3.9 Distinction between SIDS and Smothering in Infants

Symptom	SIDS	Smothering
Previous episodes of apnea or seizures	No	Yes
Death of more than one child in family	<10% of cases	More than 50% of cases
Nasal hemorrhage	15% of cases	May be found (% unknown)
Intra-alveolar pulmonary hemorrhage	47% of cases	May be found (% unknown)
Conjunctival petechiae	2.4% of cases	21.9% in trauma cases
Pulmonary emphysema	In vomit aspiration or CPR	May be found (% unknown)
Petechial thymus hemorrhages	87%	May be found (less or same as SIDS)

Table 3.10 Lung Findings in Asphyxia Due to Obstruction

Acute pulmonary emphysema
Intra-alveolar hemorrhages (in >5% of lung)
Microembolism syndrome
Intra-alveolar siderosis

Postobstructuve pulmonary edema may present with apnea, unresponsiveness, cyanosis, bloodstained mucus, radiological signs of florid bilateral pulmonary edema without cardiomegaly, and profuse amounts of bloodstained froth from the larynx on bronchoscopy or at autopsy in cases of death. Similar cases of postobstructive pulmonary edema have occurred in, for example, laryngospasm, croup, and epiglotitis.[51] Proposed mechanisms by which airway obstruction may cause pulmonary edema include negative intrathoracic pressure causing transiently low pulmonary interstitial pressure or impaired left ventricular function, or both, and hypoxic postcapillary and venous constriction.[52]

Hemorrhagic pulmonary edema appears to be associated with those cases in which the suffocation process had been interrupted and the perpetrators reported that the children had temporarily started breathing again spontaneously.[23]

Delmonte et al. (2001) published a histologic lung study that looked at diagnostic differences of sudden deaths from asphyxia, including aspiration, suffocation, drowning, and strangulation. Stepwise discrimination analysis of the resulting data showed that lung necropsies from victims of these four events could be distinguished from one another in 85% of the cases. Lung autopsies with congestion, septal hemorrhage, and foreign body showed a specificity of 100% for victims of aspiration, whereas ductal overinsufflation, interstitial edema, and bronchiolar constriction showed a specificity of 81.8% in victims of suffocation. Intraalveolar edema and dilatation of the alveolar spaces with secondary compression of the septal capillaries characterized drowning. Victims of strangulation showed a strong alveolar hemorrhage, with alveolar collapse and overinsufflation, associated with bronchiolar dilatation. Therefore the diagnosis of asphyxia might be supported by the semiquantitative analysis of lung autopsies. Additional studies, including macroscopic characteristics, clinical data, and electron microscopy studies, are needed for better identification of asphyxia (Table 3.11).[1]

3.3.6 Hemosiderosis and Asphyxiation

Bleeding from the mouth or nose observed in acute life-threatening events (ALTE) is well described in imposed infant suffocation, also as an aspect of

Table 3.11 Lung Findings in Different Causes of Asphyxia

Cause	Lung Findings
Aspiration	Congestion
	Septal hemorrhage
	Foreign body
Suffocation	Ductal overinsufflation
	Interstitial edema
	Bronchiolar constriction
Drowning	Intra-alveolar edema
	Dilatation of alveolar septa with compression of septal capillaries
Strangulation	Alveolar hemorrhage
	Alveolar collapse and overinsufflation with bronchiolar dilatation

Münchausen syndrome by proxy child abuse. When there is bleeding from the mouth or nose, there may also be intrapulmonary hemorrhage, and intra-alveolar siderophages can be a marker for previous abuse. The lungs should be stained for iron in all cases of sudden infant death.[50] There are many causes of diffuse intra-alveolar hemorrhage: accidental, non-accidental, and iatrogenic trauma; congestive heart failure; systemic bleeding disorders; pulmonary vascular, infectious and neoplastic diseases; idiopathic pulmonary hemosiderosis; and immunological abnormalities including Goodpasture's syndrome. Apart from the pulmonary complications of prematurity and neonatal intensive care, these conditions are uncommon in infancy. Intrapulmonary hemorrhage has the radiological appearance of increased markings in the lung or lung base or abnormal opacity in the lung lobe (Table 3.12).[33–35,50]

Krous et al. (2006) presented a study that compared pulmonary intra-alveolar siderophage (PS) counts between cases of SIDS and infants whose deaths were attributed to accidental or inflicted suffocation. Only 6% of each

Table 3.12 Causes of Intrapulmonary Hemorrhage and Siderophages

Accidents
Non-accidental trauma
Iatrogenic trauma
Congestive heart failure
Systemic bleeding disorders
Pulmonary vascular disease
Infections
Neoplastic disease
Idiopathic pulmonary hemosiderosis
Immunologic abnormalities
Prematurity

group had a history of prior apparent life-threatening events. The number of PS varied widely in cases of sudden infant death caused by SIDS and accidental or inflicted suffocation, and cannot be used as an independent variable to ascertain past attempts at suffocation. Although the median PS counts were not statistically significantly different, SIDS cases demonstrated a significantly wider range of PS counts. The highest PS count was observed in a SIDS case with no known history of prior ALTEs or CPS referral.[53]

3.3.7 Hypoxic-Ischemic Brain Injury and Asphyxiation

An infant found to have hypoxic-ischemic encephalopathy with no readily identifiable cause should be further evaluated for the possibility of abuse by near-fatal suffocation. Signs of hypoxic-ischemic brain injury include irritability, hyperthermia, bulging fontanel, seizures, and poor feeding.[24] A noncontrast computed tomography (CT) scan of the brain will show extensive, well-defined, hypodense lesions in the temporal, parietal, and occipital regions bilaterally, consistent with ischemic cerebral infarctions, after 24 hours postevent. The widespread bilateral distribution of these infarctions in vascular watershed areas is most consistent with severe hypoxic-ischemic encephalopathy.[24]

3.3.8 Epidural Cervical Hemorrhages and Smothering

Francisco (1970) noted that epidural hemorrhage of the cervical cord is a common accompaniment of death by smothering (Figure 3.8, Figure 3.9). There were a greater number of deaths having epidural hemorrhage in smothering-overlying groups than in the clearly natural category. The trauma group had a smaller number of epidural hemorrhages than the overlying groups. Epidural hemorrhage is a manifestation of abnormal altered visceral hemodynamics. The pressure exerted on the chest and abdomen of a child impairs the venous return to the heart, which in turn causes an increase in flow (and possibly an increase in pressure) in the perivertebral (epidural) venous plexus of Batson. There is a relatively direct communication between the large veins in the

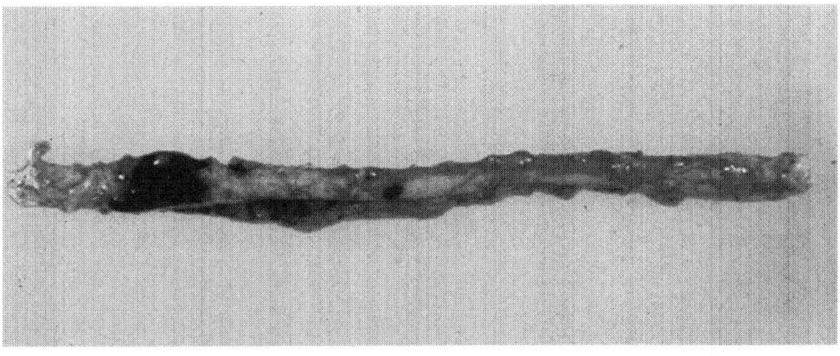

Figure 3.8 Epidural hemorrhage of the cervical spinal cord.

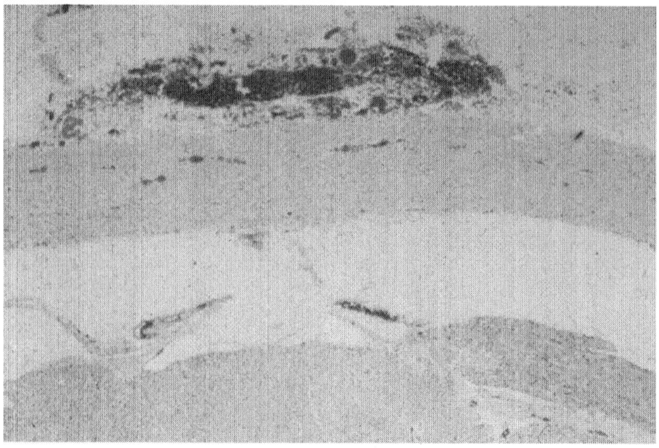

Figure 3.9 Microscopic view of epidural hemorrhage of the spinal cord (H&E).

chest and this plexus in the epidural space. This increase in flow (and possibly pressure) coupled with the associated anoxia is a reasonable mechanism for bleeding in this very loosely supported area. There may be many causes which could elevate epidural venous flow, with or without anoxia, and produce this hemorrhage. Death by overlying does not always have epidural hemorrhage.[54] If overlying causes an occlusion of the nose and mouth of an infant but not pressure on the chest or abdomen, then lethal systemic anoxia can occur without any significant change in venous pressure in the epidural space.[55]

3.3.9 The Temporal Bone and Asphyxia

Ito and Kimua (1990) studied the histology of the temporal bone in cases of various asphyxial fatalities. In drowning, the primary finding is hemorrhage in the mastoid air cells of the bilateral temporal bones. In cases of strangulation by ligature, hemorrhage and edema of the cochlear duct in the inner ear as well as hemorrhage in the mastoid air cells are demonstrated bilaterally. In contrast, congestion and edema in the mastoid air cells and inner ear are found in cases of manual strangulation, but there was no hemorrhage. Thus the histological examination of the temporal bone may be useful as an adjunct procedure for diagnosing the cause of asphyxia. Differentiation between drowning, strangulation by ligature, and manual strangulation may be possible by observing hemorrhages or their absence in the mastoid air cells and inner ear. Hemorrhage of the inner ear may be the result of increased pressure in the inner ear or common jugular vein, because the main venous system for the inner ear is the transversal sinus via the labyrinth vein which is one of the branches of the inner jugular vein.[56] Niles (1963) suggested that the pathogenesis of hemorrhage of the temporal bone is as follows: The soft tissue lining these cavities swells by virtue of its ability to accept fluid from

Table 3.13 Histology of the Temporal Bone in Different Causes of Asphyxia

Cause	Temporal Bone Findings
Drowning	Hemorrhage in mastoid air cells
Strangulation by ligature	Hemorrhage and edema of the cochlear duct of inner ear Hemorrhage in the mastoid air cells
Manual strangulation	Congestion and edema in mastoid air cells and inner ear but no hemorrhage

the rest of the body, and vascular engorgement of this tissue is followed by hemorrhage into the chambers (mainly supplied by the basilar artery via the labyrinth artery and the artery of anterior and inferior cerebellum), in addition to the direct effects of increased pressure.[57] There is no definite explanation as to why hemorrhage is found in ligature strangulation but not in manual strangulation. However, it might possibly depend on the amount of pressure to the neck. In ligature strangulation, the jugular arteries and veins, with the exception of the vertebral artery, may be obstructed completely by strong pressure. On the other hand, in manual strangulation, unstable and incomplete obstruction of the jugular arteries and veins may arise during struggling to escape from the grip (Table 3.13).[56]

3.3.10 Vitreous Humor Studies and Asphyxia

Although there appears to be a wide range of lactic acid levels in vitreous humor from deaths by natural causes and traumatic asphyxia, the mean values, assessed with history, circumstances, and other findings, especially the presence or absence of petechiae, might be useful in distinguishing traumatic asphyxia cases from SIDS cases. Therefore decreased lactic acid concentrations in vitreous humor appear to be an additional diagnostic marker in cases of infant deaths from traumatic asphyxia.[58] Most infants dying from asphyxia (anoxia) have a rapid terminal episode and so do not undergo a chemical imbalance (sodium, chloride, potassium, calcium, urea nitrogen, and glucose concentrations).[58]

3.3.11 Unusual Presentations of Asphyxia

Cohle (1986) reported a case of homicidal asphyxia by pepper aspiration. The case concerned a 5-year-old boy who was punished for lying by having pepper poured into his throat by his foster mother. He immediately became dyspneic, then apneic, and was pronounced dead about one hour later. At autopsy, the main stem and several smaller bronchi were occluded with pepper. Mechanisms of asphyxia by pepper include mechanical obstruction of the tracheobronchial tree and mucosal edema caused by the irritant effect of volatile oils in pepper. Two other cases of asphyxia by pepper have been reported. The other powdery or granular substance implicated in fatal and near-fatal asphyxia is talc, the constituent of baby powder. There is a characteristic clinically silent period between aspiration of talc and the onset of respiratory distress. These cases were reportedly accidental, sometimes as a result of a sibling pouring the powder into the infant's mouth or by self-administration.[59]

Krugman et al. (2007) presented four cases of infants who presented with aspiration of a baby wipe that were actually victims of abuse. All of the children were aged between 3 to 4½ months The perpetrator in each case was a father who was caring for the infant. The forcible nature of the insertion is demonstrated by the mouth injuries. Three of the children had a posterior pharyngeal tears, and the dissected wipe was covered in blood. Although some of the posterior pharyngeal tearing may have resulted from attempts at intubation around the baby wipe, the degree of injury would not be seen in an accidental swallowing of a soft object such as a baby wipe. In addition, three of the children had evidence of other abusive injuries. Also, young infants are developmentally unable to swallow a baby wipe. Infants younger than 5 months old have prominent extrusor reflexes and have a tendency to push objects out of their mouths, rather than aspirate inward. Additionally, each of the wipes was found deeply imbedded and balled up in the posterior pharynx. It seems likely that the force required to embed a balled-up baby wipe is much greater than an infant can produce by swallowing or breathing.[60]

3.4 Distinction of Intentional from Accidental Strangulation, Suffocation, and Compression Asphyxia

Bergeson et al. (1977) presented a case of accidental strangulation in a 7-month-old male who was found suspended by the neck on a retaining string to a toy mobile. The child was leaning forward with the neck placed over the sagging string. He had only recently learned to pull himself up and had apparently fallen forward, draping his neck over the string. A linear mark was found over the anterior part of the neck.[61] Cases have been reported of strangulation from strings or cords attached to toys suspended by a horizontal string across the top of the crib and tied to the crossbars on each side.[61]

The United States Consumer Product Safety Commission (USCPSC) reported eight cases that involved ribbons or strings attached to a pacifier. Commonly the pacifier was hung around the infant's neck by a ribbon that became entangled on part of the crib such as a corner post. Apparently, the relatively large head and poor muscle control characteristic of young children made it impossible for them to free themselves.[61]

Three reported cases of strangulation involved an infant slipping between the mattress and side rails. The most common situation involving strangulation is entrapment between the crib mattress and slats. The USCPSC reviewed 126 death certificates of crib-related deaths that occurred in the United States between January 1970 and August 1972. In 50 of these, the space between the mattress and slats was large enough for the infant's head to become lodged. In four of these cases a missing slat was contributory. In one, the mattress was folded, and in another a side rod securing the bottom of the crib was out of its hole. Mattresses are priced separately from cribs and may be purchased at a different time than the crib. The mattress may, therefore, not fit tightly against the headboard or crib sides. Current law requires strict warnings on the crib's headboard, assembly instructions, and packing carton advising the owner to use only a mattress that fits snugly.[61]

Other cases of infant strangulation have involved the crib side rails. One crib was repaired with wires placed horizontally between the side rails so that the neck was compressed between them. Recorded in the work of the USCPSC are 42 cases of entrapment of an infant's head between slats in the sides or foot of a crib. It was noted that one child worked his body through a 11.43-cm opening at the head of the bed, and another died as a result of slipping through slats that were 7.94 to 8.57 cm apart. In three cases a slat was missing, and in another the child became entangled in a cord used to replace a missing slat. In another instance the victim caught his neck between the headboard and a vertical guide bar that had become detached at the top. Two others involved loose or detached guide bars. A study done by the University of Michigan indicates that a distance of 6.03 cm between crib slats is appropriate. The study was done primarily of infants who were 2½ to 6½ months of age. It was believed that this group is most susceptible to slipping feet first through the slats. This recommendation has become law.[61]

Two cases have been reported in which infants were hanged to death by means of a protruding screw in a crib. The collar or the infant's clothes had become entangled on the screw.[61]

The dangers of strap-type restraining devices used in cribs have been reported. L'Hirondel (1961) mentions two fatalities that occurred in hospitals.[62]

Several deaths have been associated with items in close proximity to cribs. One child became wedged between two cribs. One child became wedged between two cribs placed side by side. Another child was suspended between the crossbar of his crib and a chair. Deaths have been caused by toddlers who accidentally hang themselves on the cord of venetian blinds. The USCPSC found eight deaths in which the child was wedged between the crib and a window sill and another between the crib and a dresser.[61]

Two episodes of fatal strangulation have involved high chairs. In one case the safety strap was not fastened, and the child slid beneath the tray and caught her head between the seat and tray. In the other case the tray was not in place, but a single safety strap was secured. The child slipped under the loose strap and was found hanging by the neck.[61]

The age range of all the children in the above cases was 17 days to 2 years, but the majority were 2 to 9 months. In this age range children become increasingly agile, but may lack the ability to extricate themselves from potentially dangerous situations. The head is large relative to the body, and may become entrapped if a child's body slides through an opening.[61]

Jay (1978) reported the case of a 1-week-old male who was outside in his pram wrapped in an infant's sleeping bag with the hood loosely drawn around his head. His mother found him white, rigid, and not breathing when she checked on him. The nylon lining of the sleeping bag was damp and stuck across his nose and mouth. The sleeping bag was made of two layers of closely woven nylon with a safety lining between. When wet, the nylon sticks to the face and is impossible to breathe through.[63]

3.5 Autopsy Protocol in Childhood Suffocation Cases

An editorial in the *Lancet* (1999) states that investigations into the pathology and circumstances of sudden infant death are often inadequate and inexpert. Generally accidental or deliberate suffocation of an infant produces no significant or characteristic findings at autopsy. The presence of blood in the nose or mouth should initiate further investigation. Oronasal secretions in SIDS, while often being tinged with blood, are rarely if ever frankly hemorrhagic. Similarly, facial petechiae should suggest asphyxiation rather than SIDS. Poisoning cannot be dismissed as a possible cause of death unless a toxicological screen for prescription medications or illicit substances has been performed. Even then, panels of toxicology tests do not cover all substances. The biological significance of particular levels of substances is often unknown in infants. The finding of recent or old inflicted injury, multiple cutaneous bruises, and bone fractures should raise questions about the cause and manner of death. Infants who have been physically abused are often at high risk for SIDS; they are also at increased risk for lethal injury. Even though the death remains unexplained after an autopsy has been performed, the presence of non-lethal inflicted injury is still a significant finding. Rather than "SIDS," a more suitable designation for the cause of death in these cases is "undetermined" or "unascertained." The best available way of dealing with these cases is to follow standardized autopsy and scene protocols. If standard protocols are followed, such as those endorsed by professional bodies such as the Society for Pediatric Pathology, the SIDS Global Strategy Task Force, and the National Association of Medical Examiners, the best possible investigation for these types of cases will be performed.[64–66]

References

1. Delmonte C, Capelozzi VL. 2001. Morphologic determinants of asphyxia in lungs. *Am J Forensic Med Pathol* 22:139–49.
2. Sadler DW. 1994. Concealed homicidal strangulation first discovered at necropsy. *J Clin Pathol* 47:679–80.
3. Jain V, Ray M, Singhi S. 2001. Strangulation injury, a fatal form of child abuse. *Indian J Pediatr* 68:571–72.
4. Perper JA, Sobel MN. 1981. Identification of fingernail markings in manual strangulation. *Am J Forensic Med Path* 2:45–48.
5. Khokhlov VD. 1997. Injuries to the hyoid bone and laryngeal cartilages: effectiveness of different methods of medico-legal investigation. *Forensic Sci Int* 88:173–83.
6. Katsumata Y, Suzuki O, Oya M, et al. 1980. Plasma thyroglobulin as an indicator of mechanical asphyxia—comparison of plasma thyroglobulin level by radioimmunassay and the results of precipitation–electrophoresis. *Med Sci Law* 20:84–88.
7. Katasumata Y, Sato K, Kido A, et al. 1983. Changes in plasma thyroglobulin-level in experimentally aged blood. *J Forensic Sci Soc* 23:143–46.
8. Katasumata Y, Sato K, Oya M, et al. 1984. Detection of thyroglobulin in bloodstain as an aid in the diagnosis of mechanical asphyxia. *J Forensic Sci* 29:299–302.
9. Müller E, Erfurt C, Franke WG. 1990. Thyroglobulin gehalt im lut und erhangen. *Z Rechtsmed* 103:361–67.
10. Tamaki K, Katsumata Y. 1990. Enzyme-linked immunosorbent assay for plasma thyroglobulin following compression of neck. *Forensic Sci Int* 44:259–65.
11. Coe JI. 1993. Postmortem chemistry update. *Am J Forensic Med Pathol* 14:91–117.
12. Senol E, Demirel B, Akor T, Gülbahar Ö, Bakar C, Bukan N. 2008. The analysis of hormones and enzymes extracted from endocrine glands of the neck region in deaths due to hanging. *Am J Forensic Med Path* 29:49–54.
13. Hori A, Hirose G, Kataoka S, Tsukada K, et al. 1991. Delayed postanoxic encephalopathy after strangulation. Serial neuroradiological and neurochemical studies. *Arch Neurol* 48:871–74.
14. Bird CR, McMahan JR, Gilles FH, Senac MO, Apthorp JS. 1987. Strangulation in child abuse: CT diagnosis. *Radiology* 163:373–75.
15. Stevens RR, Lane GA, Milkovich SM, Stool D, Rider G, Stool SE. 2000. Prevention of accidental childhood strangulation. A clinical study. *Ann Otol Rhinol Laryngol* 109:797–802.
16. Maxeiner H, Bockholdt B. 2003. Homicidal and suicidal ligature strangulation—a comparison of the postmortem findings. *Forensic Sci Int* 137:60–66.
17. Brockholdt B, Hempelmann M, Maxeiner H. 2003. Experimental investigation of fractures of the upper thyroid horns. *Leg Med (Tokyo)* 5 Suppl 1:S252–55.
18. Maxeiner H. 1998. "Hidden" laryngeal injuries in homicidal strangulation: how to detect and interpret these findings. *J Forensic Sci* 43:784–91.
19. Brockholdt B, Maxeiner H. 2002. Hemorrhages of the tongue in the postmortem diagnostics of strangulation. *Forensic Sci Int* 126:214–20.

20. Quan L, Zhu B, Ishida K, Oritani S, et al. 2003. Hemorrhages in the root of the tongue in fire fatalities: the incidence and diagnostic value. *Leg Med (Tokyo)* 5 Suppl 1:S332–34.
21. Tabata N. 1998. Morphological changes in traumatized skeletal muscle: the appearance of "opaque fibers" of cervical muscles as evidence of compression of the neck. *Forensic Sci Int* 96:197–214.
22. Meadow R. 1989. ABC of child abuse. Suffocation. *BMJ* 298(6687):1572–73.
23. Bohnert M, Große Perdekamp M, Pollak S. 2004. Three subsequent infanticides covered up by SIDS. *Int J Legal Med* 119:31–34.
24. McIntosh BJ, Shanks DE, Whitworth JM. 1994. Child abuse by suffocation presenting as hypoxic-ischemic encephalopathy. Report of a patient. *Clin Pediatr (Phila)* 33:561–63.
25. Oehmichen M, Gerling I, Meißner C. 2000. Petechiae of the baby's skin as differentiation symptom of infanticide versus SIDS. *J Forensic Sci* 45:602–7.
26. Kleemann WJ. 1997. Intrathorakale aund subkonjunktivale Petchien bei Säuglingstodesfällen. *Rechtsmedizin* 7:139–46.
27. Ely SF, Hirsch CS. 2000. Asphyxial deaths and petechiae: a review. *J Forensic Sci* 45:1274–77.
28. Betz P, Hausmann R, Eisenmenger W. 1997. A contribution to a possible differentiation between SIDS and asphyxiation. *Forensic Sci Int* 91:147–52.
29. Banaschak S, Schmidt P, Madea B. 2003. Smothering of children older than 1 year of age—diagnostic significance of morphological findings. *Forensic Sci Int* 134:163–68.
30. Meadow R. 1999. Unnatural sudden infant death. *Arch Dis Child* 80:7–14.
31. Pollak S, Saukko PJ. 2003. *Atlas of Forensic Medicine*. CD-ROM. Amsterdam: Elsevier.
32. Becroft DM, Thompson JM, Mitchell EA. 2001. Nasal and intrapulmonary haemorrhage in sudden infant death syndrome. *Arch Dis Child* 85:116–20.
33. Bamford FN, MacFayden UM, Meadow SR, et al. 1994. Chapter 4, Investigation. In *Evaluation of Suspected Imposed Upper Airway Obstruction: Report of a Working Party*, London: Royal Society of Medicine Press.
34. Krous HF. 1995. Chapter 16. The differential diagnosis of sudden unexpected death. In *Sudden Infant Death Syndrome: New Trends in the Nineties*. Oslo: Scandinavian University Press.
35. Oren J, Kelly D, Shannon DC. 1986. Identification of a high-risk group for sudden infant death syndrome among infants who were resuscitated for sleep apnea. *Pediatrics* 77:495–99.
36. Boos SC. 2000. Constrictive asphyxia: a recognizable form of fatal child abuse. *Child Abuse Negl* 24:1502–7.
37. Martin RJ, DiFiore JM, Jana L, Davies RL et al. 1998. Persistence of the biphasic ventilatory response to hypoxia in preterm infants. *J Pediatrics* 132:960–64.
38. Brinkmann B, Fechner G, Puschel K. 1984. Identification of mechanical asphyxiation in cases of attempted masking of the homicide. *Forensic Sci Int* 26:235–45.
39. Cashell AW. 1987. Homicide as a cause of sudden infant death syndrome. *Am J Forensic Med Path* 8:256–58.
40. Risse M, Weiler G. 1989. Differential diagnosis SIDS/non-SIDS on the bases of histological findings of petechial thymus hemorrhages. *Forensic Sci Int* 43:1–7.

41. Di Maio DJ, Di Maio VJM. 1989. In *Forensic Pathology,* 209–13. New York: Elsevier.
42. Davis P, McClure RJ, Rolfe K, Chessman N, Pearson S, Sibert JR, Meadow R. 1998. Procedures, placement, and risks of further abuse after Münchausen syndrome by proxy, non-accidental poisoning, and non-accidental suffocation. *Arch Dis Child* 78:217–21.
43. Meadow R. 1998. Münchausen syndrome by proxy abuse perpetrated by men. *Arch Dis Child* 78:210–16.
44. Starling SP, Holden JR. 2000. Perpetrators of abusive head trauma. A comparison of two geographic populations. *S Med J* 93:563–65.
45. Stein LB, Brodsky SL. 1995. When infants wail: frustration and gender as variables in distress disclosure. *J GenPsychology* 122:19–27.
46. Southhall DP, Stebbens VA, Rees SV, Lang MH, et al. 1987. Apnoeic episodes induced by smothering: two cases identified by covert video surveillance. *BMJ* 294:1637–41.
47. Valdes-Dapena M, McFeeley PA, Hoffman HJ et al. 1993. Chapter 8, The gray zone. In *Histopathology Atlas for the Sudden Infant Death Syndrome,* Washington, DC: Armed Forces Institute of Pathology.
48. Wolkind S, Taylor EM, Waite AJ, Dalton M, Emery JL. 1993. Recurrence of unexpected infant death. *Acta Paediatr* 82:873–76.
49. Kleemann WJ, Wiechern V, Schuck M, Tröger HD. 1995. Intrathoracic and subconjunctival petechiae in sudden infant death syndrome (SIDS). *Forensic Sci Int* 72:49–54.
50. Becroft DMO, Lockett BK. 1997. Intra-alveolar pulmonary siderophages in sudden infant death: a marker for previous imposed suffocation. *Pathology* 29:60–63.
51. Boykett M. 1989. Pulmonary oedema after acute asphyxia in a child. *BMJ* 298:928.
52. Brown M. 1986. Negative pressure pulmonary edema. In *Anesthetic Management of Difficult and Routine Pediatric Patients,* ed. FA Berry, pp. 168–79. New York: Churchill Livingstone.
53. Krous HF, Wixom C, Chadwick AE, Haas EA, Silva PD, Stanley C. 2006. Pulmonary intra-alveolar siderophages in SIDS and suffocation: a San Diego SIDS/SUDC research project report. *Ped and Develop Pathology* 9:103–14.
54. Francisco JT. 1970. Smothering in infancy: its relationship to the "crib death syndrome." *South Med J* 63:1110–14.
55. Harris LS, Ademson L. 1969. "Spinal injury" and sudden infant death—a second look. *Am J Clin Path* 49:562–67.
56. Ito Y, Kimua H. 1990. Histological examination of the temporal bone in medicolegal cases of asphyxia. *Forensic Sci Int* 44:135–42.
57. Niles NR. 1963. Hemorrhage in the middle-ear and mastoid in drowning. *Am J Clin Pathol* 40:281–83.
58. Sturner WQ, Sullivan A, Suzuki K. 1983. Lactic acid concentrations in vitreous humor: their use in asphyxial deaths in children. *J Forensic Sci* 28(1):222–30.
59. Cohle SD. 1986. Homicidal asphyxia by pepper aspiration. *J Forensic Sci* 31(4):1475–78.

60. Krugman SD, Lantz PE, Sinal S, De Jong AR, Coffman K. 2007. Forced suffocation of infants with baby wipes: a previously undescribed form of child abuse. *Child Abuse Negl* 31:615–21.
61. Bergeson PS, Hernried LS, Sonntag PL. 1977. Infant strangulation. *Pediatrics* 59 Suppl (6 Pt 2):1043–46.
62. L'Hirondel J. 1961. La sécurité de l'enfant au berceau et dans les chaises hautes: la strangulation par les moyens de contention et les chutes. *Rev Hyg Med Soc* 9:653.
63. Jay A. 1978. Suffocation and sudden infant death. *Br Med J* 1(6111):511.
64. Editorial. 1999. Unexplained deaths in infancy. *Lancet* 353:161.
65. Krous HF. 1995. An international standardized autopsy protocol for sudden unexpected infant death. In *New Trends in the Nineties*, pp. 81–95. Oslo: Scandinavian University Press.
66. Byard RW. 1999. Center for Disease Control and Prevention (CDC). Guidelines for death scene investigation of sudden infant death syndrome. *Morb Mortal Wkly Rep.*, June 21, 1996.

Inflicted Fatal Thoracic and Abdominal Injuries in Infants and Young Children

4

KAREN J. GRIEST

Contents

4.1 Inflicted Fatal Thoracic Injuries in Infants and Young Children

4.1.1 Overview of Fatal Thoracic Injuries in Children

Primary and contributing causes of fatal thoracic injuries in infants and children can be summarized as follows:

- Penetrating thoracic injuries in children are rare and usually result from fractured ribs or fractured clavicles.
- Blunt thoracic trauma in children is much more common than penetrating injuries.[2,3]
- Rib fractures are the most common thoracic injury in inflicted trauma in children.[1]
- Injury to the oral pharynx in children can result in upper airway obstruction from aspiration of large quantities of blood or foreign objects, like teeth.
- Partial or complete rupture of the trachea or bronchi due to trauma can result in rapidly increasing subcutaneous emphysema and progressive cyanosis.
- Major pulmonary and hilar vessels can be injured by fractured ribs or clavicles.
- Multiple rib fractures can cause pneumothorax, hemopneumothorax, or flail chest.
- Traumatic asphyxia is a result of sudden compression of the thoracic cage. The sudden increase in pressure drives the venous blood into the capillaries, resulting in extravasations in the neck and head and hemorrhages in brain tissue with loss of consciousness, convulsions, and occasionally other significant neurologic sequelae.[1]
- Major thoracic trauma may be associated with concomitant abdominal, cranial, or orthopedic injuries.
- Hypoxia and hypotension from blood loss are the immediate potentially fatal sequelae of thoracic injuries in children.[2,3]

Fatal thoracic inflicted injuries in children are usually easily diagnosed. Abusive heart injuries, however, may be subtle and pose a diagnostic dilemma. With nonpenetrating cardiac trauma, the cardiovascular signs are often initially absent or overlooked.[4]

4.1.2 Inflicted Fatal Heart Injury in Children

4.1.2.1 Atrioventricular Junctional Traumatic Defects

Marino and Langston (1982) examined the relationship of cardiac trauma and subsequent conduction defect in an 18-month-old boy. The child sustained cardiac trauma 4 to 6 weeks prior to presenting to the emergency department, asystolic with no blood pressure or respirations. He required cardiovascular and ventilatory support until his death 36 hours later. At autopsy, the pericardium was distended by 50 mL of blood. There were healing centrally located right ventricular and upper interventricular septal myocardial infarctions. The atrioventricular (AV) junctional tissues were serially sectioned at autopsy and showed that the segment of the AV bundle that penetrates the right fibrous trigone gradually narrowed and that the right fibrous trigone was thickened. It was possible that the traumatic blow to the chest affected the annulus fibrosus, which may have been in a particularly crucial stage of postnatal development.[5] Brechenmacher et al. (1976) and James (1970) postulated that there is an interplay between the AV conduction tissues and the annulus fibrosus during the postnatal period. This interplay results in the molding and reshaping of the AV node and bundle during the first two years of life. If this postnatal molding goes awry, an abnormal collagenous template may give rise to an anomalous disposition of the AV bundle. In its most extreme cases, this can lead to conduction disturbances and possibly death.[6,7] Intraventricular and atrioventricular conduction defects often are associated with nonpenetrating cardiac trauma. These effects can be permanent or transient.[8,9]

4.1.2.2 Intimal Tears of the Right Atrium from Abdominal Injuries

A mechanism of intimal tears of the right atrium of the heart was postulated to be due to blunt force injuries of the abdomen in a study of six cases, three teenagers and three children younger than 3 years of age. The three teenagers received injuries from motor vehicle crashes, and the three younger children died from inflicted injuries; two were stomped, and one had a fist blow to the abdomen. All six victims had injuries to the abdomen and pelvis. All six cases had partial-thickness intimal tears of the right atrium of the heart in an area along the posterior wall just below the right auricle. The authors postulated that the increased intra-abdominal pressure brought about by the blunt force injury resulted in a hydrostatic force transmitted to the column of blood in the inferior vena cava. This force, in turn, is transmitted into the thoracic cavity to the right side of the heart, where the relatively fixed right atrium must absorb the hydrostatic forces. If the force exceeds the right atrium's capacity to balloon and stretch, intimal lacerations will result. Because of its location in the right atrium, the laceration and localized hematoma can result in electrical conduction abnormalities in the heart by either destroying the sinoatrial node or impeding the depolarization impulse traveling through the right atrium to the atrioventricular node (Figure 4.1). Two of the teen cases showed refractory bradycardia in spite of progressive hypotension. The immature abdominal muscles in young children may predispose them to right atrial lacerations.[10]

4.1.2.3 Traumatic Cardiac Contusions and Lacerations

Heart injury can occur following chest or abdominal injury in children (Table 4.1).[1] The incidence of cardiac injury in children after blunt trauma ranges between 0.8% and 5%, with myocardial contusion being the most common injury.[11] Cardiac injury is believed to be underreported because of the high incidence of prehospital fatality, failure to diagnose myocardial contusion, or delay in symptoms (Figure 4.2).[11,12]

In a large retrospective review of 184 children with blunt cardiac injuries, 95% of the patients had myocardial contusion, 1.5% had myocardial concussion, 2% developed cardiac laceration and/or rupture, and less than 1% had traumatic ventricular septal defect (VSD).[35]

In ventricular septal defects due to blunt trauma to the chest in children, the most common location is the apex of the muscular septum.[9]

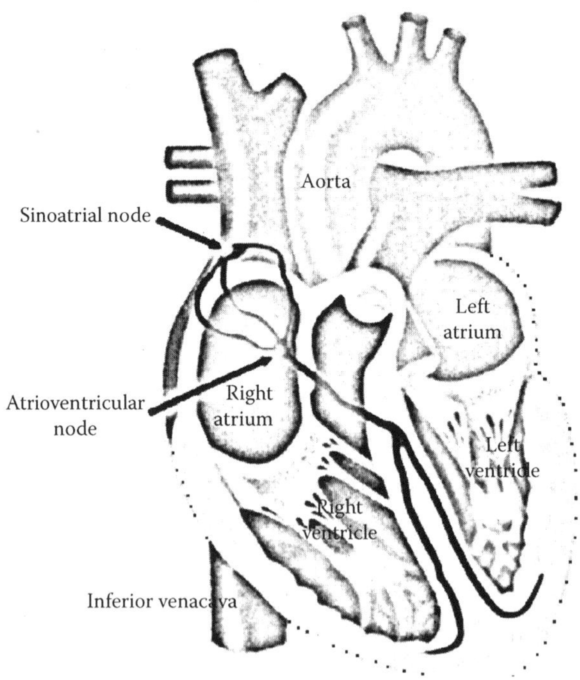

Figure 4.1 Location of SA node and AV node in heart.

Table 4.1 Injuries Due to Inflicted Cardiac Trauma in Children

Cardiac contusions
Arrhythmias
Atrioventricular junctional defects
Right atrium intimal tears
Cardiac lacerations
Right atrium
Left atrium
Right ventricle
Left ventricle
Ventriculoseptal defect
Delayed cardiac rupture
Healing cardiac contusions/lacerations
Cardiac scars
Sudden death (comotio cordis)

Presumably the apex of the heart is crushed against the vertebrae during the blunt impact.[12]

Cohle et al. (1995) presented six cases of inflicted cardiac lacerations in children and a review of similar cases in the medical literature in order to determine the mechanisms, types, and causes of blunt force injury to the heart in children. The ages of the six cases ranged from 9 weeks to 2½ years. In five of the six patients, the ruptured chamber was the right atrium. Confessed mechanisms included striking the baby with a fist, stomping on the infant, and drop-kicking the infant. Four of the cases had multiple histories given for the injuries, none of which were consistent with the injuries. Ribs were

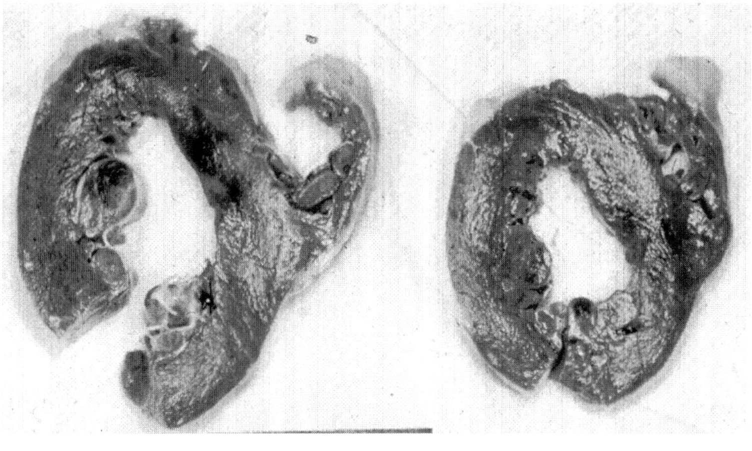

Figure 4.2 Cardiac contusions.

fractured in four out of six victims. One child had a healed myocardial contusion, and one a healing myocardial contusion.[13]

There are several mechanisms of blunt force-induced cardiac rupture. (1) A direct blow to the anterior chest is the most common mechanism. (2) Compression of the heart between the sternum or ribs and spine is especially common in individuals with a pliable chest, such as children. (3) When the legs are forcefully pressed into the abdomen, the abdominal compression can cause increased hydrostatic pressure in the heart. (4) The freely movable heart, tethered by the great vessels, can undergo tears of the atria at their venous attachments with sudden acceleration/deceleration. (5) The pointed end of a fractured rib or sternum can puncture the heart. (6) Blast forces can impact against the heart, similar to a direct blow.[13] A cardiac chamber with a transmural contusion may rupture as the injured myocardium becomes necrotic.[9,14–18] Ventricular distention, and thus rupture (including the septum), is most likely to occur at the end of diastole, while the atria are more vulnerable late in systole; in both of these situations the valves are closed.[19,20]

Whatever the mechanism, the rate at which the pressure is applied to the heart is a critical determinant in whether rupture will occur. If a blood-filled cardiac chamber is compressed slowly, the applied energy can be absorbed by deformation without rupture, but with rapid loading the chamber cannot change shape fast enough to accommodate the increased pressure and will rupture.[21]

Review of large clinical and autopsy series of patients of all ages sustaining blunt cardiac trauma showed no one chamber involved more than the others. Whether the atria or ventricles are ruptured depends on the phase of the cardiac cycle when the trauma is inflicted.[9,14,22,23] The chambers injured in cases of children 15 years of age and younger with cardiac lacerations were described by 13 authors reporting 16 cases. The right atrium was involved in five cases, the right ventricle was lacerated in one case, the interventricular septum in six cases, and the left ventricle in four.[10,12,16,17,20,24–30]

There are numerous reported accidental causes of cardiac lacerations including motor vehicle accident, pedestrian struck by motor vehicle, accidental direct blow to the chest, struck by a falling object, fall from the first floor of a building, fall 2.5 meters onto a hard surface, jumped on by playmates, struck or stomped in the abdomen, jumped on while on a sled, bicyclist who struck her precordium on the handlebar during a fall, kicked in the chest by an adult, hit by a tree limb, thrown off a rapidly moving sled, and hit in the chest with a barbell that fell 1 meter (Table 4.2).[14,16,23]

Delayed traumatic cardiac rupture has been reported in seven cases. The interval between rupture and clinical presentation ranged from 12 hours to 14 months. In three cases, the left ventricle was injured, and the other four had traumatic ventricular septal defects.[12,16,17,26,28–30]

Table 4.2 Mechanisms of Traumatic Cardiac Injury in Children

Accidental Trauma
Motor vehicle accident
Bicycle accident
Falling object
Fall to hard surface
Thrown from sled
Jumped on by playmates
Blast injury
Cardiopulmonary resuscitation
Inflicted Injury
Fist blow to chest
Fist blow to abdomen
Kick to chest
Kick to abdomen
Stomped
Drop-kicked
Compression of chest
Compression of abdomen
Acceleration/deceleration

Cardiopulmonary resuscitation (CPR) may cause rib fractures and rupture of the interventricular septum and right ventricle.[31–33] A fractured rib from CPR can perforate the heart (at least in adults).[31,34]

4.1.2.4 Diagnosis of Traumatic Cardiac Injury

External evidence of chest trauma is present infrequently, and the initial cardiac examination is most often normal.[35] In some cases there may be signs of heart failure, heart murmurs, or cardiac arrhythmias.[11] Currently, no "gold standard" for establishing the diagnosis of blunt force cardiac injury has been identified. Serial echocardiograms may help to identify evolving cardiac abnormalities. Laboratory evidence of elevated cardiac enzymes can be useful in detection of cardiac injury. The CK-MB fraction is commonly used; however this enzyme is also present in skeletal muscle and may not be a sensitive indicator in the case of multisystem trauma. Cardiac troponin I (cTnI) has proven to be a more accurate and reliable indicator of myocardial contusion. In blunt cardiac injury, elevated levels of cTnI (>2.0 ng/ml) correlated with a high likelihood of cardiac contusion. Cardiac troponin I also offers improved specificity because of the exclusive cardiac source. In adults, cTnI elevation has been documented 6 to 12 hours after injury. The timing of cTnI elevation after cardiac trauma in children has not been well established. If blunt cardiac injury is suspected, the child should be observed for at least

Table 4.3 Diagnostic Testing for Cardiac Trauma in Children

Laboratory Studies
CK-MB
Cardiac troponin I (cTnI), 6 to 12 hours after injury
Diagnostic Tests
12-lead electrocardiogram (ECG)
Echocardiogram
24-hour observation
Serial echocardiograms, with persistent symptoms
Cardiac catheterization, with persistent symptoms

24 hours. The suggested diagnostic workup should include a 12-lead ECG, echocardiography, and cTnI level at 6 to 12 hours after injury. If the patient remains symptomatic, serial echocardiography and cardiac catheterization should be considered (Table 4.3).[36–39]

4.1.2.5 Commotio Cordis in Children

Baker et al. (2003) reported a case of inflicted commotio cordis in a 7-week-old boy. This was the first report of commotio cordis in an infant, although there are three previous reports of inflicted commotio cordis in toddlers. In the reported infant case, the father, who was alone with the child, became so frustrated that he hit the infant with his fist on the center of the chest. He heard his son gasp for air then stop breathing.[40] Commotio cortis, or cardiac concussion, results from a blow to the precordial chest that disrupts the electrical activity of the heart. Sudden death, or near sudden death, results. It most commonly takes place during sporting events, usually baseball, involving children or adolescents. Ventricular fibrillation (VF) is the most commonly reported dysrhythmia in commotio cordis.[41,42] Survival following cardiac concussion, though rare, has been reported when resuscitation is initiated promptly.[43] In an experimental model of commotio cordis, chest blows timed to the cardiac electrical cycle and occurring in a 15-ms window just before the peak of the T-wave produced VF in 9 of 10 animals.[44] Relative to adults, commotio cordis is more common in children due to thinner, less muscular chest walls and a more compliant chest cage. Energy transfer to the heart from a precordial blow is therefore more complete.[43,45] Determination that a child died of commotio cordis relies heavily on witness and caretaker statements, circumstances and temporal sequence of the death, emergency medical records, and a complete autopsy to exclude other possible causes of death. Other chest injuries, such as contusions and rib fractures, may be

Table 4.4 Diagnosis of Commotio Cordis

Witness and caretaker statements
Circumstances of death
Temporal relationship between circumstances and death
Emergency medical records
Complete autopsy
Associated findings
Skin contusions
Thoracic wall contusions
Rib fractures

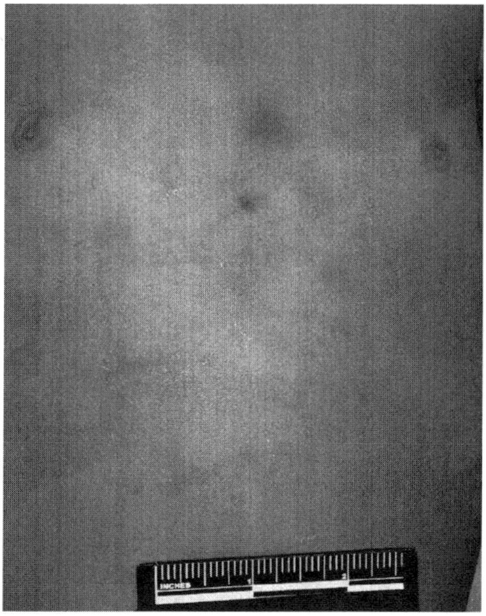

Figure 4.3 Contusion of anterior chest.

markers of previous inflicted chest trauma, or acute injuries concurrent with the fatal blow (Table 4.4, Figure 4.3).

4.2 Inflicted Abdominal Injuries in Infants and Young Children

4.2.1 Introduction

Abdominal trauma accounts for 6% to 8% of all cases of physical child abuse.[46] The incidence of inflicted injury in children with abdominal trauma from all causes ranges from 4% to 15%.[47] Only 1% of children hospitalized for child abuse have sustained intra-abdominal injury, but the mortality rate for children sustaining inflicted abdominal injury is 45% to 50%, making abdominal trauma the second most common form of fatal physical child abuse.[46,48–51] Child abuse leads to higher death rates compared to all other mechanisms of abdominal injury (i.e., accidents).[52] The high mortality rate of abusive abdominal injuries is due to the resulting hemorrhage, shock, and peritonitis.[46]

Early diagnosis is problematic, given the rarity of intentional blunt abdominal trauma in pediatric patients, the misleading and inaccurate histories often given by caregivers, and the frequent lack of abdominal skin bruising, even in cases of severe internal injuries. Another factor that may contribute to increased mortality is the delay in care that occurs frequently after an inflicted pediatric abdominal injury.[49–54] Canty et al. (1999) reported that a third of abused children in their study with blunt trauma to the gastrointestinal tract presented after more than 24 hours since injury.[53]

4.2.2 Causes of Abdominal Trauma in Children

Blunt force abdominal injuries in children under 6 years of age can occur during high-velocity accidents (HVA), low-velocity accidents (LVA), and inflicted injury.[55] High-velocity accidents include a motor vehicle crash or a fall from greater than 10 feet. Low-velocity accidents include such events as household trauma, a bicycle crash, or a fall from less than 10 feet, for example a fall from a jungle gym or a fall onto a rock. Inflicted trauma in this context was diagnosed if there were multiple unexplained injuries, confession by a perpetrator, or disclosure by the victim. Of the 121 children in the Wood et al. (2005) study, 77 (64%) had HVA injuries, 31 (26%) had LVA injuries, and 13 (11%) had inflicted injuries (Figure 4.4, Table 4.5).[55]

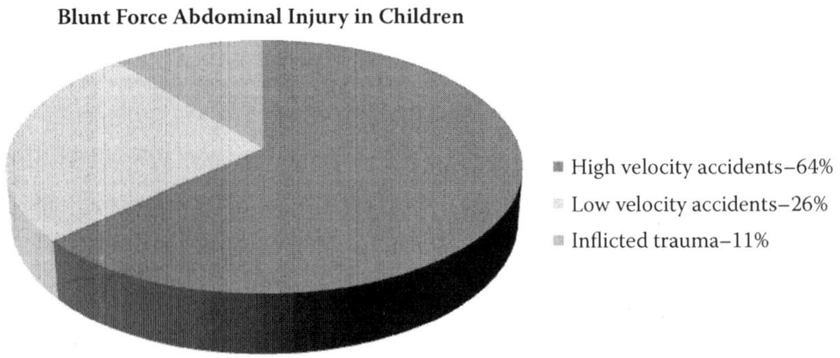

Figure 4.4 Causes of blunt force abdominal injury in children.

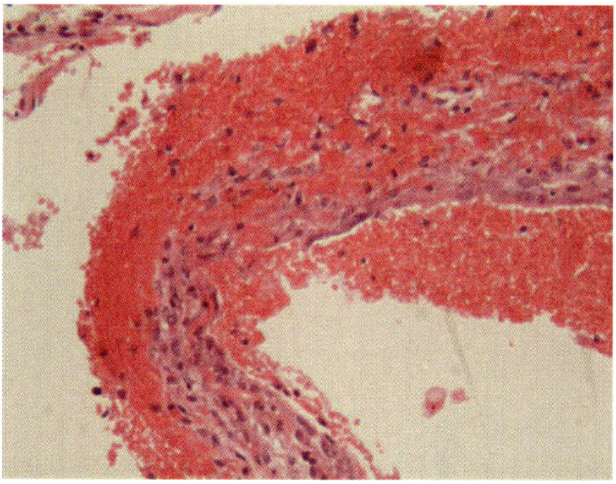

Figure 1.4 Histology of recent and older subdural hematoma with areas of membrane formation. (Courtesy of Dr. W. Squier.)

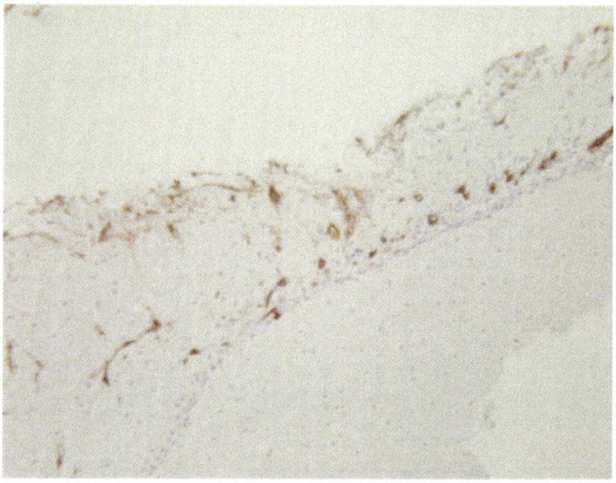

Figure 1.5 Histology of CD68 highlighting macrophages in an area of older subdural hematoma. (Courtesy of Dr. W. Squier.)

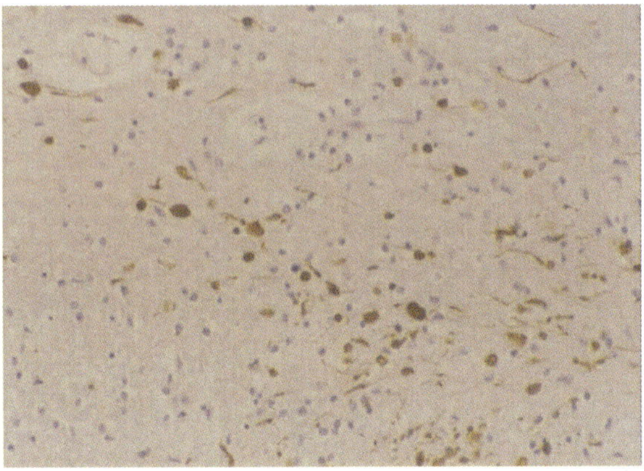

Figure 1.6 High power histology of APP staining in traumatic axonal injury.

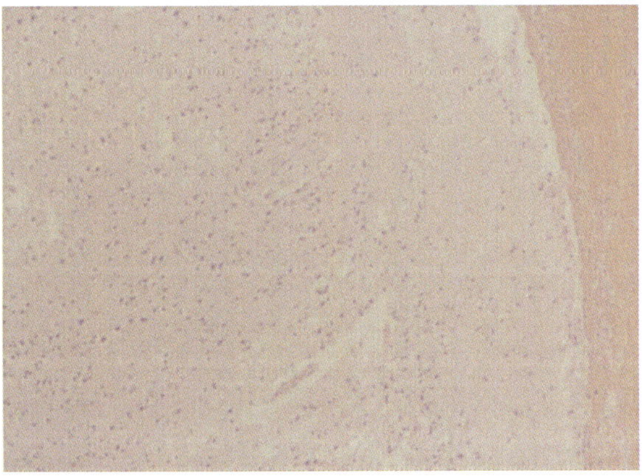

Figure 1.10 Histology of hypoxic-ischemic injury with adjacent subarachnoid hemorrhage.

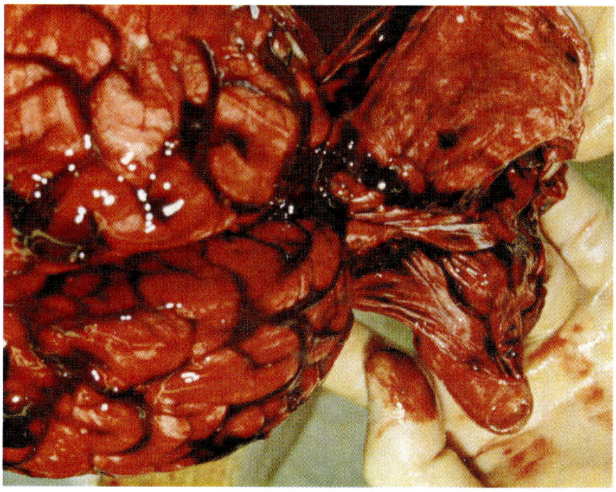

Figure 1.11 Brain and dura showing a thin film of subdural hemorrhage in a 2-month-old. (Courtesy of Dr. W. Squier.)

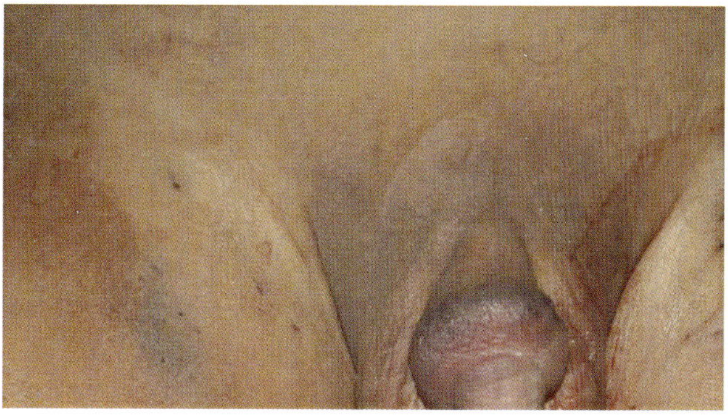

Figure 4.13 Bruising of lower abdomen in a case of sexual abuse. Note bruising of penis. There are therapeutic needle puncture marks in the groins.

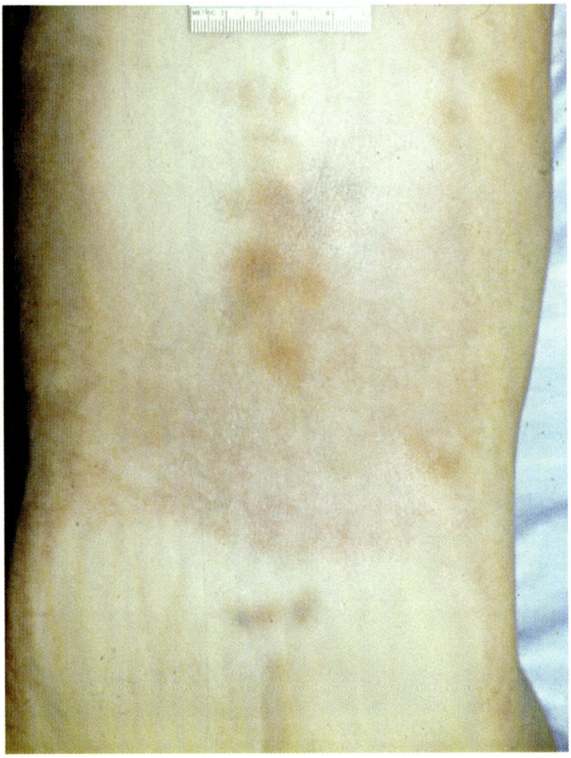

Figure 6.2 Multiple bruises of different colors. All these bruises occurred during one incident. Note the numerous bruises and clustering of bruises. The reddish band of color on the lower back and left side are due to livor mortis.

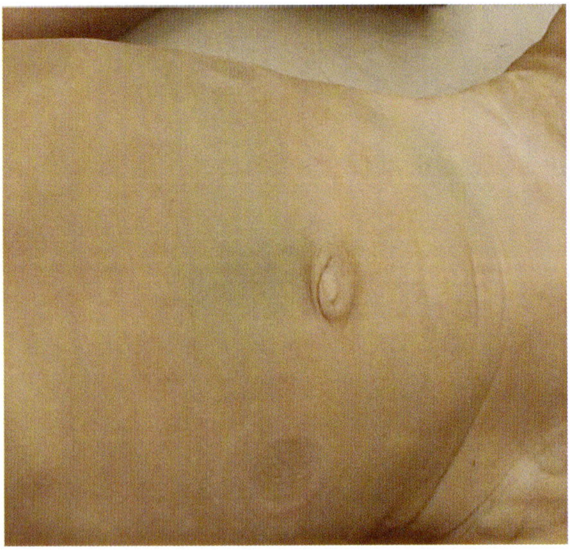

Figure 9.6 Green discoloration of skin at umbilicus and in left lower quadrant of abdomen.

Table 4.5 Causes of Blunt Force Abdominal Trauma in Children

Cause	Incidence (%)
High-velocity accidents	64%
Motor vehicle accidents	
Fall greater than 10 feet	
Low-velocity accidents	26%
Household trauma	
Bicycle accident	
Fall less than 10 feet	
Inflicted injury	11%

4.2.3 Age, Gender, and Race at Time of Injury

Among all causes of traumatic abdominal injury, the mean age of all children was 49 months; 21% of those children were younger than 3 years of age.[55] Abused children were significantly younger than accidentally injured children. More than half of the abused children in the Wood et al. study (2005) were younger than 36 months old, but only 22% of the HVA group and 3% (one child) in the LVA group were younger than 36 months old.[55] In a study of major abdominal injury due to child abuse, the average age was 24 months.[49] The ages of 10 children in one study presenting in acute, unexplained abdominal crises ranged from 5 to 30 months.[56] The victims of child abuse are typically infants and toddlers, while victims of accidental trauma are more likely to be school age.[46,57,58]

Child abuse as a cause of injury decreases with age, whereas falls increase with age. After excluding all motor vehicle injuries, child abuse accounts for a majority of injuries up to 24 months of age.[52]

In a study of major abdominal injury due to child abuse, 14 of the victims were boys and 8 girls.[49] In another study of 10 infants or small children suffering unexplained visceral trauma, 7 were boys and 3 girls.[56] One-third were girls in a study by Trokel et al. (2006) of 644 children with suspected inflicted blunt abdominal trauma.[58] Wood et al. (2005) found no statistically significant difference in gender or race between abused and accidentally injured children.[55]

4.2.4 Location of Injury and Mechanism

4.2.4.1 Location of Injuries

In the Wood et al. study (2005), of all causes of traumatic abdominal injury, most children sustained injuries to solid organs (68%), whereas a minority of children had hollow viscus injuries (19%) or isolated hematuria or adrenal injury (25%). A small group of children (5%) had combined injury to hollow viscus and solid organs. The frequency of solid organ injuries was similar among the HVA, LVA, and abuse groups, but hollow organ injuries were significantly more likely to occur in the abused children. The presence of both a hollow organ and solid organ injury occurred exclusively in the abused group. There were also significantly more children with severe injuries in the inflicted than in the accidental injury groups.[55] Ledbetter et al. (1988) studied 156 pediatric patients with abdominal trauma. Only 8% of the accidentally injured children, compared with 65% of the intentionally injured children, had hollow viscus injuries.[54]

Trokel et al. (2006) studied patient and injury characteristics associated with suspected inflicted blunt abdominal trauma in children aged 0 to 4 years; motor vehicle accidents were excluded. Six hundred sixty-four cases were analyzed. The four most common mechanisms of injury were suspected child abuse (40.5%), fall (36.6%), struck—not child abuse (9.7%), and bicycle-related injuries (4.2%). Hepatic injury (46.1%) was the most common intra-abdominal injury, followed by splenic (26%), hollow viscus (17.9%), and pancreatic (8.6%) injuries. Eighty-four percent of deaths were related to suspected child abuse. In a regression model including age, undernourishment, pancreatic injury, hollow viscus injury, traumatic brain injury, and mortality, all variables were significantly associated with suspected abuse. Hollow viscus injury had the highest odds ratio, whereas traumatic brain injury had the lowest (Table 4.6).[58]

4.2.4.2 Mechanism of Injury

The mechanism for abdominal injury is not always clear.[59] Abdominal injuries in children from a direct blow due to a punch or kick appear to be caused by acute compression against the vertebral column of hollow and/or solid upper abdominal viscera (Figure 4.5).[49] Sudden acceleration/deceleration forces have also been implicated.[59] Injuries may involve the liver, intestinal tract, spleen,

Table 4.6 General Characteristics of Accidental and Abusive Abdominal Injury

Abusive Injury	Accidental Injury
Younger age, <3 years	School age
Hollow and solid organ	Solid organ
Severe injury	LV and HV injuries
Less common	LV and HV more common
Duodenal injury	Small bowel trauma (MVA)
Punch or kick	Direct blow, acceleration/deceleration
Few bowel perforations	Bowel perforation more common
Delay in seeking care, 13 hours	LV, 2 to 12 hours; HV immediate
Associated abusive injuries	MVA, multiple injuries

Note: LV = low velocity; HV = high velocity; MVA = motor vehicle accident

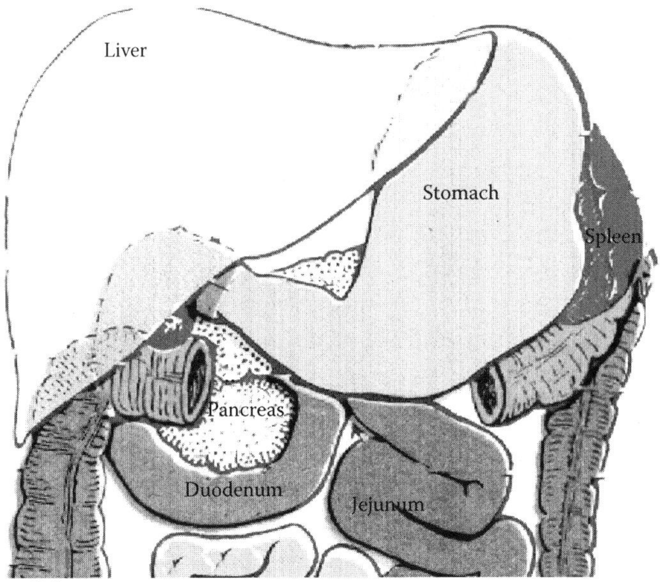

Figure 4.5 Diagram of abdominal organs.

pancreas, kidney, bladder, vascular supply, or lymphatic drainage system, with superficial organs and fixed organs more easily damaged than deeper structures or mobile structures.[46] In infants and young children, the force of the impact from an adult hand or foot covers a large percentage of body surface area and is likely to cause damage to multiple structures.[46] Most often, there is no bruising or other cutaneous sign of abdominal trauma because the smaller subcutaneous fat pads and more pliable abdominal musculature in children fail to absorb the blow. Instead, the force is transmitted to the internal organs.[46]

Perforation of the small bowel can occur at any level and may be a direct result of compression between the blunt traumatic force and the spine or the delayed result of bowel wall necrosis. The most common cause of small bowel trauma is a motor vehicle accident, but it also results from bicycle accidents and child abuse. In motor vehicle accidents, this external blunt force typically is generated by sudden deceleration, causing the seat belt or lap belt to compress the abdomen. In child abuse, this force is commonly the result of a punch or kick.[46] There are 15 well-documented cases of small bowel perforation in association with child abuse, approximately half of which involved the duodenojejunal flexure. Sixty percent of all intestinal perforations occur in the proximal jejunum just beyond the ligament of Treitz.[60] Also involved were the jejunum and ileum. Perforation in this part of the bowel is due to a shearing force produced by a sudden deceleration-acceleration injury tearing the bowel at the antimesenteric border close to its point of attachment to the posterior abdominal wall. Another proposed explanation of this injury is that, while the relatively thick duodenojejunal junction can withstand a blow to the abdomen, the thinner proximal jejunum is more vulnerable to perforation.[60]

The duodenum is an intestinal segment that is particularly vulnerable to blunt abdominal trauma. The duodenum is fixed in its retroperitoneal location and crosses the spine; therefore it is less likely than other portions of bowel to become displaced and protected from blunt force trauma. It is also more susceptible to compression against the spine.[46]

Mesenteric avulsion is not an uncommon sequela in children receiving blunt force abdominal trauma. Decelerating or whipping forces tear the mesentery and may disrupt the small intestine at the sites of ligamentous support (Figure 4.6 through Figure 4.9).[6]

Abusive parents often report that their children's injuries resulted from a fall on stairs. Huntimer et al. (2000) examined the medical literature covering a 29-year period for reports of the types of injuries sustained in falls on stairs and for reports of the types of blunt abdominal trauma that result in small intestine perforations in infants and children. Falls on stairs were not reported to cause any of the 32 cases of small intestine perforations in the literature. There were no reports of any intra-abdominal injuries, including small intestine perforations, in any of the 677 cases of falls on stairs reviewed. Falls on stairs rarely result in any type of truncal injury.[62]

4.2.5 Delay in Seeking Care

In the Wood et al. study (2005), all but one child involved in HVA trauma presented within 2 hours after injury. Thirteen of the children (42%) in the LVA groups presented within 2 hours, and only two (15%) of the abused

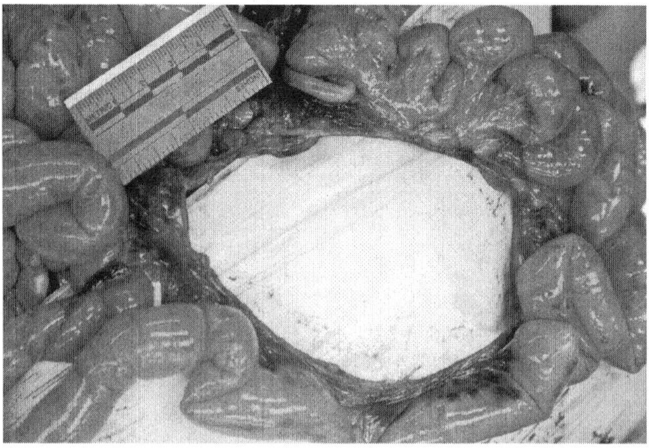

Figure 4.6 Mesenteric avulsion in inflicted abdominal trauma.

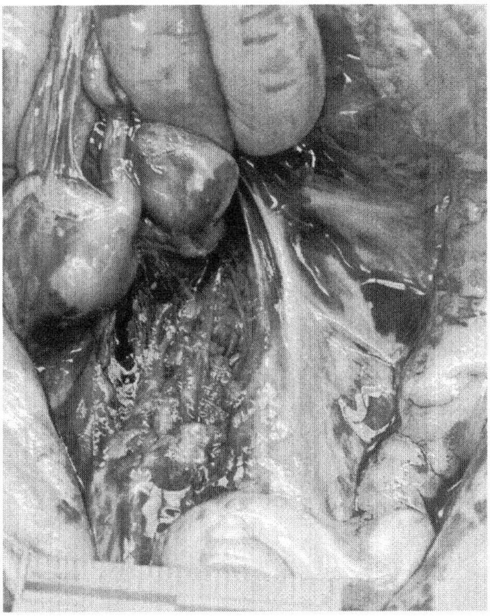

Figure 4.7 Mesentery torn from posterior wall of abdomen.

children were brought to medical attention within 2 hours. By 12 hours, the majority, or 20, of the LVA-injured children (65%) were brought to medical care, but only six (46%) of the abused children had sought medical care.[55] In a review of eight cases of severe abdominal trauma, four had delayed presentation.[63] In the study of Cooper et al. (1988) of children with severe abdominal injury from child abuse, failure of the parent(s) to seek immediate medical care delayed treatment by a mean of 13 hours.[49] As a single indicator of abuse, delay in care has a specificity of only 65% which, given the prevalence of only 30% overall inflicted injury in the cohort studied, results in only a modest predictive value of 39%. When the group is further restricted to only those children with severe intra-abdominal injury, the specificity improved to 90%, but the predictive value increased to only 67%.[55]

For fear of recrimination, or for simple lack of understanding the consequences of their actions or of knowledge of the situation (hurt by another person), most seriously abused children are not brought to the hospital by their parents until physical signs of deterioration are so obvious that even the layman recognizes a threat to life so immediate that death may soon occur. Since it may take several hours to develop fever or peritoneal signs following hollow viscus injury, and given the remarkable capacity of children to compensate for hypovolemia, it appears that a delay of at least this long is probably inevitable.[46,49]

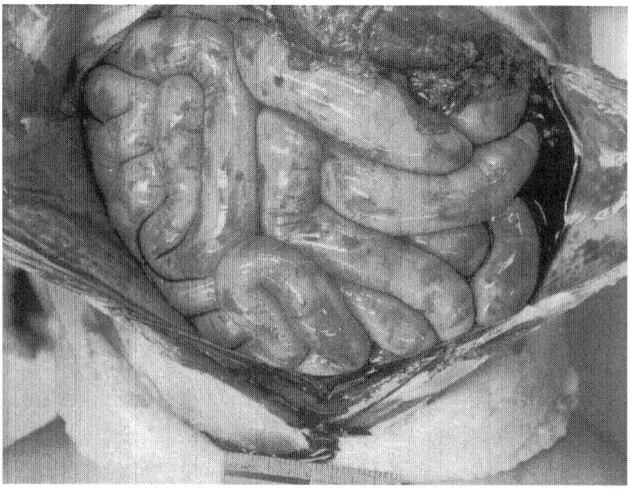

Figure 4.8 Hemoperitoneum due to torn mesentery.

4.2.6 Associated Injuries

In the Wood et al. (2005) study, 12 of 13 cases of inflicted abdominal injury had multiple injuries.[55] In the Cooper et al. study (1988) of severe abdominal injuries due to child abuse, associated injuries were present in all cases and followed the patterns typically observed in the syndrome of child abuse and neglect. They included soft-tissue trauma, head trauma, bony and skull

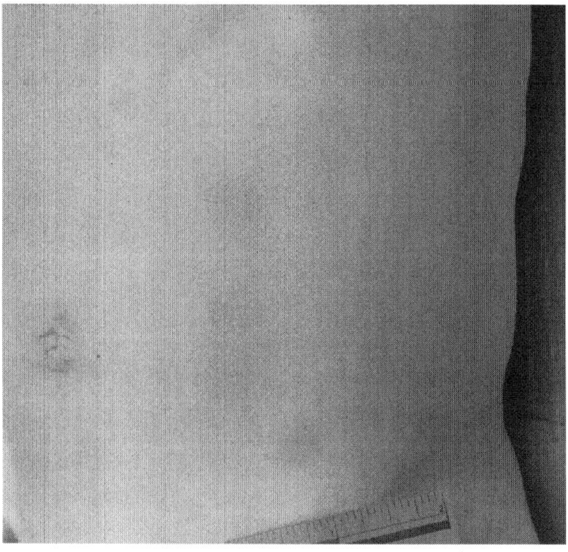

Figure 4.9 Small bruise in left lower quadrant of the abdomen was the only external injury in the case of inflicted mesenteric avulsion illustrated in Figure 4.6 through Figure 4.8.

fractures, hemothorax, hemomediastinum, renal contusion, genital hematoma, and human bites.[49] Cooper et al. (1988) found that in victims of abuse-related abdominal trauma, 95% also had soft tissue injury, 45% had evidence of head trauma, and 45% had a skeletal fracture. Most battering injuries are repetitive and follow fairly specific patterns, e.g., contact or immersion burns, long bone and rib fractures.[49] In the Barnes et al. study (2005), other injuries due to abuse were noted in 17 children and were vital in making the diagnosis of abuse. All 17 children with other injuries had bruises, and seven had fractures. Other injuries included torn frenulum, bites, and multiple burns.[64] Ng and Hall (1998) presented three children with anterior rib fractures which involved the sixth to ninth costochondral junctions (incidence of 4% in over 300 referrals). The fractures were bilateral in two children and symmetrical in one. These fractures were associated with major abdominal visceral injuries.[65] There are many other reported cases of inflicted abdominal trauma with multiple associated injuries (Figure 4.10, Figure 4.11).[46,57,60,61]

Although the presence of multiple injuries and a delay to care are associated with child abuse, neither approaches the specificity required to rely on those features alone for a diagnosis of abuse. Rather, such findings must be interpreted in light of other features of a child's history: the age of the child,

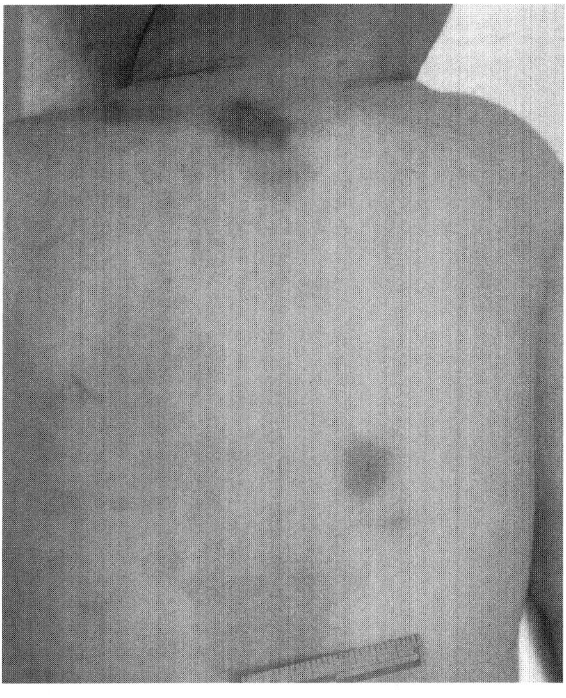

Figure 4.10 Bruise on midback and abrasions on upper back in case of fatal abdominal trauma.

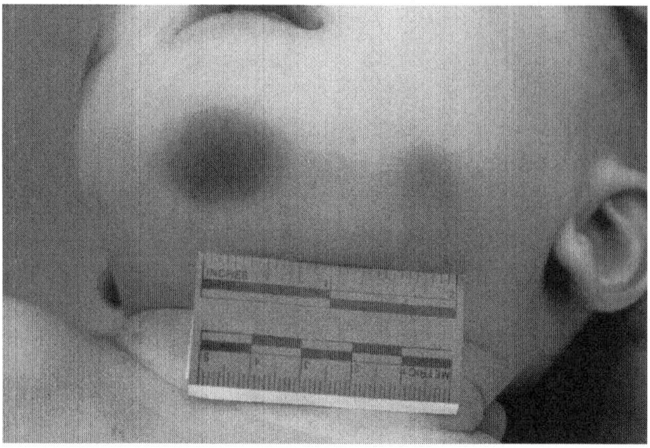

Figure 4.11 Multiple chin bruises and cheek bruise/abrasion in case of fatal abdominal injury.

the mechanism of injury, and the presence of other injuries suspicious for abuse. Although occurring more frequently among abused children, delay in seeking medical care and multiple injuries may also occur among children with significant injuries from low-velocity accidental trauma.[54]

An association between the "neglected child" and the "battered child" is apparent when the nutrition and development of these patients are studied.[56–58,66,67] In one study of ten children with inflicted abdominal injuries, three were poorly developed, one was malnourished, and two had severe anemia. In six of the ten cases supporting evidence was present (bruises, fractures, etc.) (Figure 4.12).[56]

The suspect case for inflicted abdominal trauma is any child, particularly under 3 years of age, with bruising or who appears undernourished, presenting with vomiting or other symptoms, however vague, relating to the alimentary tract.[57]

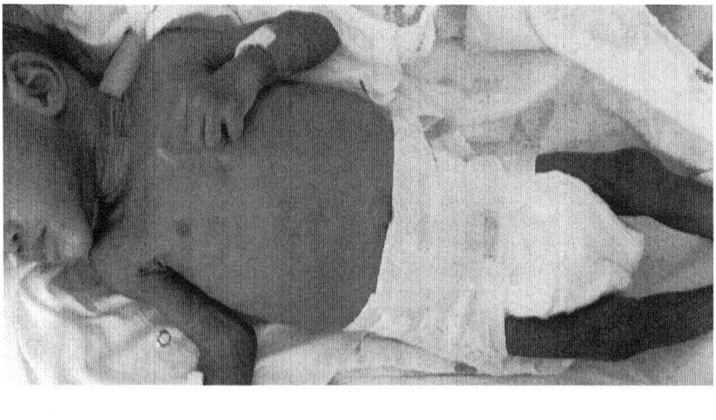

Figure 4.12 Malnourished infant.

4.2.7 History

Cooper et al. (1988) reviewed all childhood trauma cases examined over a 15-year period at two hospitals for the circumstances and presentations of major blunt abdominal trauma due to child abuse, 22 cases. In only two instances was the family intact, and in both of those cases, the child was abused by the babysitter. Otherwise the father or the mother's boyfriend was responsible for the injuries. More than half of the families had been involved with the civil authorities from previous documented episodes of child abuse. The histories proffered by the child's caretakers followed regular patterns. The history given may be implausible or insufficient to explain the seriousness of the observed symptoms.[49]

In the Barnes et al. study (2005), evidence of identity of the alleged perpetrator was available for 18 children. In 11 cases, the perpetrator was a male cohabitee of the mother (not the biological father). Only two women (mothers) were identified as perpetrators. For the remaining five children, the alleged perpetrator was the biological father in three cases, an older brother in one, and an uncle in one. The exact cause of the injury was unknown in most abused children; however, two cohabitees admitted punching the child's abdomen. In ten children, there was previous concern about abuse, but only three had been on the child-protection register.[64]

Disturbance of the parent–child relationship is often reported. Unstable homes are usual, and there may be reported excessive use of alcohol or a pattern of neurotic or psychotic behavior in one or both parents (Table 4.7).[56]

4.2.8 Clinical Presentation and Diagnosis

Clinically, children with inflicted abdominal trauma may present with hemodynamic instability, altered mental status, abdominal pain, abdominal distention, fever, or emesis.[46] Other possible symptoms include abdominal tenderness, hematuria, abdominal bruising or ecchymoses, decreasing or low hematocrit, hyperactive or absent bowel sounds, palpable abdominal mass, jaundice, and the presence of blood in the nasogastric aspirate or on rectal examination.[68,69] Tenderness alone is not a reliable sign, particularly when there is bruising of the abdominal wall.[70] The mean number of physical signs in the Sivit et al. study (1989) was 3.1 per child (range, 1–8).[69]

In the Cooper et al. study (1988), hemodynamically stable patients with injuries affecting the integrity of the gastrointestinal organs usually presented with dysfunctional complaints related to the particular structure that was damaged. Patients with injuries affecting the integrity of the circulation, particularly if hemodynamically unstable, usually presented with lethargy and/or coma, either of "unknown" cause, or which develop following a seemingly trivial episode of head trauma, often reportedly due to a fall from the bed.

Table 4.7 Presenting History and Clinical Presentation in Inflicted Abdominal Injury

History
Family not intact/unstable homes
Excessive use of alcohol
Neurotic or psychotic behavior in one or both parents
Previous encounters with police or CPS
Unknown cause
Trivial episode of head trauma, i.e., fall from bed
Inconsistent history
Abuser
Mother's boyfriend
Father
Babysitter
Mother
Older brother/uncle
Clinical Presentation
Hemodynamically Stable
Dysfunctional complaints related to organ damaged
Nonspecific general illness
Abdominal pain/tenderness
Right should pain (Kehr's sign) (hepatic injury)
Fever
Epigastric mass (pancreatic pseudocyst)
Abdominal mass
Emesis/Bilious vomiting (duodenal hematoma)
Jaundice
Peritonitis (intestinal rupture)
Septic shock
Hypovolemia
Low hematocrit
Anemia
Abdominal distention
Abdominal bruising
Neglect and malnourishment
Hematuria
Hyperactive. hypoactive or absent bowel sounds
Blood in nasogastric aspirate or rectal exam
Absent bowel movement for days
Hemodynamically Unstable
Lethargy and/or coma
Profound shock
Dead on arrival to hospital

Occasionally the histories were misleading enough, given the subtlety or relative lack of specific localizing signs of intraperitoneal hemorrhage, to direct the attention of the physician away from the abdomen until a hematocrit was obtained. One child presented with an epigastric mass due to a pancreatic hematoma, which progressed to a pseudocyst. Three children presented with bilious vomiting due to duodenal hematoma. Five children had peritonitis due to duodenojejunal rupture; one presented in profound septic shock at greater than 24 hours after injury. Three presented with hypovolemia due to moderate hemorrhage. Six presented in profound shock due to massive hemorrhage. Four were dead on arrival to the hospital; all of these children had intra-abdominal hemorrhage exceeding 50% estimated blood volume. Overall mortality was 45%. The mortality rate was higher in patients who presented with intra-abdominal bleeding. There was no difference between survivors and nonsurvivors with respect to a delay in seeking medical attention. Of the three children who presented with hypovolemia due to moderate hemorrhage (liver tear, spleen tear, kidney avulsion) all survived. In six children who presented in profound shock due to massive hemorrhage (massive hepatic laceration, hepatic and hepatocaval disruption, cavomesenteric disruption), all but one died. Four were dead on arrival from massive hepatic laceration, ruptured viscus, renal fracture, caval disruption, or retroperitoneal hematoma. In general, vital signs and hematocrits on admission were reliable predictors of the type and seriousness of the injury. Blunt abdominal injuries, as a rule, are more difficult to assess accurately and usually require sophisticated invasive and/or noninvasive diagnostic tests to guide further therapy. Unequivocal abdominal distention and/or bruising, although not always present, are obviously helpful pathognomonic signs.[49]

Just as in cases of accidental abdominal trauma, injury to the liver, pancreas, kidneys, and spleen can be seen after inflicted intentional trauma. The liver is the most commonly injured solid organ, and common symptoms of *hepatic injury* include abdominal pain and right shoulder pain (Kehr's sign). Major hepatic trauma is best visualized with an abdominal computed tomography (CT) scan. Minor liver trauma is associated with elevated hepatic transaminases. Positive radiographic findings such as lacerations and hematomas have been correlated with an aspartate aminotransferase (AST) level greater than 450 U/L and an alanine aminotransferase (ALT) level greater than 250 U/L. *Pancreatic injury* may present as major damage, such as a transection, but more commonly presents as a laceration or contusion or as posttraumatic pancreatitis. Although the pancreas is a deep organ, it is susceptible to abuse-related injury because of its fixed location and its susceptibility to compression against the spine. Abdominal CT and measurement of pancreatic enzymes remain the best methods of diagnosing pancreatic injury. An amylase level of greater than 200 IU/L and a lipase level of greater than 1,800 IU/L have been correlated with the presence of major pancreatic injury.

However, normal amylase and lipase levels do not rule out the possibility of pancreatic trauma, and an abdominal CT should be obtained if abdominal trauma is suspected. *Renal and splenic injuries* are seen less frequently with inflicted abdominal trauma. Splenic laceration or rupture may be associated with injury to the lower ribs, and renal damage may include not only the kidney but also its vascular supply. Both of these injuries are best diagnosed with abdominal CT scan. A diagnosis of *intestinal perforation* can be difficult to make, but clinical signs include abdominal tenderness, cutaneous findings of abdominal trauma, and free peritoneal air on x-ray or CT scan. Untreated, a patient with intestinal perforation will progress to frank peritonitis or shock. *Intramural duodenal hematomas* are also sequelae of blunt trauma to the epigastrium.[46] An intramural hematoma is the characteristic form of duodenal injury in battered children. The hematoma may involve the entire duodenum and may cause partial or complete intestinal obstruction, which becomes maximal several days after the injury. A barium study demonstrates dilation of the duodenum proximal to the obstruction and usually shows a "coiled-spring" appearance of the edematous mucosal folds.[70] An abdominal CT scan may also be diagnostic.[46]

Jejunal intramural hematoma has been reported in child abuse. The delay time between trauma or symptoms and presentation for medical treatment was reported to be 1 hour and 3 days, respectively, in two reported cases of child abuse. Rare causes of intramural hematoma include anticoagulant therapy, blood dyscrasia, ruptured aneurysm, mesenteric cyst, acute pancreatitis, and carcinoma of the pancreas. The site of bleeding may be retroperitoneal, intramural, subserosal, or submucosal. The most typical patient, based on frequency of reports, is a young male with a history of blunt trauma to the abdomen dating from 1 to 12 days prior to admission. This delayed onset of symptoms can be explained by continued bleeding with associated edema or by late enlargement of the hematoma due to osmotic imbibing of water. The most common symptoms encountered are pain and vomiting. The former is usually present in the epigastric or mid-abdominal region. Vomiting results from mechanical obstruction by the intramural mass, is usually persistent, and eventually becomes bile-stained. Gastric distention may be present, but since the intestine distal to the obstruction is collapsed, the abdomen may remain relatively scaphoid. Bowel sounds are usually present—hyperactive at first, but possibly markedly reduced later. A mass is occasionally palpable, and may lead one to the mistaken diagnosis of chronic intussusception. Jaundice is rarely encountered, but can result either from hemolysis of the entrapped blood or from obstruction of the bile duct if the hematoma is in the area of the ampulla of Vater. Shock, tachycardia, anemia, and leucocytosis may also be present as evidence of hidden blood loss. Diagnosis is often confirmed on x-ray. Supine film of the abdomen may be sufficient, but a thin barium or Lipiodol swallow will sometimes help show the characteristic picture of an intramural mass associated with crowding together of the valvulae conniventes and production of a "coiled-spring pattern." Frequently there is total obstruction to the passage of the contrast material and there may be x-ray evidence of extrinsic pressure on surrounding organs. The obstruction tends to be complete and prolonged, leading to electrolyte imbalance and other complications.[68]

X-ray films of the abdomen and chest, with the child in an upright position, should be obtained because of the possibility of an intestinal rupture, with free air under the diaphragm. Skeletal x-ray studies to detect healed or healing fractures are recommended, even if there are no changes in limb length, thickness, or contour. The blood count is not a dependable diagnostic aid because anemia or leukocytosis, though compatible with visceral injury, may be the result of chronic deprivation and soft-tissue bruising.[70]

In inflicted abdominal injuries, CT scan shows that injuries to solid abdominal organs are most common, followed by pulmonary contusion or laceration and pneumoperitoneum due to duodenal transection. In the group diagnosed by emergency surgery, injuries to the intestinal tract and mesentery are most common, followed by solid organ injury, and pulmonary contusion. Intestinal, mesenteric, and pancreatic injuries are associated with a poor outcome. CT should be the examination of choice in abused children with suspected intra-abdominal injury. CT reveals abdominal injury in abused children that might otherwise go undetected. At autopsy of children who did not survive, injuries to the intestinal tract and mesentery were most common and included extensive small bowel laceration, rectal laceration, and mesenteric laceration. Although injuries to solid abdominal viscera occur more frequently, bowel or mesenteric injuries appear to be associated with poor outcome.[69]

Ultrasonography is helpful in the diagnosis of retroperitoneal hematoma, acute traumatic pancreatitis, and pancreatic pseudocyst. Nuclear scintigraphy is valuable if injury is limited to the liver or spleen. CT is the imaging modality of choice for assessing generalized blunt abdominal trauma as well as evaluating the extent of injuries to the liver, spleen, pancreas, kidneys, and mesentery (Table 4.8).[71]

Table 4.8 Diagnostic Studies in Inflicted Abdominal Injuries

CT scan of abdomen
Radiology of the abdomen
Ultrasound of abdomen
Emergency laparotomy
Serum transaminases (AST, ALT, amylase)
CT and x-ray of head/chest
Barium study
Nuclear scintigraphy

In fatal cases, part of the autopsy should be microscopic examination to support the diagnosis of traumatic abdominal injury and to date any injuries. Histologic examination of the region of acute injury may also establish the presence of unexpected older injuries in the form of fibroblast proliferation, early scar formation, increased vascularity, and hemosiderin-laden macrophages. Another region of interest to look for previous injury is the retroperitoneum, particularly around the head of the pancreas.[87]

4.2.9 Less Common Presentations in Inflicted Abdominal Injury

Shah et al. (1997) reported in a 15-month-old for the first time a small-bowel stricture secondary to abdominal trauma in child abuse, although it has been reported in lap-belt injury.[60]

The stomach is a relatively mobile organ and can avoid serious injury in most cases by moving about in response to nonpenetrating forces. In a large series of blunt abdominal trauma cases, gastric rupture is generally felt to comprise from 1.3% to 7.1% of visceral injuries, with most authors reporting about 2.1%.[72,73] Schechner and Ehrlich (1974) reported two cases of gastric rupture following episodes of proved or strongly suspected child abuse. One was a 4-year-old boy admitted with a stomach ache. According to his stepfather, he had been spanked on the buttocks while lying across the stepfather's knee at about 9 p.m. on the day of admission, shortly after the ingestion of a large picnic meal of hot dogs and beans. Ten minutes later the child began to complain of abdominal pain, nausea, and respiratory distress. At laparotomy, a 10- to 12-cm laceration was found through the anterior gastric wall near the greater curvature. Case 2 concerned a 5-year-old boy who was reported to have been kicked in the abdomen by his father earlier that evening, apparently following the ingestion of a large amount of water. A laparotomy showed a 13-cm linear tear along the lesser curvature of the stomach through the anterior wall. In each of the reported cases, the child presumably had a full stomach, and the compressing force applied squeezed the gastric contents into a small area of the stomach, thus resulting in a bursting of the gastric wall outward.[74]

Acute gastric dilatation may occur as a complication of child abuse and neglect. Acute gastric dilatation is a paralytic phenomenon which is due to loss of muscle tone rather than mechanical gastric outlet obstruction. The pathogenesis of this acute gastric dilatation in the deprived child is related to structural and functional changes in the stomach due to chronic starvation with subsequent ingestion of a large meal in the hospital.[75]

Boysen (1975) reported the case of chylous ascites in a battered 20-month-old child. The child had a history of enlarging abdomen for 2 weeks. A diagnostic paracentesis yielded chylous fluid. A definite leak in the abdominal lymphatic system was visualized by lymphangiogram.[76] In one large series of chylous ascites, 12% of the cases were due to trauma. By far, the most common cause of chylous ascites in children is a congenital abnormality. Other causes include obstruction to the mesenteric lymphatic vessels by enlarged retroperitoneal lymph nodes due to neoplasm or tuberculosis or mesenteric adenitis. In about one-third of cases no cause can be found.[77]

Both direct and indirect forces have been implicated in the cause of abdominal pseudoaortic aneurysms, although child abuse is a rare cause. Direct force, the major component of injury, occurs when the aorta is compressed against a relatively fixed vertebral column. An example is an improper seat belt position. Indirect force occurs with acute deceleration; the abdominal vasculature, especially the mesenteric vessels, are sheared from the aorta. There are often accompanying injuries to the abdominal viscera and vertebrae. A striking feature of pediatric pseudoaneurysms is delayed presentation at greater than 24 hours.[78]

Only four cases of bladder rupture have been reported in child abuse. The bladder remains an abdominal organ for the first 6 years of life; as a result, it is more vulnerable to external trauma. After age 6, the bladder assumes a more protected position beneath the symphysis pubis. The superior surface, or dome, of the bladder is the least supported and the weakest part of the bladder. It extends upward and is the only surface completely covered by peritoneum. Intraperitoneal bladder ruptures account for approximately one-third of all bladder injuries. The rupture classically appears as a large horizontal tear in the dome of the bladder. The tear is believed to occur when a blow is delivered to the lower abdomen in the presence of a full bladder. Peritoneal resorption of urine produces electrolyte imbalance, acidosis, and uremia (i.e., pseudorenal failure). The recognition of a possible relationship between an elevated BUN and intraperitoneal rupture of the bladder may be the only indication of this diagnosis in clinically unsuspected cases. Along with laboratory findings suggestive of acute renal failure, the patient with bladder rupture may also present with symptoms such as suprapubic pain, genital pain, bilateral shoulder tip pain, anuria, abdominal distention, peritonitis, nausea, decreased bowel sounds, and gross hematuria. Peritoneal signs cannot be relied upon for early diagnosis of bladder rupture because extravasated urine is sterile, invoking little peritoneal reaction. The diagnostic test of choice is a retrograde cystogram radiograph. Abdominal CT scan is used for evaluation of bony injury and can substitute for diagnostic peritoneal lavage and intravenous pyelogram. Delayed diagnosis may lead to abscess and urinary fistula formation. True renal failure in the abused child may also occur. This can result from direct trauma to renal parenchyma and extensive muscular injury with rhabdomyolysis. Bladder rupture should be suspected in the setting of blunt trauma with hematuria, and in a child with abdominal distension, oliguria, hyperkalemia, and apparent renal failure.[79]

Hopkins et al. (1994) presented an unusual case of a 2½-year-old boy who had a 100-kg tombstone fall on him. The left renal vein was transected. The left renal vein is especially susceptible to blunt trauma because of its longer length and its course across the midline. Probable lateral displacement of the kidney in this incident led to the venous injury. Ligation of the left renal vein is possible because of collateral drainage by the adrenal and gonadal veins. Blood loss is severe with a renal vein injury because there is not the intense vasospasm that occurs with arterial injuries.[80]

Complete avulsion of the common bile duct from the duodenum has been reported in inflicted abdominal trauma. Avulsion of the common bile duct has not been reported before, but is in keeping with injuries in battered children to relatively fixed viscera in the epigastrium, the duodenum, the pancreas, the root of the mesentery, and the liver.[57]

Perforation of the pelvic colon has also been reported in abdominal injury from child abuse.[57]

DiGiacomo et al. (2000) reported a case of periportal fluid tracking in a case of child abuse with abdominal injury. Laboratory studies showed marked elevations of liver enzymes.[81] In another study of pediatric blunt abdominal injury, 40% of children with periportal fluid tracking had no other abnormal findings by CT.[82]

Periportal venous gas and pneumatosis intestinalis are rare findings in child abuse. They have been associated with hematoma of the small bowel mesentery, duodenal hematoma, hemoperitoneum, tear of the peritoneum, mesenteric abscesses, and liver laceration. Portal venous gas may be seen in a variety of conditions, including mucosal damage from such causes as inflammation, ischemia, or causes of increased intraluminal gas pressure such as trauma or obstruction. Peripheral location of portal venous gas within the liver has been attributed to centrifugal portal venous flow. Biliary air, on the other hand, is more central within the liver, presumably because of the centripetal flow of bile. Both CT and ultrasonography are more sensitive than conventional radiography for detection of portal venous flow.[83–85]

Van Winckel et al. (1997) reported the case of a 21-month-old boy who had unremitting bilious vomiting and elevated serum amylase and lipase levels. Sonographic examination of the abdomen revealed a cystic mass in the epigastric region; fluid collection in the lesser sac; fluid collection bordered by the pancreas, liver, and stomach; distended intestinal loops surrounded by ascites. Fluid collection in the lesser sac and ascites surrounding distended intestinal loops indicated remote subacute hemorrhage. Fluid in the lesser sac can be differentiated from a pancreatic pseudocyst by the absence of pancreatic tissue surrounding the fluid collection, by cranial and lateral extension of the fluid collection, and by the presence of ascites.[85]

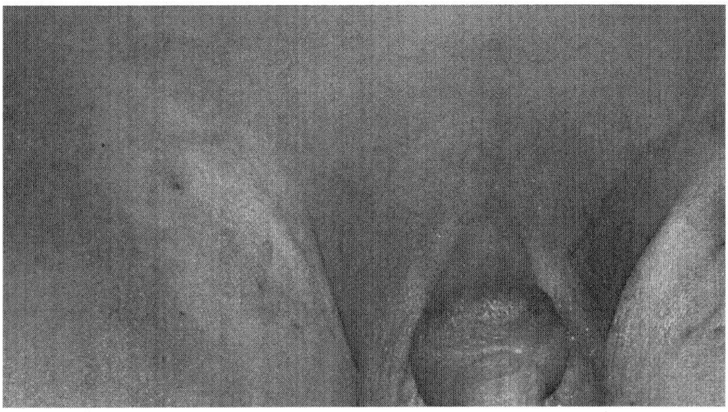

Figure 4.13 (see color insert following page 80) Bruising of lower abdomen in a case of sexual abuse. Note bruising of penis. There are therapeutic needle puncture marks in the groins.

4.2.10 Child Sexual Abuse and Abdominal Injury

It is important to consider and examine the possibility of sexual abuse. A case of rectal injury from sexual abuse was excluded from the Barnes et al. study. Cases have been identified where abdominal injury and sexual abuse have coexisted.[86] The presence of bruising of the lower abdominal wall in a child is suggestive of sexual abuse (Figure 4.13).

References

1. Ellis PS. 1997. The pathology of fatal child abuse. *Pathology* 29:113–21.
2. Haller JA, Shermeta DW. 1975. Major thoracic trauma in children. *Pediatr Clin North Am* 22:341–47.
3. Sarihan H, Abes M, Akyazici R, Cay A, et al. 1996. Blunt thoracic trauma in children. *J Cardiovasc Surg* 37:525–28.
4. Prim RK, Karp RB, Shrank JP. 1979. Multiple cardiovascular injuries and motor vehicle accidents. *JAMA* 241:2540–41.
5. Marino TA, Langston C. 1982. Cardiac trauma and the conduction system: a case study of an 18-month-old child. *Arch Pathol Lab Med* 106:173–74.
6. Brechenmacher C, Coumel P, James TN. 1976. De Subitaneis mortibus: XVI. Intractable tachycardia in infancy. *Circulation* 53:377–81.
7. James TN. 1970. Sudden death in babies: new observations in the heart. *Am J Cardiol* 25:213–26.
8. Dolara A, Morando P, Pampaloni M. 1967. Electrocardiographic findings in 98 consecutive nonpenetrating chest injuries. *Dis Chest* 52:50–56.
9. Parmley LF, Manion WC, Mattingly TW. 1958. Nonpenetrating traumatic injury of the heart. *Circulation* 18:371–96.
10. Cumberland GD, Riddick L, McConnell CF. 1991. Intimal tears of the right atrium of the heart due to blunt force injuries to the abdomen. *Am J Forensic Med Path* 12:102–4.

11. Karpas A, Yen K, Sell LL, Fommelt PC. 2002. Severe blunt cardiac injury in an infant: a case of child abuse. *J Trauma* 52:759–64.
12. Rees A, Symons J, Joseph M, Lincoln C. 1975. Ventricular septal defect in a battered child. *Br Med J* 1(5948):20–21.
13. Cohle SD, Hawley DA, Berg KK, Kiesel EL, et al. 1995. Homicidal cardiac lacerations in children. *J Forensic Sci* 40:212–18.
14. Bright EF, Beck CS. 1935. Nonpenetrating wounds of the heart. A clinical and experimental study. *Am Heart J* 10:293–321.
15. Getz BS, Davies E, Steinberg SM, Beaver BL, Koenig FA. 1986. Blunt cardiac trauma resulting in right atrial rupture. *JAMA* 255:761–63.
16. Jebara VA, Acar C, Dervanian P, Farge A, et al. 1992. Traumatic ventricular septal defects. Report of 3 cases with tricuspid valve rupture in 2 cases. *J Card Surg* 33:253–55.
17. Pollak S, Stellwag-Carion C. 1991. Delayed cardiac rupture due to blunt chest trauma. *Am J Forensic Med Path* 12:13–16.
18. Stein W, Revitch E. 1942. Traumatic rupture of the right ventricle—an unusual case. *Am Heart J* 24:703–5.
19. Fulda G, Rodriguez A, Turney SZ, Cowley RA. 1990. Blunt traumatic pericardial rupture: a ten-year experience 1979 to 1989. *J Card Surg* 31:525–30.
20. Knapp JF, Sharma V, Wasserman G, Hoover CJ, et al. 1986. Ventricular septal defect following blunt chest trauma in childhood: a case report. *Ped Emerg Care* 2:242–43.
21. Viano DC, King AI, Melvin JW, Weber K. 1989. Injury biomechanics research: an essential element in the prevention of trauma. *J Biomechanics* 22:403–17.
22. Baumgartel ED. 1992. Cardiac rupture from blunt trauma with atrial septal defect. *Arch Surg* 127:347–48.
23. Fulda G, Brathwaite CEM, Rodriguez A, Turney SZ, et al. 1991. Blunt traumatic rupture of the heart and pericardium. A ten-year experience (1979–1989). *J Trauma* 31:167–73.
24. Dieter RA III, Anderson AE. 1991. Ventricular septal defect caused by nonpenetrating trauma in a 3-year old child: use of extracorporeal membrane oxygenation in preoperative stabilization. *J Tenn Med Ass* 84:492–93.
25. Golladay ES, Donahoo JS, Haller JA. 1979. Special problems of cardiac injuries in infants and children. *J Trauma* 19:526–31.
26. Merzel DI, Stirling MC, Custer JR. 1985. Massive fatal ventricular septal defect due to nonpenetrating chest trauma in a six-year-old boy: the role of early invasive monitoring in an evolving lesion. *Ped Emerg Care* 1:138–42.
27. Mozzetti MD, Devin JV, Susselman MS, Lammert GR, et al. 1990. A pediatric survivor of left ventricular rupture after blunt chest trauma. *Ann Emerg Med* 19:386–89.
28. O'Reilly RJ, Kazenelson G, Spellberg RD. 1970. Traumatic pseudoaneurysm of the left ventricle. *Am J Dis Child* 120:252–54.
29. Rosenthal A, Parisi LF, Nadas AS. Isolated interventricular septal defect due to nonpenetrating trauma. Report of a case with spontaneous healing. *New Eng J Med* 283:338–41.
30. Smith D, Walker D, Sturridge M. 1981. Traumatic left ventricular aneurysm in an 8-year-old child. *Br Heart J* 45:22–24.
31. Bodily K, Fischer RP. 1979. Aortic rupture and right ventricular rupture induced by closed chest cardiac massage. *Minn Med* 62:225–27.

32. Engleman RM, Rousou JA, Schweiger M. 1984. Traumatic ventricular septal defect following closed-chest massage: a new approach to closure. *Ann Thor Surg* 38:529–32.
33. Powner DJ, Holcombe PA, Mello LA. 1984. Cardiopulmonary resuscitation-related injuries. *Crit Care Med* 12:54–55.
34. Agdal N, Jorgensen TG. 1973. Penetrating laceration of the pericardium and myocardium and myocardial rupture following closed chest cardiac massage. *Acta Med Scan* 194(5):477–79.
35. Dowd DM, Krug S. 1996. Pediatric blunt cardiac injury: epidemiology, clinical features, and diagnosis. *J Trauma* 40:61–67.
36. Adams JE III, Davila-Roman VG, Bessey PQ, Blake DP, et al. 1996. Improved detection of cardiac contusion with cardiac troponin I. *Am Heart J* 131:308–12.
37. Helm M, Hauke J, Weiss A, Lampl I. 1999. Cardiac troponin I as a biochemical marker of myocardial injury early after trauma. *Chirurg* 70:1347–52.
38. Hirsch R, Landt Y, Porter S, Canter CE, et al. 1997. Cardiac troponin I in pediatrics: normal values and potential use in the assessment of cardiac injury. *J Pediatr* 130:872–77.
39. Swaanenburg JC, Klaase JM, DeJongste MJ, Zimmerman KW, et al. 1998. Troponin I, troponin T, CKMB-activity and CKMB-mass as markers for the detection of myocardial contusion in patients who experienced blunt trauma. *Clin Chim Acta* 272:171–81.
40. Baker AM, Craig BR, Lonergan GJ. 2003. Homicidal commotio cordis: the final blow in a battered infant. *Child Abuse Negl* 27:125–30.
41. Abrunzo TJ. 1991. Commotio cordis: the single most common cause of traumatic death in youth baseball. *Am J Dis Child* 145:1279–82.
42. Perron AD, Brady WJ, Erling BF. 2001. Commotio cordis: an underappreciated cause of sudden cardiac death in young patients: assessment and management in the ED. *Am J Emerg Med* 19:406–9.
43. Maron GJ, Link MS, Wang PJ, Estes NA III. 1999. Clinical profile of commotio cordis: an under appreciated cause of sudden death in the young during sports and other activities. *J Card Electophysiology* 10:114–20.
44. Link MS, Wang PJ, Pandian NG, Bharati S, et al. 1998. An experimental model of sudden death due to low-energy chest-wall impact (commotio cordis). *New Eng J Med* 338:1805–11.
45. Boglioli LR, Taff ML, Harleman G. 1998. Child homicide caused by commotio cordis. *Ped Card* 19:436–38.
46. Thompson S. 2005. Accidental or inflicted? *Peadiatr Ann* 34:372–81.
47. Ludwig S. 2001. Visceral manifestations of child abuse. In *Child Abuse Medical Diagnosis and Management,* eds. RM Reece and S Ludwig. Philadelphia: Lipincott, Williams and Wilkins.
48. Caniano DA, Beaver BL, Boles ET. 1986. Child abuse: an update on surgical management in 256 cases. *Ann Surg* 203:219–24.
49. Cooper A. Floyd T., Barlow B., et al. 1988. Major blunt abdominal trauma due to child abuse. *J Trauma* 28:1483–87.
50. Schmitt BD. 1987. The child with nonaccidental trauma. In *The Battered Child,* eds. ME Helfer, RS Kempe, RD Krugman, 180, 189–90. Chicago, Illinois: The University of Chicago Press.

51. Rothrock SG, Green SM, Morgan R. 2000. Abdominal trauma in infants and children: prompt identification and early management of serious and life-threatening injuries. Part 1: injury patterns and initial assessment. *Pediatr Emrg Care* 16:106–15.
52. Fossum RM, Descheneaux KA. 1991. Blunt trauma of he abdomen in children. *J Forensic Sci* 36:47–50.
53. Canty Sr TG, Cant Jr TG, Brown C. 1999. Injuries of the gastrointestinal tract from blunt abdominal trauma in children: a 12-year experience at a designated pediatric trauma center. *J Trauma* 46:234–40.
54. Ledbetter DJ, Hatch EI, Feldman KW, Flinger CL, et al. 1988. Diagnostic and surgical implications of child abuse. *Arch Surg* 123:1101–5.
55. Wood J, Rubin DM, Nance ML, Christian CW. 2005. Distinguishing inflicted versus accidental abdominal injuries in young children. *J Trauma* 59:1203–8.
56. McCort J, Vaudagna J. 1964. Visceral injuries in battered children. *Radiology* 82:424–28.
57. Gornall P, Ahmed S, Jolleys A, Cohen J. 1971. Intra-abdominal injuries in the battered baby syndrome. *Arch Dis Child* 47:221–24.
58. Trokel M, DiScala C, Terrin NC, Sege RD. 2006. Patient and injury characteristics in abusive abdominal injuries. *Pediatr Emerg Care* 22:700–704.
59. Hobbs CJ. 2005. Abdominal injury due to child abuse. *Lancet* 366(9481): 187–88.
60. Shah P, Applegate KE, Buonomo C. 1997. Stricture of the duodenum and jejunum in an abused child. *Pediatr Radiol* 27:281–83.
61. Dworkind M, McGowan G, Hyams J. 1990. Abdominal trauma—child abuse. *Pediatrics* 85:892.
62. Huntimer CM, Muret-Wagstaff S, Leland NI. 2000. Can falls on stairs result in small intestinal perforations? *Pediatrics* 106:301–5.
63. Amin A, Alexander JB, O'Malley KF, Doolin F. 1993. Blunt abdominal aortic trauma in children: case report. *J Trauma* 34:293.
64. Barnes PM, Norton CM, Dunstan FD, Kemp AM, et al. 2005. Abdominal injury due to child abuse. *Lancet* 366(9481):234–35.
65. Ng CS, Hall CM. 1998. Costrochondral junction fractures and intra-abdominal trauma in non-accidental injury (child abuse). *Pediatr Radiol* 28:671–76.
66. Karp RJ, Scholl TO, Decker E et al. 1989. Growth of abused children. Contrasted with the non-abused in an urban poor community. *Clin Pediatr* 28:317–20.
67. Skuse DH, Gill D, Reilly S, et al. 1995. Failure to thrive and the risk of child abuse: a prospective population survey. *J Med Screen* 2:145–49.
68. Eisenstein EM, Delta BG, Clifford JH. 1965. Jejunal hematoma: an unusual manifestation of the battered-child syndrome. *Clin Pediatr (Phila)* 4:436–40.
69. Sivit CJ, Taylor GA, Eichelberger MR. 1989. Visceral injury in battered children: a changing perspective. *Radiology* 173:659–61.
70. Touloukian RJ. 1969. Battered children with abdominal trauma. *GP* 40:106–9.
71. Kirks DR. 1983. Radiological evaluation of visceral injuries in the battered child syndrome. *Pediatr Ann* 12:888–93.
72. Allen RB, Curry GJ. 1957. Abdominal trauma. A study of 297 consecutive cases. *Am J Surg* 93:398–404.
73. Watkins GL. 1960. Blunt trauma to the abdomen. *Arch Surg* 80:106–9.

74. Schechner SA, Ehrlich FE. 1974. Gastric perforation and child abuse. *J Trauma* 14:723–25.
75. Franken Jr EA, Fox M, Smith JA, et al. 1978. *AJR* 130:297–99.
76. Boysen BE. 1975. Chylous ascites. Manifestation of the battered child syndrome. *Am J Dis Child* 129:1338–39.
77. Vasko JS, Tapper RI. 1967. The surgical significance of chylous ascites. *Arch Surg* 95:355–68.
78. Roche KJ, Genieser NB, Berger DK, Ambrosino MM. 1995. Traumatic abdominal pseudoaneurysm secondary to child abuse. *Pediatr Radiology* 25:S247–48.
79. Yang JW, Kuppermann N, Rosas A. 2002. Child abuse presenting as pseudorenal failure with a history of a bicycle fall. *Pediatr Emerg Care* 18:91–92.
80. Hopkins RL, Frieberg EM, Bonis SL. 1994. Traumatic asphyxia—curious cause and consequence. *Am J Emerg Med* 12:384–85.
81. DiGiacomo JC, Frankel H, Haskell RM, Rotondo MF, et al. 2000. Unsuspected child abuse revealed by delayed presentation of periportal tracking and myoglobinuria. *J Trauma* 49:348–50.
82. Patrick LE, Ball TI, Atkinson GO, Winn KJ. 1992. Pediatric blunt abdominal trauma: periportal tracking at CT. *Radiology* 183:689–91.
83. Wu JW, Chen MYM, Auringer ST. 2000. Portal venous gas: an unusual finding in child abuse. *J Emerg Med* 18:105–7.
84. Mueller GP, Cassady CI, Dietrich RB, Pais MJ, et al. 1994. Pediatric case of the day. Occult child abuse (manifesting with pneumatosis intestinalis and portal venous gas). *Radiographics* 14:928–30.
85. Van Winckel M, Robberecht E, Afschrift M, Smets, et al. 1997. Radiological case of the month. Battered child syndrome. *Arch Pediatr Adolesc Med* 151:621–22.
86. Barnes, PM, Norton, CM, Dunstan, FD, et al. 2005. Abdominal injury due to child abuse. *Lancet* 366(9481):234–35.
87. Dye DW, Peretti FJ, Kokes CP. 2008. Histologic evidence of repetitive blunt force abdominal trauma in four pediatric fatalities. *J Forensic Sci* 53:1430–33.

Child Abuse by Drowning

5

KAREN J. GRIEST

Contents

5.1 Introduction

The incidence, location, and circumstances surrounding drowning and near-drowning in children are dependent on the age of the child and the child's environment. The highest incidence of drowning from all causes in any age group occurs in 0- to 4-year-old children, and drowning is the second highest cause of unintentional death in this age group.[1–3] In 0- to 4-year-old children, the sites of drowning are predominantly bathtubs, buckets, small bodies of fresh water, and swimming pools.[1–3] Drowning during child abuse is also found in the 0- to 4-year-old group of children and occurs predominantly in bathtubs, buckets, and secluded, small bodies of fresh water (Table 5.1).[1,2,4–6] Distinguishing between accidental and non-accidental drowning in infants

Table 5.1 Characteristics of Accidental and Inflicted Drowning in Children

	Accidental Drowning	Inflicted Drowning
Age	0–4 years old	0–4 years old
Location	Bathtub, buckets, small bodies of fresh water, swimming pools	Bathtubs, buckets, secluded small bodies of fresh water
Contributing factors	Inadequate supervision Cobathing Infant bath seats Coexisting medical disorders	Other signs of child abuse

and young children can be difficult. Therefore, knowledge of the circumstance, autopsy findings, and clinical aspects of both accidental and abusive drowning are necessary to make the diagnosis of child abuse by drowning.

5.2 Overview of Drowning in Infants and Young Children

Drowning is the second most common cause of accidental deaths in children. Children from 0 to 4 years old make up 22% of all drowning deaths. The most common sites for preschool children drowning are swimming pools. Children who drown in open water are significantly older than children who drown in pools (6 years 6 months versus 4 years 6 months). Most boys drown in open water (53%), whereas most girls drown in pools (50%). For infants and toddlers, the most common sites of drowning are bathtubs and buckets, with up to 10% of bucket drownings due to child abuse. Sixty-five percent of drownings in victims aged 0 to 4 years occurs in urban rather than rural locations, such as in lakes, rivers, and irrigation ditches. Contributing factors include cardiac disease, neurological disease including epilepsy, metabolic disease including hypoglycemia, and child abuse.[1–3,6,7]

The drowning event is witnessed least often among children 0 to 4 years (28%), as compared to older age groups. Medical care (prehospital, emergency department, or hospital) is most often received in drowning victims aged 0 to 4 years (79%).[3]

Of bathtub submersion victims, all were bathing unattended or with another child less than 5 years of age. Although supervisors could be identified for 84% of 1- to 4-year-old victims, only 18% were present to witness the event.[2]

5.3 Overview of Bathtub Drowning in Young Children

Drowning in family tubs involves children exclusively under the age of 14 months, with the exception of those who are victims of non-accidental injury

Table 5.2 Characteristics of Bathtub Drownings in Children

Less than 14 months of age
Majority female
Males older than females
Contributing factors: inadequate adult supervision, cobathing, use of infant bath seats, seizure disorder

and those with medical conditions, like epilepsy.[1,2,5] Most cases involve infants aged 12 months or less (72%), and 89% are aged 2 years or less. Bathtub drowning occurs in significantly younger children when compared with other sites of drowning, with an average age of 1 year 5 months (open water, 6 years 6 months; pools, 4 years 6 months). The male drowning victim tends to be older than the female victims (mean, 23 months versus 11 months, respectively). The largest single group of bathtub drowning victims are females aged 12 months or less. Contributing factors include inadequate adult supervision (89%), cobathing (39%), the use of infant bath seats (28%), and coexistent medical disorders predisposing the infant or child to the drowning episode (17%), such as seizure disorder. In the majority of bathtub drowning cases, the child is left unsupervised by an adult for up to 20 minutes.[8] The cobathing children are usually older siblings, with an age range of 19 to 48 months, and the siblings usually survive.[8] Common caregiver activities when leaving the child unsupervised included getting a towel or diaper, answering the phone, and cooking. There were no significant differences in cases of children being left unattended in the tub based on the race or education level of the families (Table 5.2).[9]

5.4 Pathophysiology of Drowning

In order to make the determination of drowning, whether intentional or accidental, it is necessary to know the pathophysiology of drowning and the clinical signs of drowning and near-drowning.

Near-drowning is defined as submersion in a liquid in which the victim survives, at least temporarily.[10]

The main problems in drowning are caused by hypoxia.[1,5,11,12] The hemodynamic effects are similar in both seawater and fresh water. With both there is a rapid drop in cardiac output and an increase in pulmonary capillary wedge pressure, central venous pressure, and pulmonary vascular resistance. The reduction in the dynamic compliance of the lungs is the same following inspiration of fresh or salt water and is the main cause of morbidity and mortality.[1] Water osmolality has no significant effect in the near-drowned child, and very few electrolyte abnormalities occur.[1,5,11]

Table 5.3 Pathophysiology of Drowning

Hypoxia
Drop in cardiac output
Increase in pulmonary capillary wedge pressure
Increase in central venous pressure
Increase in pulmonary vascular resistance
Atelectasis
Intrapulmonary shunting
Pulmonary edema

In freshwater aspiration the pulmonary surfactant has been shown to be "washed out" to an extent sufficient to increase the surface tension properties of the gas–fluid interface of the alveolar membrane. This results in alveolar collapse and atelectasis with portions of lung being perfused but not ventilated. The net result is intrapulmonary shunting and hypoxemia. Loss of surfactant activity has been experimentally shown to be associated with lesions resulting in pulmonary edema, a common clinical finding in patients with near-drowning.[10,11]

In saltwater aspiration the surface tension properties of the lung are not significantly altered. The primary mechanism for hypoxia appears to be intrapulmonary shunting resulting from fluid-filled alveoli which are perfused but not ventilated. Pulmonary edema further contributes to the problem and is explained as the influx of fluid into the alveolus from the circulatory system due to hypertonic fluid in the airspace (Table 5.3).[10,11]

5.5 Clinical Aspects of Drowning

5.5.1 Clinical Findings in Drowning

In children under the age of 14 years (the majority under 5 years of age), the most common clinical findings on hospital admission after near-drowning were found to be a history of cardiopulmonary resuscitation (44% of cases), tachypnea (50% of cases), pulmonary edema (40%), and acidosis. One-fourth of patients were in stage 3 or 4 coma on admission to the hospital.[11] The acidosis is caused by the hypoxia.[1] Eighty-two percent of patients survived. Thirty-five percent required mechanical ventilation, of whom half died or had severe neurological sequelae (Table 5.4).[11]

Fifty percent of the drowning victims develop fevers of 101°F or greater, and spiking temperatures occur in 20%.[7]

In cases of delayed drowning deaths, the victims are unconscious but quickly resuscitated. After resuscitation, they initially have spontaneous respiration, but these patients will suddenly develop cardiac shock, tachycardia gallop rhythm, hypertension and apnea.[13,14]

Table 5.4 Clinical Presentation of Drowning

General Aspects	CPR
	Fever
	Abdominal distension
	Vomiting
	Splenic necrosis
	Renal tubular necrosis
	Death
Pulmonary Aspects	Tachypnea
	Apnea
	Pulmonary edema
	Pleural pain
	Rales and wheezes
	Stridor
	Acidosis
	Aspirated particles
	Frothy, blood-tinged sputum
	Foam in the respiratory passages
	Cyanosis
	ARDS/post immersion syndrome
	Dry drowning
Cardiovascular Aspects	Hypervolemia in freshwater drowning
	Hypovolemia in saltwater drowning
	Q-T changes and atrial fibrillation of the heart
	Tachycardia
	Hypertension
	Cardiac failure
Neurologic Aspects	Brain edema
	Laminar necrosis of cerebral and cerebellar cortex
	Cerebral anoxia
	Hyperactivity and confusion
	Convulsions
	Coma
	Survival in vegetative state or death
Laboratory Findings	Leukocytosis
	Anemia
	Hypoxia
	Hypercapnia
	Acidosis

Abdominal distention is common due to the swallowing of large amounts of fluid, and there may be delayed vomiting after drowning.[7]

Focal necrosis of the spleen and renal tubular necrosis are occasionally found in victims of delayed drowning deaths. These findings are attributed to hypoxia and pulmonary edema secondary to aspiration.[13,14]

Hemolysis and hemoglobinuria have been documented in freshwater near-drowning. The significance of the hemoglobinuria as a potential cause of acute renal failure is uncertain, because many patients with this finding also have acute tubular necrosis secondary to hypoxia.[11]

Immersion accidents in the sea have special characteristics, not specifically as a result of differences in water osmolality, but related to hypothermia, secondary lung complications, and immersion times.[5]

5.5.2 Pulmonary Aspects of Drowning

In saltwater aspiration improvement in pulmonary function appears to be more rapid than in freshwater aspiration. The reason for this may be that the regeneration of surfactant, which is depleted in freshwater near-drowning, takes almost 24 hours.[10,11]

Radiologic findings in near-drowning show varying degrees of pulmonary edema.[11] The radiologic examinations show fluffy, nodular confluent infiltrations, chiefly of the medical third of the lung fields, in 80% of cases. There may also occur sporadic homogeneous infiltrations. The lesion can vary in size from quite small isolated to quite large confluent densities.[7] From one- to two-thirds of patients have abnormal radiologic findings, which show clearing by three to five days. Most patients have radiologic abnormalities at the time of admission, and the degree of change seems to be related to the severity and course of the illness. Some patients, however, may have minimal changes initially and then become seriously ill.[11] Occasionally a patient may aspirate significant foreign particles in the water, causing lesions that may not resolve for 3 or 4 weeks.[7]

Autopsy of victims of delayed drowning deaths demonstrate hemorrhagic desquamative pneumonia. Empyema and multiple abscesses in those surviving more than a few days are often found.[13,14]

Bronchospasm is a common finding, with diffuse rales and wheezes secondary to the aspiration of fluid.[7]

Pulmonary symptoms of rapid and shallow respirations frequently are aggravated by the presence of pleural pain. There may be stridor and pharyngeal spasm. Frequently there is expectoration of a frothy, blood-tinged sputum. Cyanosis, especially of fingers and toes, is present.[7]

Adult respiratory distress syndrome (ARDS) has been reported after near-drowning and usually occurs within six hours of admission.[1] The classic postimmersion syndrome is characterized by widespread intra-alveolar polymorphonuclear leukocyte infiltrates and edema. Hyaline membranes may be present. Superimposed bronchopneumonia has a characteristic microscopic pattern that is distinct from postimmersion syndrome.[15]

In 70% of drowning cases, aspirated particles are found in the lung, 24% showed aspirated gastric contents, 60% showed aspirated vegetation, and 33% showed diatoms, algae, or flagellates in lung sections at autopsy. At autopsy, the lungs are found to contain a stiff, leathery, white or pinkish foam in the respiratory passages and there is characteristic watery emphysema of the lungs in which the organs are overexpanded and heavy, showing petechial hemorrhages in the pleura and parenchyma. On microscopic examination, there is characteristically distention of the alveoli–alveolar ducts or terminal bronchioles, and some alveolar walls appear to have been ruptured. The blood vessels are congested, and saccular dilation of alveolar capillaries is seen. Erythrocytes within the capillaries and alveoli frequently are hemolyzed in cases of either fresh- or saltwater drowning. Diatoms are the most commonly encountered aquatic microorganisms in the lungs. Occasionally, fat or marrow emboli are seen; they are thought to be agonal in nature.[13,14]

5.5.3 Dry Drowning

Aspiration is usual in drowning and near-drowning, although in approximately 10% to 20% of cases laryngeal spasm occurs and aspiration is prevented or occurs in minute amounts (dry drowning).[1,7,10,11]

5.5.4 Neurologic Aspects of Drowning

With no cerebral blood flow, the brain suffers irreparable damage. Death or severe neurological impairment occurs after submersion of more than 5 to 10 minutes.[1]

Brain examination of victims of delayed drowning deaths reveals edema with laminar necrosis of the cerebral and cerebellar cortex. Typical changes of cerebral anoxia are found in the frontal and parietal cortex, with patchy loss of neurons and spotty necrosis in the hippocampus and thalamus.[13,14]

Initial hyperactivity and confusion in drowning victims may be followed by tonic or clonic convulsions and marked depression, which may accompany the vascular collapse as the patient lapses into a coma. The development of persistent cyanosis on oxygen breathing is a sign of impending cardiovascular–central nervous system death. Muscular hypertonicity, decerebrate spasms, and rigidity may occur, indicating irreversible neural damage. Electroencephalographic changes often are indications of the extent of hypoxic injury; especially ominous is a widely spread slow wave pattern. Deep tendon reflexes are depressed or absent, depending on the extent of neural damage. Mental deterioration with involuntary spasms may increase progressively as the effects of necrosis of neural tissue increases. Survival in a vegetative and decorticate state has been reported.[7]

5.5.5 Cardiovascular Aspects of Drowning

In freshwater aspiration, large amounts of hypotonic fresh water are rapidly absorbed into the circulation around the alveoli and cause initial acute hypervolemia. Within an hour, redistribution of fluid and pulmonary edema occurs, which results in decreased circulating blood volume. Conn et al. (1995) calculated that almost 10% of body weight of water could be reabsorbed from the lungs in freshwater drowning. Aspiration of large volumes of hypertonic seawater draws fluid from the circulation to the lung by osmosis causing hypovolemia.[1,10,16] Saltwater hypovolemia may persist for as long as two days and require vigorous fluid therapy.[11]

Ventricular fibrillation is rarely reported in humans after drowning events, but frequently there is evidence of mild cardiac anoxia of the asphyxia type in which Q-T changes and atrial fibrillation are reported in both fresh- and saltwater drownings. These changes usually respond to oxygen.[7,14]

A marked tachycardia is usually present, and there is often transient hypertension. The presence of extrasystoles may herald the onset of gallop rhythm and cardiac failure. As the pulmonary disease increases in severity, with resulting marked hypoxia, greater cardiac decompensation may occur, followed by coma and death from cardiovascular collapse and respiratory failure.[7]

5.5.6 Laboratory Findings in Drowning

Examination of the blood reveals a shift to the left in the white blood cell count and a marked leukocytosis, with counts ranging from 20,000 to 30,000 cells/mL. Hemoglobin in victims drowned in fresh or salt water initially is at a normal level, but with fluid therapy a marked anemia may develop due to hemolysis. Hypoxia and hypercapnia are noted, with a decrease in the pH, depending on the amount of fluid aspirated. The severe metabolic acidosis that is present in these victims increases in severity with time if oxygen is not supplied. There is a rise in the lactic acid level in the body and a decrease in the bicarbonate level of the blood.[7]

5.5.7 Frothy Exudate, Pleural Effusion, and Lung Weight in Drowning

A retrospective review of autopsy records of child drowning, excluding bathtub drowning, of victims ranging in age from 9 months to 17 years, showed an incidence of frothy exudate, pleural effusion, and increased lung weight of 43%, 36%, and 80%, respectively. Frothy exudate was defined as a visible frothy exudate within or proximal to the major stem bronchi. Pleural effusion was defined as greater than 5 mL of fluid in any one pleural cavity. Significantly increased lung weight was defined as greater than the 95% confidence limit for age 16 years. The incidence of frothy exudate and the combination of all three factors was significantly higher in cases with no resuscitation compared with those cases with attempted resuscitation with or without delayed death. As the interval between the drowning episode and autopsy increased, the incidence of frothy exudate decreased significantly. There was no relationship between these findings and the age and sex of the decedent.[17]

In one 20-year review (18 cases), the presence of frothy exudate, pleural effusion, and increased lung weight in bathtub drowning was not significantly different from that found in nonbathtub drowning.[17]

5.5.8 Petechial Hemorrhages in Drowning

Petechial hemorrhages involving the periorbital region and the conjunctivae are thought to be uncommon in drowning. A study in children who drowned indicated that 13% had periorbital/conjunctival petechial hemorrhages. The age and gender of the victim, site of drowning, resuscitation history, and the presence of other drowning pathological findings were not significantly associated with the presence of periorbital/conjunctival petechiae. However, as the interval between the drowning episode and autopsy increased, (due to maintenance on life-support) the incidence of periorbital/conjunctival petechiae decreased (28% for <24 h; 7% for >24 h). Petechial hemorrhages involving the thoracic viscera (thymus, visceral pleura, epicardium) were found in 28%, and two victims had petechiae involving the mucosa of the oral and upper airway. The presence of periorbital and/or conjunctival petechiae was significantly associated with the presence of petechiae on the thoracic viscera.[18]

5.5.9 The Temporal Bone in Drowning

The middle ear and sinuses were examined in 50 cases of drowning in one study. The middle ear was unremarkable in 94% of cases, and there was otitis media in three cases (6%). No hemorrhage was detected in any case. All sinuses were normal without evidence of petechial hemorrhage overlying the mastoid air cells.[17]

Ito and Kimua (1990) studied the histology of the temporal bone in 23 cases of various asphyxial fatalities. In drowning, the primary finding in the temporal bone was hemorrhage in the mastoid air cells of the bilateral temporal bones.[19]

5.5.10 Organ Weights in Drowning

Nishitani et al. (2005) compared the weight ratio of the lungs and pleural effusion to the spleen in the diagnosis of drowning. The control group consisted of cases of deaths by mechanical asphyxia and cardiac deaths. In the case of males, there were significant differences in the weight of the spleen and the total weight of the lungs and pleural effusion between drowning and other causes of death; however, there was no such significant difference in females. There were significant differences in the lungs and pleural effusion/spleen weight ratio between drowning and the other causes of death for both sexes.[20]

Hadley and Fowler (2003) compared organ weights of victims of drowning, asphyxiation, and trauma. The effects of drowning compared to asphyxiation resulted in elevated mean organ weights only with the lungs and kidneys (with mean increases of 30.0% and 4.4%, respectively). Only the mean heart and brain weight remained constant across all experimental groups. A picture of drowning is suggested when elevated lung and kidney weights are the result of both asphyxiation and the aspiration of water that occurs with drowning, whereas elevated spleen and liver weights in drowning victims are associated with only the effects of asphyxiation. In addition, the common autopsy finding of a small, anemic spleen in drowning was hypothesized to be a postmortem phenomenon (Table 5.5).[21]

5.5.11 The Autopsy in Drowning

Drowning is one of the most difficult modes of death to prove at autopsy. Pulmonary edema, pleural effusion, and frothy exudate in the airways are neither sensitive nor specific for the diagnosis of drowning. The combination of all three features is seen in 12% of drowning cases.[17] Chemical tests are nonspecific and unreliable, for instance using the gravity of blood on the

Table 5.5 Other Signs That May Be Useful in the Diagnosis of Drowning

Presence of frothy exudate, pleural effusion, increased lung weight
Petechial hemorrhages in periorbital region and conjunctivae, thoracic petechiae
Mastoid air cell hemorrhage
Increased weight ratio of lung and pleural effusion to spleen
Increased weight of lungs and kidneys

right and left atrias to determine drowning or the amount of chloride on each side of the heart to determine if the drowning was in fresh or salt water or by using the presence microscopically of diatoms to determine drowning because diatoms can be found throughout the environment.[22]

Comparing river diatom populations with diatom genera found in tissues of drowning victims may indicate the site of drowning.[23]

The mean difference of blood iron concentration in the left ventricle and right ventricle of the heart was significantly higher in drowning cases compared with controls in one study. All drowning cases showed hemodilution. No overlap was found between the two groups. Resuscitation attempts seemed to have no effect on the results. Iron seems to be a good biochemical marker in freshwater drowning with a short postmortem interval.[24]

Hemolytic intimal staining of the aortic root has been documented in 5% of drowning cases at autopsy. This consists of reddened discoloration of the proximal portion of the aortic root, without any significant staining of the proximal pulmonary artery.[25]

A retrospective study of the association of drowning in children and the presence of myocarditis found 5 of 22 children (23%), aged 23 months to 13 years, had myocarditis. None of these patients had premortem symptoms of myocarditis. Subclinical myocarditis is a well-described cause of sudden unexpected death in children and adults. Both myocarditis and swimming increase the risk of arrhythmias; the combination of both may predispose an individual to sudden cardiac death.[26]

A study comparing the results of total-body multidetector computed tomography (MDCT) of drowning victims to that of controls (victims of coronary artery disease) found that MDCT was useful in diagnosing death by drowning. On MDCT, all of the drowning victims had fluid in the paranasal sinuses and ears and ground-glass opacity in the lungs; 93% had fluid in the subglottic trachea and main bronchi; 50% had sediment in the subglottic airways; 21% had frothy fluid in the airways; 89% had ground-glass opacity and thickening in the lungs; and 89% exhibited swelling of the stomach. No members of the control group had frothy fluid or sediment in the airways or sinuses; 92% had subglottic, tracheal, and bronchial fluid. All members of the control group exhibited collapsed stomachs. Airway froth and sediment on MDCT were specific to drowning, confirming the findings seen at autopsy.[27]

Finally, Zhu et al. (2003) looked at using postmortem serum markers to try to differentiate freshwater from saltwater drowning and from acute cardiac deaths. They sampled left and right cardiac blood for sodium (Na), chloride (Cl), magnesium (Mg), blood urea nitrogen (BUN), creatinine, pulmonary surfactant-associated protein A (SP-A), and cardiac troponin T (cTn-T). The most efficient markers were the left-right cardiac BUN ratio for determination of drowning (hemodilution) and the left heart blood magnesium level for differentiation between fresh- and saltwater aspiration. A characteristic feature of saltwater drowning was a low left-right BUN ratio and a marked elevation in the serum Cl, Mg, and Ca levels of the left heart blood. Serum cTn-T level was usually low in drownings, showing a difference from most cases of acute myocardial infarction/ischemia. Freshwater drowning showed a significant elevation of serum SP-A, although there was considerable overlapping with saltwater drowning and acute myocardial infarction/ischemia.[28]

5.6 Child Abuse by Drowning

There are very few medical articles that deal predominantly with drowning in child abuse, a reflection of both the difficulty in the diagnosis and the scattered occurrence of this manner of death.[15,29–33] Calculations of the incidence of drowning resulting from child abuse range from 1.2% to 10% of drowning cases.[5,8,30,34] The incidence is higher when only bathtub submersions are considered.[2,15,30]

Studies from Australia found that bathtub and bucket drownings affected infants and toddlers under the age of 12 months, and some 10% of fatal bucket–tub immersions affecting infants were the result of child abuse.[5]

In abusive bathtub submersions, where the child is less than 5 years old, 19% had other signs of child abuse. These signs of child abuse included prolonged absent supervision, delay in seeking help, the child refuses to see the parent at the hospital, and head injury.[2]

Pearn and Nixon (1977) reported two cases of non-accidental bathtub submersions of children. One was a 3-year-old girl who was left unattended in the bath for five minutes according to the mother, who was alone in the house with the child. Later the mother admitted to deliberately holding the child under the water in the bathtub but panicking when the child lost consciousness. The mother was known to child protective services because she had previously abandoned the child. The child survived with resuscitation, but had an IQ of 99 on follow-up. The second case was of a 14-month-old boy who was left unattended in the bathtub for 10 to 15 minutes with sheets that he had soiled. He was found by his father submerged under the sheets with the tap water running. The father administered mouth-to-mouth resuscitation successfully. The child was not taken to the hospital. The stepmother was reported to have been severely depressed at the time. Eight months later, the child suffered an unexplained compound fracture of the skull. The history was that he was found under his home with a brick lying nearby. His IQ on follow-up was 55. The authors believed that many cases of deliberate immersion of children were being missed because there was no associated specific physical trauma. Even with nonfatal pulmonary edema or subsequent pneumonia, the diagnosis would be difficult without a history of immersion.[33]

Griest and Zumwalt (1989) reported six cases of child abuse by drowning that demonstrated the importance of the scene investigation and a thorough autopsy with microscopic examination. The first case involved a 2½-year-old boy who was found unresponsive in his bed. His front upper body was wet. The parents were known abusers of drugs and alcohol. There was no history, but the father said the boy's head may have been submerged in water. At autopsy, there were bruises of the lips, lacerations and abrasions of the buccal mucosa, and frontal subscalpular hemorrhages. There was edema of the brain and lungs. The only significant microscopic finding was a few polymorphonuclear leukocytes in alveolar spaces.[15]

The second case was a 3-year-old girl found apparently dead on the couch in the living room. The girl's clothing was wet and her hands and feet were waterlogged. The police found a group of nude women, including the mother and grandmother, in the home conducting a religious ritual. At autopsy, there were contusions of the lips and cheeks. There were prominent petechiae on the conjunctivae, eyelids, and upper face. The brain and lungs showed edema. Microscopically, there was amorphous pale-staining foreign material in some bronchioles. The vitreous sodium was 119 mEq/L and the chloride 105 mEq/L. The grandmother admitted to conducting a religious cleansing of the devil from the child by forcing water from a soft drink container down her throat until the child became unresponsive.[15]

The third case was of a 2-year-old boy brought to the emergency department in a coma by his father. The child survived in a coma for two days. The history was that the boy had fallen from the monkey bars in the park earlier in the day, striking the back of his head, but did not lose consciousness until later that evening. At autopsy, there were several contusions of the chest, abdomen, and extremities, as well as numerous white small scars on the abdomen, back, helix of the left ear, and extremities. The brain was markedly edematous with microscopic signs of hypoxia. The lungs were moderately edematous with moderately abundant numbers of foamy macrophages in the alveoli, extensive intra-alveolar polymorphonuclear leukocyte infiltrates in all lobes, and hyaline membranes. When confronted with the autopsy finding consistent with postimmersion syndrome, the father admitted to holding the child's head under water in the bathtub until he lost consciousness. The father had a prior history of abusing his sons.[15]

The fourth case concerned a newborn infant boy found in the toilet of a private home. His 17-year-old, unwed mother was bleeding from the vagina and had fainted. At autopsy, it was determined that the infant was 34 to 35 weeks gestation, viable, and without congenital malformations or disease. A hematoma occupied approximately one third of the maternal surface of the placenta. Microscopically the lungs were mature and contained eosinophilic amorphous-appearing vegetable cell walls in bronchi, bronchioles, and alveoli consistent with the toilet paper in the water sampled from the toilet.

The lungs were edematous. The position of the infant in the toilet was not consistent with delivery into the toilet (the placenta was under the infant).[15]

The fifth case involved a 3-month-old girl whose body was recovered from a shallow grave in a rural area. The mother and her boyfriend at first claimed the child had been kidnapped but later admitted the baby had died and they buried her. At autopsy, there was edema of the lungs and brain, a healing fracture of the left eighth rib, periosteal reaction of the right humerus and left and right femora, and soft tissue swelling of the right upper arm. Microscopically, the lungs were edematous with large areas of moderately abundant intra-alveolar macrophages, intra-alveolar edema, polymorphonuclear cells in all lobes, and a few intra-alveolar giant cells. A small group of intra-alveolar vegetable cells with mild surrounding cellular reaction and several intra-alveolar vegetable spores were present. Analysis of the water from a hot spring at the last encampment site of the mother and boyfriend showed vegetable matter and spores similar to those in the child's lungs. The boyfriend had a police record in another state for attempted drowning of a child of another girlfriend in the same hot water spring.[15]

Case six was of a 9-month-old boy found unresponsive in the bathtub by his mother. He had been left in the bathtub with his 2-year-old brother for 15 minutes while his mother went to get some clothes for the children. Rescue was not called until 20 minutes later. There was a history of child abuse, including neglect and sexual abuse, in the family. At autopsy, the lungs and brain were edematous. Watery fluid was present in the small bowel. On the forehead were a few recent small abrasions associated with some subscalpular hemorrhage. Microscopically, distended alveoli alternated with partial atelectasis. The forehead injuries were acute and healing on microscopic examination. There were conflicts in the mother's story.[15]

In the six cases presented above, the age ranged from newborn to 3 years, matching the peak age for child abuse by any cause. All of the cases occurred in secluded areas, home, and rural hot springs. Three cases occurred in the bathtub, a common site of intentional drowning in infants and toddlers. There was a history of abuse or drug/alcohol use in four cases. Three of the cases had pulmonary features of postimmersion syndrome. The authors classified deliberate drowning as a form of subtle abuse, easily missed, lacking physical evidence or criteria for diagnosis (Figure 5.1).[15]

In a retrospective study of submersion in children younger than 19 years old, Gillenwater et al. (1996) found that 8% of cases were inflicted. The diagnosis of inflicted drowning was based on inconsistent histories (in 50%) and other physical findings consistent with abuse (in 69%). The other physical findings, in descending order of frequency, consisted of old and/or multiple bruises, lacerations, ocular and central nervous system injuries, burns, and scars. Fifty percent of the abuse victims had histories that were inconsistent with the developmental age of the child, varied with repetitive telling, or were

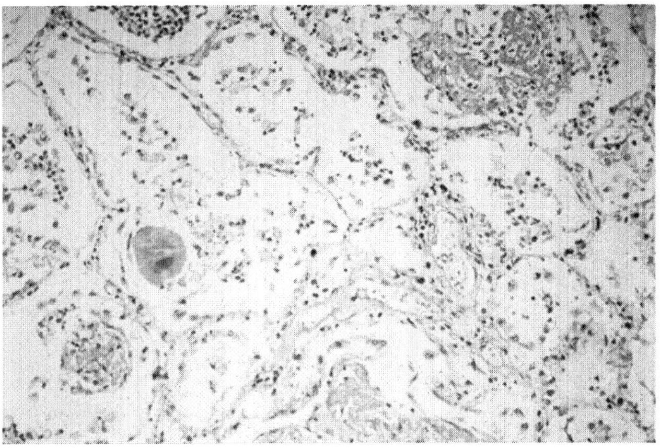

(A)

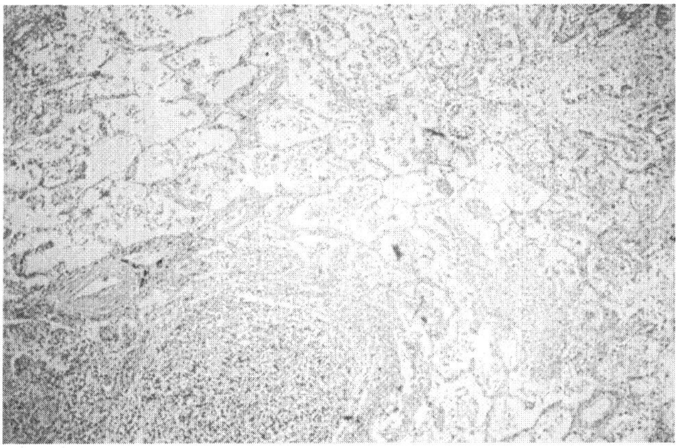

(B)

Figure 5.1 (A) Foreign body in lung, leukocyte infiltrate, microscopy. (B) Foreign body in lung, abundant leukocyte infiltration, microscopy.

inconsistent with the physical findings. Inflicted submersion victims were likely to be younger (median age, 2.1 years). There were more male victims in both inflicted and unintentional submersions. The inflicted submersion victims tended to be the youngest sibling in a large (three or more children) household. In families with only two children, two-thirds of both inflicted and unintentional submersion victims were the younger child. There were no significant differences noted in the guardian's marital status or history of previous child protective services involvement. Caretakers at the time of submersion included eight mothers, three biological fathers, and two non-biological parents. Caretaker drug and alcohol use was documented in only one of the inflicted submersions. Bathtubs were the most common site for inflicted submersions (56%), and submersions in bathtubs were frequently inflicted (26%). Both inflicted and unintentional submersions occurred with equal frequency in lakes and rivers and miscellaneous bodies of water.

Inflicted submersions in lakes and rivers, as well as pools, involved younger victims than did unintentional submersions. However, the mean age of the unintentional submersion group was skewed upward by the large number of adolescent submersions in the area's lakes and rivers. The identity of the victim's caretaker, the premorbid activity of the child, and whether the submersion event was witnessed by the child's caretaker did not differ between the inflicted and unintentional groups. The child's supervisor reported not witnessing the submersion event in 96% of unintentional and 89% of inflicted submersions. Compared with unintentional submersion victims, children who were inflicted submersion victims were less likely to be revived by bystanders and were more likely to die. The identity of the person performing resuscitation did not differ between the two groups. Inflicted submersion victims were more likely to receive nonstandard cardiopulmonary resuscitation than were unintentional submersion victims. There was no statistically significant difference in the reported total submersion duration or resuscitation duration; victims of inflicted submersions were more likely to die than were those of unintentional submersions. The poorer outcome of inflicted submersion victims suggests an increased severity of the submersion, a delay in resuscitation, and/or an inappropriate attempt at resuscitation. Submersion duration greater than 5 minutes has been associated with increased mortality. The small sample size of the inflicted submersion population might also mask a significant difference. A delay in seeking care has long been noted as a significant indicator of abuse. The historical accounts of the submersion event collected by multiple professions at the initial presentation proved invaluable in defining the abuse population. These accounts either changed over time or were inconsistent with the child's stage of development or extent of injury. The authors concluded that bathtub submersion victims and children with physical and historical findings common to other forms of abuse are most likely to be the victims of inflicted submersion. Several characteristics may help make the diagnosis of inflicted submersion. These include bathtub submersions, failed resuscitation, and a victim who is the youngest child in a large household. Unexplained physical injuries and developmentally implausible or changing histories remain the cornerstones of the recognition of inflicted submersion.[30]

Lavelle et al. (1995) performed a chart review study that looked at risk factors associated with bathtub submersion injury and their relationship with child abuse. Bathtub near-drownings accounted for 24% of near-drowning patients in the 10-year study period. The ages of the patients ranged from 4 months to 6 years; 75% were less than 24 months old and 48% were in the first year of life. More than half were boys. Following the event, approximately half died or remained in a vegetative state. Ninety-five percent of the events occurred in the child's home, with the mother as the supervisor (52%). The father or other male friend was the supervisor in only 14% of cases. Age of the caretaker was documented in only half of the cases; 58% were less than 19 years old. All children were left unattended for a brief period (80% for less than 5 minutes). In 28% of cases, there was more than one child in the tub; however, all were less than 4 years old. These events occurred at various times of day between 8 a.m. and 11 p.m. A significant number of these children had indicators for child abuse. Incompatible histories (37%) or multiple stories for the event (26%) were not uncommon. In 38% of cases, there were other physical findings indicative of abuse, including severe physical neglect, bruising, fractures, and retinal hemorrhages. A previous child abuse report had been filed for 25% of the patients. This study documented a 29% incidence of documented physical evidence or admitted intent of child abuse in bathtub near-drownings. Factors speculated to be associated with bathtub drownings such as age of the child, time of day, age and sex of the caretaker, isolated or single parent, and presence of other children in the bathtub were not good indicators in this series.[31]

Kemp et al. (1994) looked at accidental and child abuse in bathtub submersions during a 2-year period. Ten cases (six drownings and four near-drownings) had stories suggestive of abuse, with inconsistent histories, previous histories of abuse, late presentation for medical care, and inappropriate childcare giver such as a very young babysitter. The ratio of male to female victims was 8:7. All submersion incidents, accidental and abuse, occurred in the family home, and all the children were the youngest in the family. In six cases of drowning (14% of total cases) there was a diagnosis of unlawful killing or homicide. The ages of the children were 5 months to 32 months. The perpetrator was the mother in five cases and the father in one case. In four submersion cases, there were features highly suggestive of child abuse, including inconsistent descriptions of the event, history of prolonged unsupervised period in the bath (up to an hour), previous death of a sibling, subsequent fracture or death. The majority of accidental bathtub submersion victims were aged between 8 and 15 months of age, probably related to the motor developmental stage of the child. The child was able to sit but had difficulty righting him or herself. Most of the non-accidental submersion children were outside or at the limits of the age span for typical accidental bathtub immersions. There are often no positive physical findings in this type of child abuse; it is therefore helpful to identify features in the history that suggest non-accidental bath submersion. This diagnosis should be considered in the differential diagnosis of bathtub immersions without a typical accident description and in children outside the age range of 8 to 24 months in the absence of epilepsy or developmental delay. In six of the fatal cases there was an association with maternal mental illness.[32]

In a literature review of bathtub drownings including abusive drowning and neglect, Alpert (2003) suggested that the same principles used to evaluate other forms of physical abuse or neglect should be applied to bathtub submersion injuries. As with many of the other authors of abusive drownings, Alpert suggests that certain histories should raise concerns for the possibility of abuse: (1) a history of trauma that is inconsistent with an injury revealed by physical examination, imaging, or laboratory studies; (2) a history of minor or no trauma in a child with extensive injury; (3) a history that changes over time; (4) a history of self-inflicted trauma that is incompatible with the child's development; (5) the caregiver that blames a young sibling or playmate for serious injuries to a child; (6) delay in seeking medical treatment. Child victims of submersion of five minutes or less have a greater than 90% probability of survival with minimal or no brain damage. A history of a brief submersion in a child who dies or is profoundly injured by submersion should raise the question of abuse. Also, unexplained pulmonary infiltrates and respiratory distress might be an indicator of near-drowning (Table 5.6).[29]

5.7 The Investigation in Drowning

The difference between survival or death of a child after being pulled from the water may be as little as 30 seconds. There is a higher rate of immersion survival in girls, probably due to a social phenomenon whereby a missing girl toddler is sought by concerned parents one or two minutes earlier than a boy of the same age. There is also a difference in survival rate depending on the site of immersion. Saltwater immersions have a survival rate of 70% versus freshwater with a survival rate of 50%. Saltwater immersion accidents are more survivable because it takes much longer for a wandering toddler to traverse a dune strip and reach the sea before a search is started, and therefore the child is discovered in the water earlier. In contrast, most freshwater incidents involve tubs or backyard pools which are on average not farther than 3 meters from the center of the home.[5] Pearn (1992) found that the best prognostic indicator of survival was the "time to first gasp." If time to first gasp is 1 to 5 minutes, the percentage of deaths is zero. At 5 to 15 minutes, it is 1% to 5%, and if 15 to 30 minutes, it is 5% to 30%. At 60 or more minutes, the percentage of deaths becomes 60% to 100%.[5]

Inflicted immersion can be a difficult diagnosis. It not only must be distinguished from accidental drowning in children, but must be distinguished from other accidents and sudden infant death syndrome (SIDS). In a review of 170 SIDS autopsies performed over a 4-year period, eight cases (4.7%) had findings suggestive of accidental or homicidal death. Only one of those eight cases had a history suggestive of a diagnosis other than SIDS. That case was asphyxia by overlying. One other case of asphyxia, by drowning in the bathtub, had no history at the time of autopsy. After autopsy, five other cases were

Table 5.6 Reports of Child Abuse by Drowning

Author(s)	Major Findings
Pearn and Nixon (1977)	2 cases of bathtub drownings
	Aged 14 and 36 mos
	Initial false history, one case
	Known to CPS, one case
	Severe depression in stepmother, one case
	Subsequent skull fracture, one case
Griest and Zumwalt (1989)	6 cases
	Aged 2½ yrs, 3 yrs, 2 yrs, newborn, 3 mo, 9 mo
	Initial false history, 3 cases
	No history, 3 cases
	Other signs of trauma, 4 cases
	Wet body or clothing, 2 cases
	Foreign bodies in lungs, 3 cases
	Postimmersion syndrome, 3 cases
	Prior history of abuse, 2 cases
	Locations: bathtub, toilet, secluded hot spring, home
	Drug or alcohol use, 4 cases
Gillenwater et al. (1996)	8% of drowning cases were inflicted
	Inconsistent history (50%)
	Other physical signs of abuse (69%)
	Mean age 2.1 yrs
	Youngest sibling
	Drug and alcohol use, 1 case only
	Location: bathtub (56%), lakes, rivers, pools, misc.
	Less likely to receive CPR or to have failed CPR
	More likely to die
Lavelle et al. (1995)	Study of bathtub drownings
	Aged, 75% less than 24 mos
	Half died or remained in vegetative state
	95% occurred in the home
	Age of caretaker < 19 yrs in 58%
	All left unattended for a brief period
	Cobathing in 28%
	Incompatible histories 37%, multiple histories 26%
	Other signs of abusive physical injury, 38%
	Previous child abuse report in 25%
	Physical evidence or admitted abuse in 29%
Kemp et al. (1994)	Study of bathtub drownings
	10 cases (4 near-drownings)
	Outside accidental age range of 8 to 24 mos
	Inconsistent histories

Table 5.6 Reports of Child Abuse by Drowning (Continued)

Author(s)	Major Findings
	Previous history of abuse
	Previous death of another child, subsequent fracture
	Delayed medical care
	Inappropriate caregiver (young)
	Youngest child in family
	Occurred in home
	Maternal mental illness, 6 cases
Alpert (2003)	Study of bathtub drownings
	Inconsistent history
	Changing history
	Delay in medical care

considered to be due to child abuse or neglect. Since asphyxia in infants, like a number of other subtle causes of death, has few physical signs at and prior to autopsy, a thorough investigation is needed to help determine the cause of death. The investigation should begin before the autopsy so that the autopsy can be tailored to the possible cause of death, for example, myocarditis or child abuse.[35]

A 9-year review of birth/infant death files in the United States indicated that the leading cause of death during that period was homicide, suffocation, motor vehicle crashes, and choking (inhalation of food or objects). The rates of death from drowning were highest among infants born to mothers who had received no prenatal care, and among Native Americans. Other factors included maternal age <20 years, one or more previous live births, and single marital status.[36]

In a study of women who killed their children, the most frequent causes of filicide were head trauma, strangulation, suffocation, and drowning. The mean age was 3.5 years for the victim and 29.5 years for the women. There were four drowning cases. The ages of those cases were 2 months, 15 months, 20 months, and 8 years. All were girls. Two were poisoned in addition to being drowned. The sites of drowning were the bathroom and the bedroom. One child was drowned in a bowl. Two of the girls were moved to their beds after the drowning. The majority of women were married or lived with their partners. They often had an occupation. Disturbing behavior was documented in 15 of 17 perpetrators. Four perpetrators were known to have psychiatric diagnoses or symptomatology. Eight women suffered from depression thought to have been triggered by marital problems and separation, financial problems, or unknown causes. Seven women tried to commit suicide. It was often possible to identify apparent motivation for the action. Some women killed their children believing that it was better to kill them than to allow them to grow up and face constant failure, as the mothers believed they were destined to. Marital misunderstanding and financial problems were also cited as reasons. There were two types of killer mothers. The first group was made up of five mothers. These mothers killed their children in a general context of abused children and presented similarities with the neonaticide mothers. They were young and immature. They came from poor economic backgrounds. None attempted suicide. The children were below the age of 2 years. The mother only killed one child, there was no premeditation, and generally they had made no plans for the birth or care of the child. There was a generally abusive environment. There were some indications of previous maltreatment in some of the children. The other group of filicide mothers were generally older (average age 32), married, and employed. The crime was usually premeditated, committed with the direct use of hands, and sometimes very violent. They killed all the siblings. For the second group, there were altruistic filicides (eight cases) and spouse revenge filicides (two cases). Few of the mothers suffered from real psychiatric problems; however, most of them had troubling behaviors. A lot of women showed signs of suicidal tendencies prior to the event, displaying aggressive and anger behavior. In general, suicide attempts tended to prevail. These offenders acted out of an acute sensitivity to social regulation. A variety of psychosocial stressors appeared to have been a major factor. These stressors included lack of social or marital support, economic difficulties, family stress, and unrealistic expectations of motherhood. The precipitating stress may have been a dispute.[37]

In all drowning deaths in toddlers and preambulatory children, 3 to 24 months, more males are involved than females. Locations of submersion include swimming pools, baths, waterways, buckets, bins, sinks, and ponds. Drowning most often occurs in infants left in bathtubs, in toddlers who have over-balanced into heavy buckets containing water, and in children of all ages who have fallen into swimming pools or other bodies of water. Bathtub victims are younger, with an average age of 8.7 months. The peak ages of drownings are less than 4 years and between 15 and 19 years. Bathtub drownings raise the possibility of nonaccidental injury. It is possible for the child to be held under water with no evidence of bruising or trauma discernable at autopsy. Thus the autopsy assessment of a possible drowning case requires a detailed account of the events leading up to death, including a death scene examination.[38]

The depth of water in bathtub drowning had a median of 8 inches and a range of 2 to 14 inches in two review studies.[39,40]

Because so many infant drownings occur in the home, often the only witness is the parent or childcare provider. The lack of independent corroboration of the details surrounding these drowning deaths, and the nonspecificity of autopsy findings, may make exclusion of inflicted injury difficult.[38]

It is also possible that an infant could have succumbed to another form of inflicted injury such as poisoning, where there are no external findings, and then placed underwater after death to simulate drowning. For this reason, full autopsies are required in all cases, with toxicologic and radiologic screening. Laboratory studies are not reliable.[38]

The role of siblings or older children in the fatal episode is also difficult to ascertain. Rough play or deliberate attempts to hold an infant under water could easily result in an unobserved drowning episode.[38]

In cases where there is a history of a toddler being found head down in a bucket, the autopsy examination should include measurements of both the infant and the bucket. The types of buckets associated with these types of accidental drownings are usually heavy industrial buckets ranging in height from 34 to 38 cm. Toddlers who have been reported drowned in such circumstances have been between 9 to 16 months with heights of 67 to 79 cm.[42] Examination of the bucket should also be undertaken, because this may reveal additional exacerbating factors, for example, sand added to increase stability of the bucket, which was being used to provide water for the family dog (Table 5.7; Figure 5.2).[38]

The human body weighs slightly more than fresh water. Consequently, when individuals become unconscious, they sink. Generally, a drowning victim will reach the bottom of a body of water in spite of the depth unless it meets some obstruction on the way down. Almost without exception, a corpse lying on the bottom of a lake or river eventually will surface because of the gas formation in the tissues as a result of decay and the action of internal bacteria. This results in reduced specific gravity of the body so that it rises.[41]

Table 5.7 The Investigation in Drownings

Time from submersion to discovery
History, consistent with circumstances and developmental age of child
Witness statements
Age of child
Age of siblings
Location of drowning, bathtub, bucket, other body of water
Death scene examination/reconstruction
Depth of water
Signs of neglect
Signs of acute or past trauma
Prenatal care
Maternal age
Caregiver mental history
History of caregiver drug/alcohol use
History of family/social stressors
Full autopsy, with toxicology, radiographs, microscopic examination
Ancillary tests for drowning

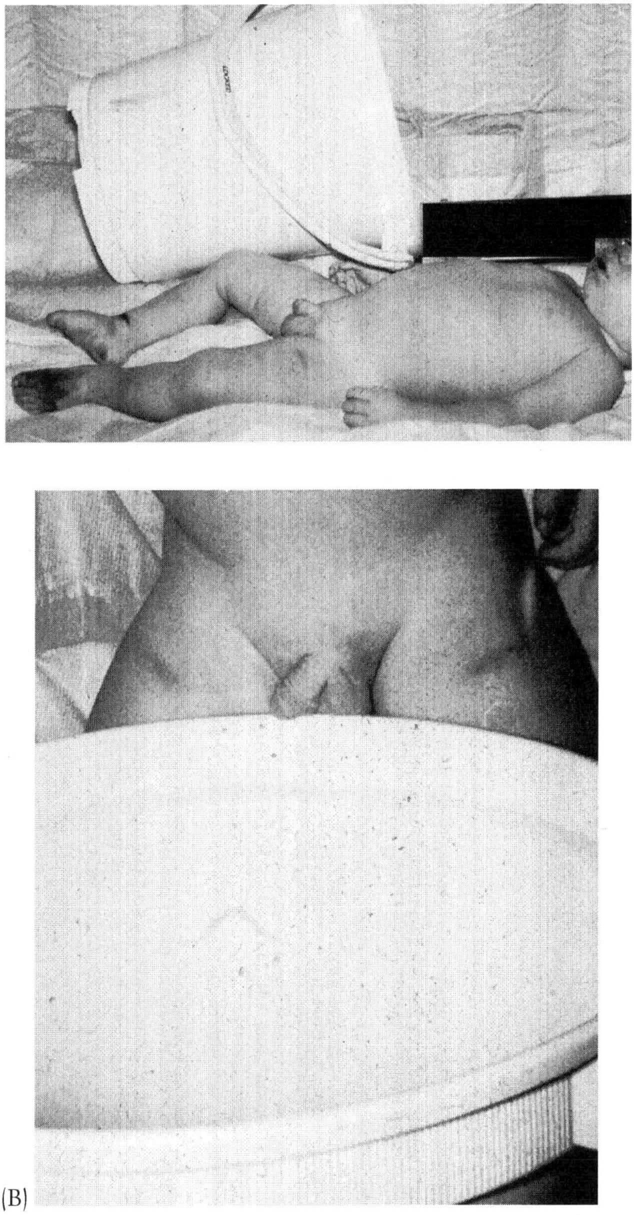

(A)

(B)

Figure 5.2 (A) Bucket drowning, comparison of bucket height with height of marks on child's legs and height of child. (B) Comparison of marks on child's anterior thighs with rim of bucket in bucket drowning.

Rivers differ from other bodies of water in two ways: They are shallow and have currents. In extremely heavy currents, the victim's body may roll on the bottom for a considerable distance. But usually the body is found near the site of submersion. After the body floats to the surface, it may drift in the current before washing ashore or coming to rest in a back eddy.[41]

Investigators should look carefully around the victim's head, face, and mouth for any signs of vomitus. Vomitus is transient and easily washed away. Vomit is a reliable indicator that the victim became submerged while alive. Foam may exude from the nose or mouth of victims of wet drownings. This froth results from a mix of mucous, air, and water during respiration. It indicates that the person became immersed while still breathing, although authorities do not consider it conclusive evidence that the individual drowned. Some blood resulting from the tearing of lung tissue by forceful breathing just prior to unconsciousness may exist with it. Decomposition can destroy the foam. This froth is similar to foam often found on individuals who have died form acute heart failure or a drug overdose, both of which result in pulmonary edema. Transient in nature, this frothy foam easily can wash away during recovery operations. It can sometimes continue to ooze from the nose and mouth for a period of time after recovery. In other cases, no visible signs of it may exist, even in confirmed drownings (Figure 5.3).[41]

Typically lividity, when present, is most evident in the head or neck, because in drowning the body normally assumes a position of head down, buttocks up, and extremities dangling downward. Blood pooling not conforming to these patterns should alert authorities to investigate further to determine if death preceded immersion.[41]

The skin on the hands and feet of a body will have a wrinkled "washerwoman" appearance if immersed for more than 1 or 2 hours. This is called maceration and does not indicate that the deceased has drowned, because it will develop whether the individual was alive or dead when entering the water. After prolonged immersion, the outer layer of skin may become completely separated from the feet and hands and comes off in a glove or sock fashion.[41]

Rigor mortis, or postmortem rigidity, usually begins to develop within 2 hours, becoming fully established in 6 to 12. Once fully established, it remains for a variable period of time and then gradually diminishes (24 to 38 hours after death). Both the onset and disappearance of rigor mortis will vary depending on water temperature. Cold water will retard the process. It may be poorly formed in infants. Cutis anserine, or goose flesh, is a spasm of the erector pilae muscles due to rigor mortis. It does not indicate whether the person was alive or dead when entering the water.[41]

Putrefaction refers to the decomposition of the body because of bacteria and fermentation. Although this process can take longer in water-submerged victims, these individuals may remain concealed longer when they become

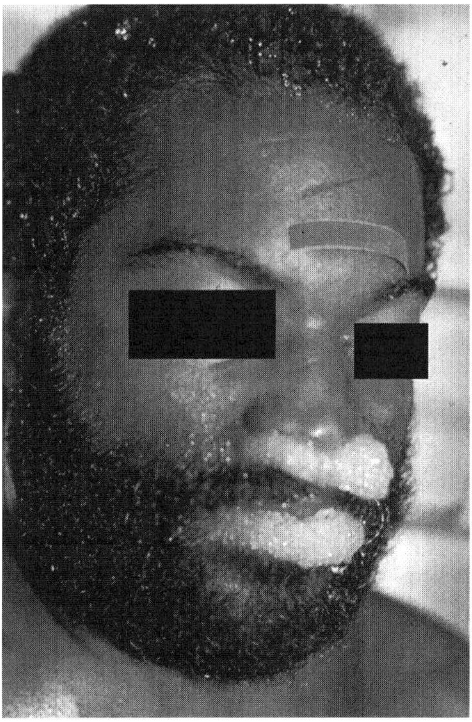

Figure 5.3 Foam and blood at nose and mouth of river drowning victim. Note linear abrasions on forehead and nose due to dragging of body along bottom of river.

hidden in water or vegetation or lost in a large body of water; this results in advanced postmortem changes before recovery. No time schedule for this stage of decomposition exists because differing water and climatic conditions will have a profound effect. Generally, cold and swiftly moving water preserves bodies, whereas heavy clothing and stagnant, warm water hasten decomposition. Advanced stages of putrefaction can lead to mummification of the skin, especially if the body refloats, becomes exposed to the drying effects of air, and remains hidden for a long time.[41]

Corpses normally exhibit a relaxed, often prone, semifetal position when discovered by divers on the bottom of a body of water. They assume this posture because of the buoyant properties of water and the buoyancy of the lungs, which lie nearer the back than the front. In this posture, the arms and legs usually are slightly bent at the elbows and knees. The head tilts slightly forward, and the spine curves slightly. Any person who has died on land and remained in a terrestrial environment during the onset of rigor mortis will display a different posture. The head likely will be rotated to one side, a position never found in a drowning victim.[41]

Sometimes investigators may find objects in the hands of victims, such a grass from an embankment. If the drowning occurred in relatively shallow water, soil or gravel commonly found on the bottom may be clutched in the hands, indicating that the individual probably entered the water while conscious.[41]

Immersion of a body in water for several hours may cause leaching of blood from injuries such as propeller cuts, lacerations, and stab wounds. Thus an individual may have a number of what appear to be bloodless postmortem injuries, which actually are antemortem or agonal and the cause of the person's demise. Legitimate postmortem injuries can occur to a body in water, especially around the head, face, knees, tops of the feet, and backs of the hands, although investigators should take care not to confuse these with defense wounds. A corpse that floats to the surface after partially decomposing is subject to currents that can repeatedly drag it across rocks and obstructions in a very strong current; the body can travel far underwater, also causing these postmortem injuries. Marine life can cause postmortem damage to a body. It is not unusual for the lips, ears, and nose to be at least partially eaten away.[41]

References

1. Fenner, P. 2000. Drowning awareness: prevention and treatment. *Aust Fam Physician* 29(11):1045–49.
2. Quan L, Gore EJ, Wentz K, Allen J, Novack AH. 1989. Ten-year study of pediatric drownings and near-drownings in King County, Washington: lessons in injury prevention. *Pediatrics* 83(6):1035–40.
3. Quan L, Cummings P. 2003. Characteristics of drowning by different age groups. *Inj Prev* 9(2):163–68.
4. Brenner RA, Trumble AC, Smith GS, Dessler EP, et al. 1995. Where children drown, United States 1995. *Pediatrics* 108:85–89.
5. Pearn J. 1992. Medical aspects of drowning in children. *Ann Acad Med Singapore* 21(3):433–35.
6. Somers, GR, Chiasson DA, Smith CR. 2005. Pediatric drowning: a 20-year-review of autopsied cases: I. demographic features. *Am J Forensic Med Path* 26(4):316–19.
7. Giammona ST. 1971. Drowning: pathophysiology and management. *Curr Probl Pediatr* 1(7):1–33.
8. Somers GR, Chiasson DA, Smith CR. 2006. Pediatric drowning: a 20-year review of autopsied cases: III. bathtub drownings. *Am J Forensic Med Path* 27(2):113–16.
9. Simon HK, Tamua T, Colton K. 2003. Reported level of supervision of young children while in the bathtub. *Ambulatory Pediatrics* 3:106–8.
10. Battaglia JD, Lockhart CH. 1977. Drowning and near-drowning. *Pediatr Ann* 6(4):270–75.
11. Fandel I, Bancalari E. 1976. Near-drowning in children: clinical aspects. *Pediatrics* 58(4):573–79.

12. Model JH. 1971. *Pathophysiology and Treatment of Drowning and Near Drowning.* Springfield, IL: Charles C. Thomas.
13. Fuller RH. 1963. The clinical pathology of human near-drowning. *Proc Roy Soc Med* 56:33
14. Swann HG, Brucer M, Moore C, Vezien BL. 1946–1947. Fresh water and sea water drowning: A study of the terminal cardiac and biochemical events during rapid anoxic death. *Texas Rep Biol Med* 6–7:604.
15. Griest KJ, Zumwalt RE. 1989. Child abuse by drowning. *Pediatrics* 83(1):41–46.
16. Conn AW, Miyasaka K, Katayama M, et al. 1995. A canine study of child water drowning in fresh versus salt water. *Crit Care Med* 23(12):2029–37.
17. Somers GR, Chiasson DA, Smith CR. 2006. Pediatric drowning: a 20-year review of autopsied cases: II. pathologic features. *Am J Forensic Med Path* 27(1): 20–24.
18. Somers GR, Chiasson DA, Taylor GP. 2006. Presence of periorbital and conjunctival petechial hemorrhages in accidental pediatric drowning. *Forensic Sci Int* 175:198–201.
19. Ito Y, Kimua H. 1990. Histological examination of the temporal bone in medicolegal cases of asphyxia. *Forensic Sci Int* 44:135–42.
20. Nishitani Y, Fujii K, Okazaki S, Imabayashi K, et al. 2005. Weight ratio of the lungs and pleural effusion to the spleen in the diagnosis of drowning. *Leg Med* 8:22–27.
21. Hadley JA, Fowler DR. 2003. Erratum to "Organ weight effects of drowning and asphyxiation on the lungs, liver, brain, heart, kidneys, and spleen." *Forensic Sci Int* 137:239–46.
22. Forged N. 1983. Diatoms and drowning—once more. *Forensic Sci Int* 21:153–59.
23. Ludes B, Coste M, Traqui A, Mangin P. 1996. Continuous river monitoring of the diatoms in the diagnosis of drowning. *J Forensic Sci* 41(3):425–28.
24. De la Grandmaison GL, Leterreux M, Lasseuquette K, Alvarez JC, et al. 2005. Study of the diagnostic value of iron in fresh water drowning. *Forensic Sci Int* 157(2–3):117–20.
25. Tsokos M, Cains G, Byard RW. 2008. Hemolytic staining of the intima of the aortic root in freshwater drowning. *Am J Forensic Med Path* 29(2):128–29.
26. Somers GR, Smith CR, Wilson GJ, Zielenska M, et al. 2005. Association of drowning and myocarditis in a pediatric population. *Arch Pathol Lab Med* 129:205–9.
27. Levy AD, Harcke HT, Getz JM, Mallak CT, et al. 2007. Virtual autopsy: two- and three-dimensional multidetector CT findings in drowning with autopsy comparison. *Radiology* 243:662–68.
28. Zhu BL, Ishida K, Taniguchi M, Quan L, et al. 2003. Possible postmortem serum markers for differentiation between fresh-, saltwater drowning and acute cardiac death: a preliminary investigation. *Leg Med (Tokyo)* 5(Suppl 1):298–301.
29. Alpert B. 2003. Bathtub drowning: unintentional, neglect, or abuse. *Med Health R I* 86(12):385–86.
30. Gillenwater JM, Quan L, Feldman KW. 1996. Inflicted submersion in childhood. *Arch Pediatr Adolesc Med* 150:298–303.

31. Lavelle JM, Shaw KN, Seidi T, Ludwig S. 1995. Ten-year review of pediatric bathtub near-drownings: evaluation for child abuse. *Ann Emerg Med* 25:344–48.
32. Kemp AM, Mott AM, Sibert JR. 1994. Accidents and child abuse in bathtub submersions. *Arch Dis Child* 70:435–38.
33. Pearn J, Nixon J. 1977. Attempted drowning as a form of non-accidental injury. *Aust Paediat J* 13(2):110–13.
34. Collins KA, Nichols CA. 1999. A decade of pediatric homicide: a retrospective study at the Medical University of South Carolina. *Am J Forensic Med Pathol* 20(2):169–72.
35. Perrot LJ, Nawojczyk S. 1988. Nonnatural death masquerading as SIDS (Sudden Infant Death Syndrome). *Am J Forensic Med Path* 9(2):105–11.
36. Brenner RA, Overpeck MD, Trumble AC, DerSimonian R, et al. 1999. *Pediatrics* 103(5):968–74.
37. Rougé-Maillart C, Jousset N, Gaudin A, Bouju B, et al. 2005. Women who kill their children. *Am J Forensic Med Path* 26(4):320–26.
38. Byard RW, Lipsett J. 1999. Drowning deaths in toddlers and perambulatory children in South Australia. *Am J Forensic Med Path* 20(4):328–32.
39. Pearn J, Nixon J. 1977. Bathtub immersion accidents involving children. *Med J Aust* 64:211–13.
40. Schmidt P, Madea B. 1995. Death in the bathtub involving children. *Forensic Sci Int* 72:147–55.
41. Haupt G. 2006. Drowning investigations. *FBI Law Enforcement Bulletin* Feb 1, 2006.
42. Jumbelic MI, Chambliss M. 1990. Accidental toddler drowning in 5 gallon buckets. *JAMA* 263:1952–53.

Supporting Evidence in Physical Child Abuse

6

KAREN J. GRIEST

Contents

Table 6.1 Supporting Evidence of Physical Child Abuse

Bruises and other cutaneous injuries
Alopecia and scalp hemorrhages
Bite marks
Orofacial injuries
Burns
Fractures

6.1 Introduction

Many of the more subtle forms of child abuse leading to death are associated with, and diagnosed due to, classical child abuse injuries, i.e., bruises, fractures, etc. (Table 6.1).[1,2]

6.2 Cutaneous Injuries in Children

6.2.1 Definitions and Differential Diagnosis

Cutaneous injuries are the most recognizable and common form of physical abuse. A bruise, or ecchymosis, or a contusion, is usually the result of blunt trauma or a squeezing that crushes the tissues and ruptures blood vessels but does not break the skin. Abrasion is scraping and removal of the superficial layers of the skin, usually limited to the epidermis, and usually caused by a tangential frictional force. Scratches are narrow and linear abrasions caused by a sharp edge, fingernail, or claw.[3]

It is important to distinguish abusive skin injuries from lesions due to other causes. The differential diagnosis includes false bruises, systemic diseases, dermatologic problems, congenital lesions, ethnic home remedies, drug-induced bruises, everyday play activities, and accidents (Figure 6.1; Table 6.2).[3]

6.2.2 Abusive versus Normal Cutaneous Injuries

Studies of cutaneous injuries in normal children reveal that:

- Bruising is the most common injury.
- Babies without independent mobility have fewer injuries compared to older mobile children. Babies do not have more injuries in warmer seasons. They rarely have bruises. Their most frequent injuries are self-inflicted fingernail scratches on their faces.

Table 6.2 Differential Diagnosis of Skin Injuries
False bruises
Systemic diseases
Dermatologic lesions
Congenital lesions
Ethnic home remedies
Drug-induced bruises
Everyday activities
Accidents
Abuse

- In children older than nine months, injuries are more frequent in warmer seasons. The prevalence of abrasions and scratches is higher at this age group, but bruises remain the most common injuries.
- Bruises caused by everyday activities are usually small, less the 15 mm in diameter.
- The mean number of injuries in children increases with age until adolescence, when it decreases.
- There is no difference in injury patterns between boys and girls in most studies.
- The location of cutaneous injuries in walking children varies with age. Despite some slight differences between the studies, location can be roughly divided into three categories according to their frequency. The shins and knees are the most common sites. Relatively common sites are the forehead, the upper arms, the forearms, the elbows, the lumbar spine, the anterior thighs, the hands, and the feet. Uncommon sites are the lower face, the ears, the neck, the chest, the abdomen and pelvis, the buttocks, the genitalia, and the posterior legs.[3–14]

A systematic review of the literature by Maguire et al. (2005) examined bruises in normal children versus abused children. The main findings in the studies on abused children were:

- Bruises on babies who are not independently mobile are suggestive of abuse.
- Numerous bruises are suggestive of abuse. The mean number of bruises varied from 5.7 to 10 in the abuse populations studied, a much higher figure than in the control groups, who had an average of 1.5 bruises.
- The measured lengths of bruises were greater in abused children than in the control groups.

(A)

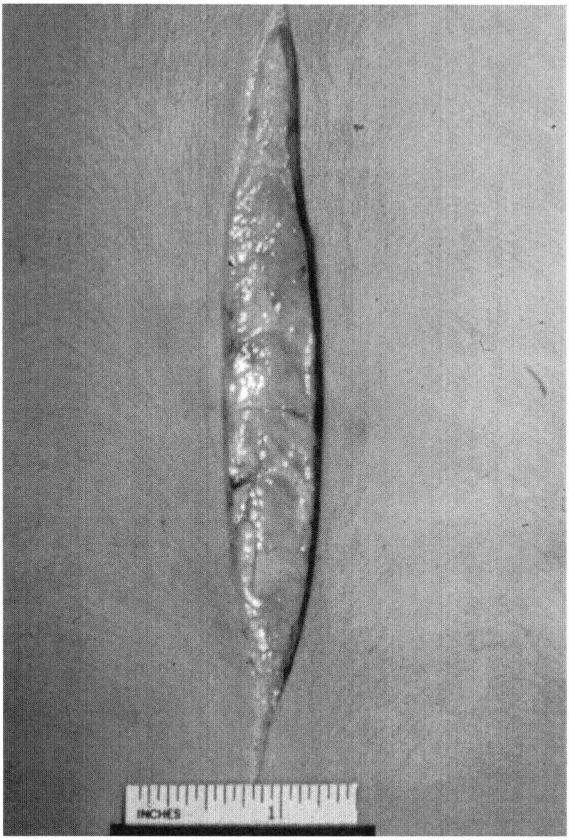

Figure 6.1 (A and B) Autopsy incision into a skin lesion can distinguish bruises from benign lesions. (A) Shows a benign lesion.

- All studies that addressed the distribution of bruises in abused children confirmed that the head was the most common site.
- Other sites that were significantly more affected in abused children were the neck, the trunk, the back, the buttocks, the abdomen, and the hands.
- In contrast to nonabused children, bruises were often seen on soft parts of the body, away from bony prominences.
- Another common feature in abused children was clustering of bruises, such as defensive injuries on the forearms or bruises on the trunk and the adjacent extremities. Bruises often carried the imprint of the implement used. For example, the typical linear parallel petechial marks of a slap and the railroad track bruising due to being hit by a rod (Table 6.3).[3,15]

(B) 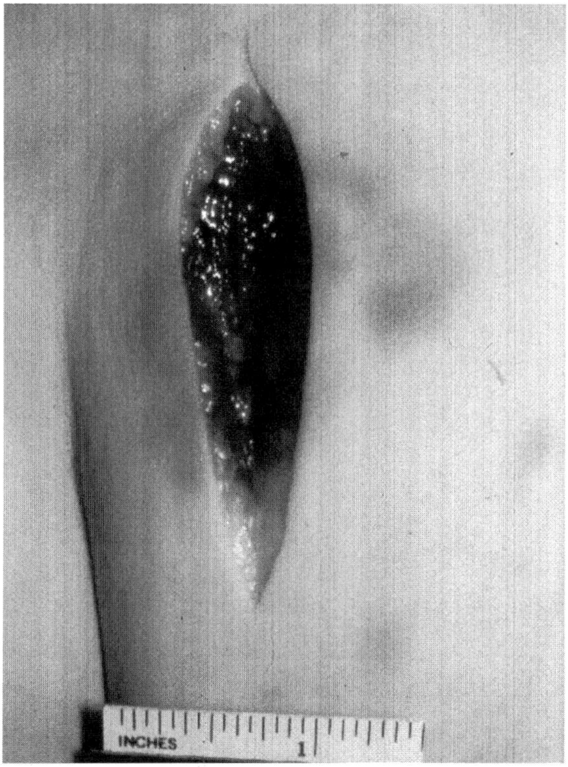

Figure 6.1 (Continued.) (B) Shows a bruise with hemorrhage into the subcutaneous tissue. Note cluster of bruises in (B).

Table 6.3 Abusive Versus Normal Cutaneous Injuries

	Abusive	Normal
Most common injury	Bruises	Bruises
Age	Less than 3 yrs	More numerous in mobile children
Season	All seasons	More frequent during warm months
Size	Larger	Less than 15 mm
Number	Average 5.7 to 10	Average 1.5
	Clustered	Individual
Location	Head, neck, chest, abdomen, back, buttocks, ears, hands, and feet	Shins, knees, forehead, upper arms, forearms, elbows, lumbar spine, anterior thighs, hands
Other characteristics	Patterned injuries	Over bony prominences

Any cutaneous injury must never be interpreted in isolation and must always be assessed in the context of medical and social history, developmental stage, explanation given, full clinical examination, and relevant investigations.[15]

6.2.3 Dating of Bruises

The ability to estimate the age of bruises would be useful in medicolegal investigations to evaluate the history given by the child's caregiver, identify the individual who was with the child at the time of injury, and to identify if there was more than one episode of injury.[3]

A bruise may be located at the area of impact and visible shortly after infliction of the injury, as is the case of a superficial bruise. It may be located at the area of impact but delayed in appearance because of its depth. It may be located at a site away from the impact area and result from tracking of blood from the impact area, as in the case of a black eye that results from gravitational movement of a forehead injury. Bruising occurs more easily where there is loose tissue and sufficient space outside the vessel for free blood to accumulate.[3]

The initial color of a bruise visible to the naked eye is the product of the child's natural skin pigmentation, the color of the pigments in the extravasated blood, the amount of hemorrhage, the depth of the hemorrhage, and any color added by the inflammatory reaction to the injury. Oxygenated blood is red, whereas venous blood is darker. The final result may include any of the following colors: red, blue, and purple/black.[3]

The immediate tissue response to traumatic injury involves an acute inflammatory reaction initiated by the trauma. This reaction involves recruitment of neutrophils and macrophages from the vascular system. Macrophages and neutrophils engulf both erythrocytes and free hemoglobin molecules and initiate the heme oxygenase system to break down the hemoglobin and produce compounds including hemosiderin, biliverdin, and bilirubin. Presence of bilirubin will cause bruises to appear yellow. Other colors may also be seen before the bruise fades, such as green and brown.[3]

Until recently, many people believed that if these changes of color followed a predictable sequence, it would be possible to date bruises or to at least give time frames for the development of different colors. Such charts for dating bruises were commonly found in child abuse textbooks of the 1980s and 1990s. The interpretation of the ages of bruises differed between the charts. None of the authors of these charts did experimental studies on the aging of bruises in living people. They expressed their own opinions based on their experience with bruises in deceased patients, who were mostly adults.[16]

Between 1977 and 2004, six different studies have been performed that indicate bruises cannot be dated (even in a general sense of fresh, intermediate, or older) by their color(s) alone on gross inspection or on photographs.

In addition, observers were in complete agreement with their own previous conclusions when looking at *in vivo* bruises versus photographs of the same bruise in only 31% of the cases.[16–21] These studies found that:

- Superficial bruises appear almost instantaneously.
- The appearance of deep bruises may be delayed for hours or days.
- The colors that used to be considered characteristics of a fresh bruise, that is red, blue, purple, and black, can in fact be seen until the complete disappearance of the bruise (21 days).
- Bruises of identical age on the same person may have different colors, and these colors may change at a very different rate (Figure 6.2).
- The presence of the color yellow indicates that the bruise is at least 18 hours old, but, unfortunately, the perception of yellow can vary considerably between individuals and even in the same individual over time. Bruises older than 48 hours are not usually confused with very fresh ones.[16–21]

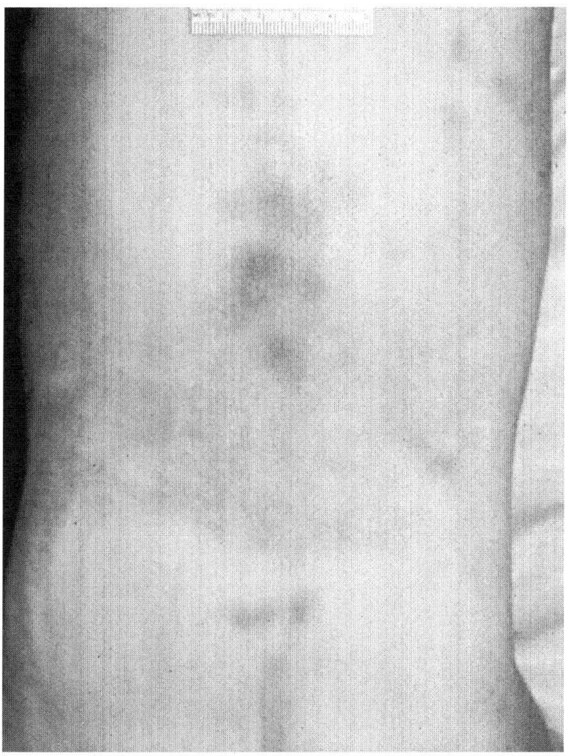

Figure 6.2 (see color insert following page 80) Multiple bruises of different colors. All these bruises occurred during one incident. Note the numerous bruises and clustering of bruises. The reddish band of color on the lower back and left side are due to livor mortis.

Table 6.4 Dating of Bruises

Superficial bruises appear almost instantaneously.
Deep bruises may appear hours or days later.
Bruises may be red, blue, purple and/or black from occurrence to resolution.
Bruises of identical age on the same person may have different colors and may change color at very different rates.
Yellow indicates a bruise of at least 18 hours old.
Perception of yellow varies significantly between individuals.
Swelling and tenderness indicate a recent bruise.

In conclusion, it is impossible to precisely date a bruise according to current scientific knowledge. The colors red, blue, and purple/black do not indicate with certainty that a bruise is fresh, unless other signs such as swelling and/or tenderness are present. A bruise is older than 18 hours if it contains the color yellow. Other signs of relatively old bruises are the colors green or brown and the absence of swelling or tenderness (Table 6.4).[3,16–21]

No experimental data exist to confirm that children heal more quickly than adults, as is sometimes asserted. There are also no data concerning the duration of swelling or tenderness associated with bruises, the minimal time for the appearance of green and brown colors, or the demarcation of the bruise with the intact skin. Fresh bruises may have a rather clear border. The demarcation with the intact skin seems to blur with time.

6.2.4 Cutaneous Injuries Due to Child Abuse

Kos and Shwayder (2006) presented a review article of the cutaneous manifestations of child abuse. Bruising of the genitalia and ears is highly suspicious for abuse, because these areas are rarely injured accidentally. No site is invariably spared in accidental bruising, and therefore site is not a pathognomonic characteristic in itself. Another helpful factor is the shape of the bruise, which can reflect the shape of the object used to inflict it. Pattern bruising is a strong indicator of abuse. Linear bruises are produced by objects such as rods, switches, or wires. They are usually found over the buttocks, posterior legs, and back. Loop marks are pathognomonic for abuse and result from striking the child with a doubled-over flexible cord such as an extension cord, rope, or belt. Another pattern mark is seen in slap-and-grab injuries. Bruises in the shape of finger marks, often seen on the upper arm, indicate the child was grabbed forcefully. When a child is slapped, blood is forced laterally by the fingers, extravasating and leaving the outline of the fingers while the actual point of impact is white (spared). This phenomenon can be seen in any high-velocity injury, such as whippings and slaps. Spanking the child on the buttocks can also produce characteristic vertical bruises along the gluteal cleft secondary to the shearing damage to the vessels along the

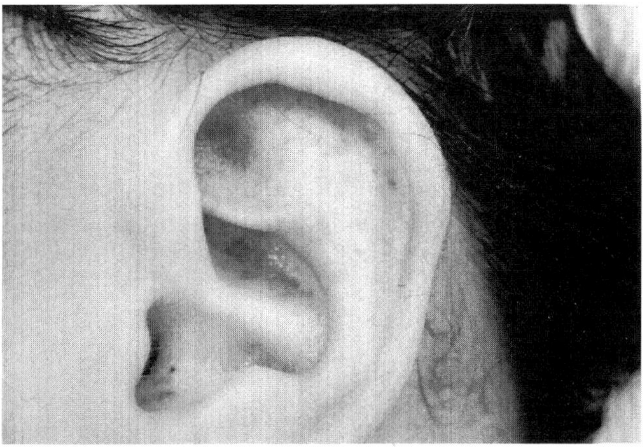

Figure 6.3 Petechial hemorrhages of the ear in a case of child abuse.

convex curvature of the buttocks. Circumferential bruises or abrasions around wrists and ankles implicate binding injuries. This type of injury can also result in distal petechiae and edema. Similar marks can be seen at the oral commissure if the child has been gagged, or around the neck after attempted strangulation. Wood lamp illumination has been reported to have an application in identifying bruises that are faint or not visible to the naked eye (Figure 6.3 through Figure 6.8).[22]

6.2.5 Postmortem Cutaneous Artifacts

Caution should be used when classifying linear marks on the front and sides of a deceased infant's neck as injuries, such as ligature marks, because the normal folds in an infant's neck can appear as white lines and indentations. These may be exaggerated as the subcutaneous fat cools after death (Figure 6.9).[23]

After death, drying of the lips, scrotum, and conjunctivae (where the eyelids are not closed) can give the false impression of bruises or injuries (Figure 6.10).[27]

6.3 Alopecia and Scalp Hemorrhages in Child Abuse

Alopecia in a child can be traumatic in origin, as seen when a parent pulls the child's hair or uses the hair to grab the child. Pulling the hair may lead to petechiae at the site of the pulled hair roots. The scalp may be boggy, a sign of subgaleal hematoma because of lifting of the scalp off the calvarium. Acute scalp tenderness may be present.[22]

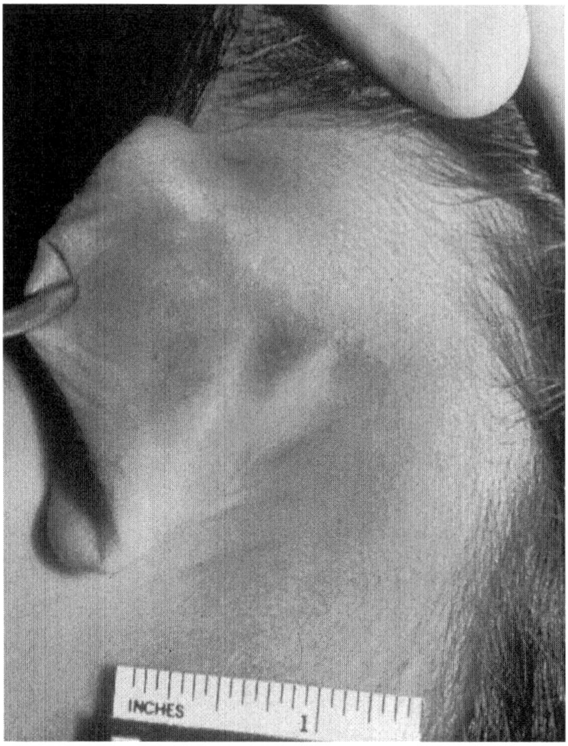

Figure 6.4 Hemorrhage behind the ear in a case of child abuse.

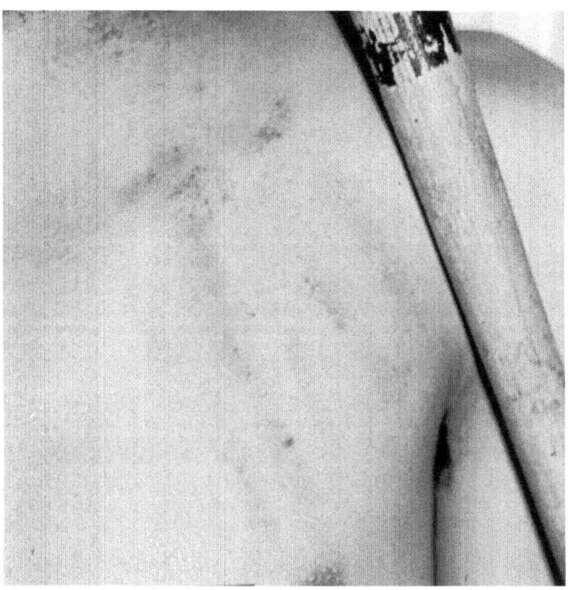

Figure 6.5 Parallel linear bruises caused by a bat.

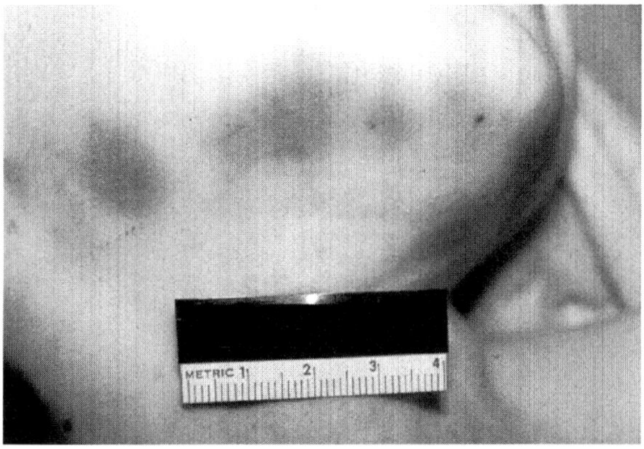

Figure 6.6 A line of rounded bruises along the jaw due to a blow by a fist in a case of child abuse.

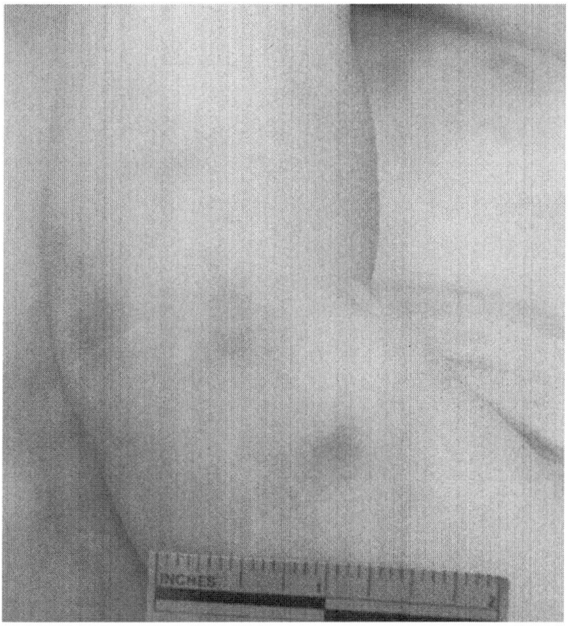

Figure 6.7 Fingertip-sized bruises on the arm of an infant.

6.4 Bite Marks in Child Abuse

6.4.1 Appearance of Bite Marks

If properly preserved and protected, bite marks can provide an important link between victim and assailant. It is important that the responding personnel protect the bite site so that the forensic odontologist or pathologist may analyze the evidence. Investigators should be suspicious of any marks or

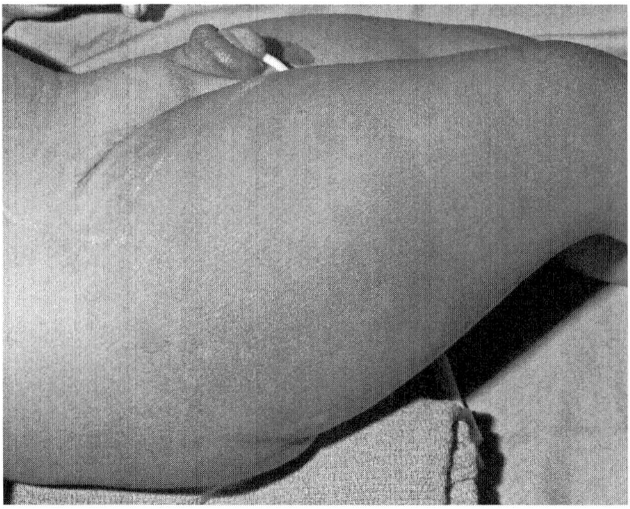

Figure 6.8 Alternating linear bruises with spared skin from forceful grabbing of the leg in a case of child abuse. There is also bruising of the penis and anterior pelvis.

bruises that appear to be bite marks on deceased or unconscious victims. The suspected bite site on a victim (or assailant) should not be washed until certain necessary steps have been taken; in addition, the suspected areas should be examined without being touched. A bite mark may reveal individual tooth marks or may appear as a double horseshoe. It may also resemble a doughnut or a solid rounded to oval marking. Another possibility is the appearance of both upper and lower teeth marks, while on other victims only the teeth of

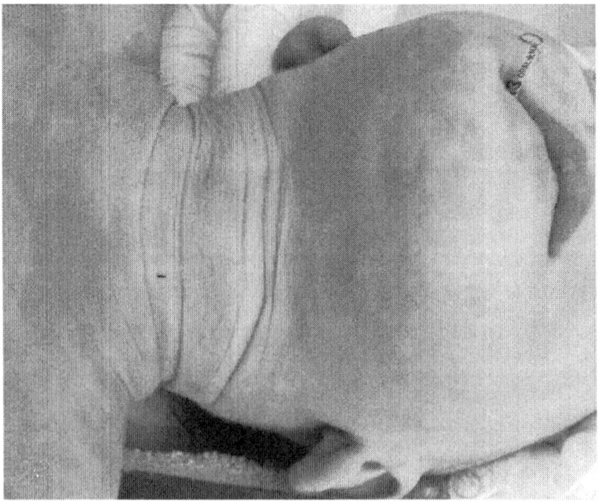

Figure 6.9 Skin fold lines on the neck of an infant. This should not be confused with an injury.

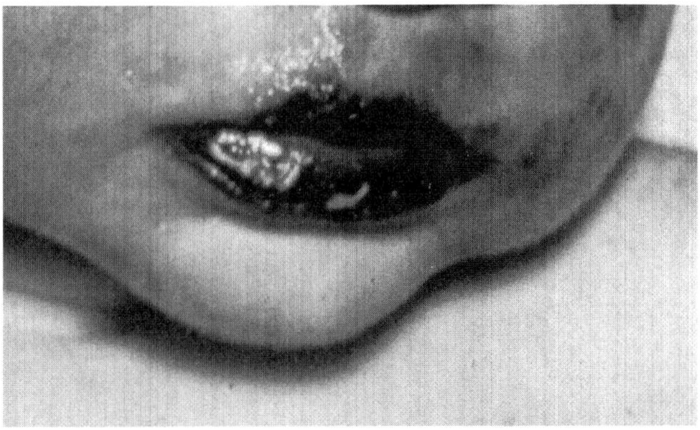

Figure 6.10 Postmortem drying of the lips. There are some postmortem abrasions on the cheek and philtrum.

the jaw may be visible. In addition, the number of teeth marks may vary from several to only one.[24]

Bite marks may have a central area of ecchymoses (contusions) caused by two possible phenomena: (1) positive pressure from the closing of the teeth with disruption of small vessels, or (2) negative pressure caused by suction and tongue thrusting.[25]

Bites produced by dogs or other carnivorous animals tend to tear flesh, whereas human bites compress flesh and can cause abrasions, contusions, and lacerations but rarely avulsions of tissue. An intercanine distance (i.e., the linear distance between the central point of the cuspid tips) measuring more than 3.0 cm is suspicious for an adult human bite.[25,26]

6.4.2 Evidence Collection from Bite Marks

Photographs may be the most valuable type of evidence and should be taken immediately after the crime. Ideally, black and white and color photographs with appropriate lighting should be used. The camera (preferably a 35 mm or other nondistorting model) is placed at right angles to the various curves of the bite. Orienting photographs are taken before cleaning or wiping the area. A scale or ruler should be placed near the bite mark in some of the photographs. After taking the initial photographs, crime laboratory personnel, using a noncontaminating technique, should swab the site with distilled water or physiological saline solution. Using sterile gloves to avoid contamination, they should work from the periphery toward the center of the bite mark, allowing the swabs to dry for a few minutes and then placing them in a sterile, sealed, marked test tube. The area should be reswabbed using a dry swab to pick up residual moisture. The swabs should be promptly sent to a qualified laboratory for analysis. Swabbing of unbitten areas, for control purposes, is recommended. As an example, in the case of a left wrist bite, the right and left wrists should be swabbed and these swabs placed in separate properly labeled test tubes. This technique is used to determine the major blood groups (if a secretor) and for DNA analysis of the assailant or victim. If there is a question as to whether an injury is a bite mark, a qualified forensic laboratory technician can perform an evaluation for the presence of salivary amylase prior to washing the area. Laboratory personnel should secure blood and salivary specimens from the victim. When a suspect is in custody, the same specimens should be obtained.[24]

6.4.3 Photographing Bite Marks

After swabbing for saliva residue, the area is debrided, cleansed, and an orienting photograph taken. An orienting photograph illustrates the relation of the bite mark to the body. A ruler is placed as close to the bite mark as possible without obscuring it. A flexible rule, e.g., tape measure, is unsatisfactory, because distortion may be introduced on curved surfaces. Then, a number of close photographs should be taken, also with the ruler in close proximity to the marks, with the camera lens placed perpendicular to the marks. This procedure is especially important if bite marks are on rounded areas, e.g., shoulders, arms, legs, or breasts. Two or more rulers may be placed in a photograph to demonstrate that there is little or no distortion. Photographs should be repeated for 5 days at 24-hour intervals on live and deceased victims, since bite marks may become more evident and distinct in the course of time. Deceased victims should be refrigerated and should not be embalmed. Embalming tends to "wash out" bite marks. An autopsy should not be performed before photographing the bite mark(s). Incisions or suturing in the proximity of bite marks are also to be avoided prior to taking photographs or bite mark impressions.[24]

6.4.4 Bite Mark Impressions

Bite mark impressions should be taken by a forensic odontologist, dentist, or experienced crime lab technician, using standard, accurate impression materials. If a suspect is in custody, impressions, photographs, and wax bites can be taken by the forensic odontologist after informed consent is obtained or following a court order. After models are constructed, they are analyzed by the forensic odontologist, who renders an expert opinion.[24]

6.5 Orofacial Trauma in Child Abuse

In a survey of 1155 pediatric dentists in the United States in 1979, the principal oral injuries in cases of suspected child abuse were (in descending order of frequency) fractures of the teeth (32%), oral bruises (24%), oral lacerations (14%), fractures of the mandible and maxilla (11%), and oral burns (5%).[28] A study by Naidoo (2000) at a children's hospital in Cape Town found that injuries to the face occurred in 59% of child abuse cases, the lips being traumatized in 54% of cases of mouth trauma, the oral mucosa in 15%, and the teeth and gingiva each in 12%.[29]

According to the American Academy of Pediatrics Committee on Child Abuse and Neglect (2005), oral injuries may be inflicted with instruments such as eating utensils or a bottle during forced feeding, or with hands, fingers, scalding liquids, or caustic substances. The abuse may result in contusions, burns, or lacerations of the tongue, lips, buccal mucosa, palate, gingiva, alveolar mucosa, or frenulum; fractured, displaced, or avulsed teeth; or facial bone and jaw fractures.[30] Discolored teeth, indicating pulpal necrosis, may result from previous trauma.[31] Gags applied to the mouth may result in bruises, lichenification, or scarring at the corners of the mouth.[32] Some serious injuries of the oral cavity, including posterior pharyngeal injuries and retropharyngeal abscesses, may be inflicted by caregivers with factitious disorder by proxy to simulate hemoptysis or other symptoms requiring medical care.[33] Unintentional or accidental injuries to the mouth are common and must be distinguished from abuse by judging whether the history, including the timing and mechanism of injury, is consistent with the characteristics of the injury and the child's developmental capabilities. Multiple injuries, injuries in different stages of healing, or a discrepant history should arouse suspicion of abuse.[30]

Although the oral cavity is a frequent site of sexual abuse in children, visible oral injuries or infections are rare.[30] Unexplained injury or petechiae of the palate, particularly at the junction of the hard and soft palate, may be evidence of forced oral sex.[34]

Tears of the labial or lingual frenulum can be a sign of a blow to the mouth, forced feeding, or forced oral sex. A torn frenulum can also be seen when a child falls on his face (Figure 6.11, Table 6.5).[22]

6.6 Burns in Child Abuse

6.6.1 Incidence and Diagnosis

Burns comprise approximately 5% to 22% of physical abuse. Burn abuse appears to be more common in children under 3 years of age. Inflicted burns account for 8% to 25% of all pediatric burns.[22] When compared with accidentally burned children, abused children were significantly younger, had longer hospital stays, and had a higher mortality.[35]

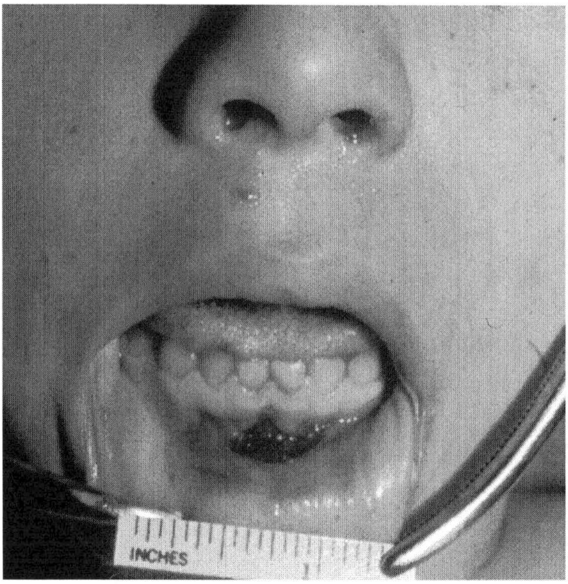

Figure 6.11 Torn frenulum.

Table 6.5 Orofacial Trauma in Child Abuse

Fractures of the teeth
Oral bruises
Oral lacerations
Fractures of the mandible and maxilla
Oral burns
Discolored teeth
Lichenification or scarring at the corners of the mouth (gags)
Posterior pharyngeal injuries and abscesses
Petechiae of the palate (oral sex)
Torn frenulum

Although the reported incidence of child abuse by burns is 4% to 39%, less than half are substantiated. Preexisting burn scars are present in 5% to 10%. Ojo et al. (2007) presented a retrospective study, the purpose of which was to ascertain the patterns of abuse by burning in children less than 6 years old. The abuser's profile, the burn pattern, and the child's history are essential components to the diagnosis. Only 6 of the 155 cases (3.8%) of burns in children less than 6 years old were confirmed to be abuse. Burns in these children were said to be confirmed to be from abuse if the Department of Children and Families investigated the incident, the perpetrator agreed to or was convicted of the abuse, and the child was placed in a safe haven. Accidental burns were more likely from liquids, including water used in

Table 6.6 Characteristics of Abusive Burns

Children under 3 years old
Scalds from tap water (50%), immersion, splash
Contact burns, less frequent
Left extremity involved
Lower extremity 87%
Upper extremity 17%
Second- or third-degree burns

cooking (42%), whereas abuse burns were more likely from tap water (50%). The gender distribution was similar. The age range was from 1 to 33 months, with 87% occurring below the age of 2 years. An extremity was involved in all abuse burns singly or in conjunction with other parts of the body. The left extremity was involved in 100% of the children in this review. The upper extremities were involved in 17% of the cases, and the lower extremities were involved in 87% of the cases, making the left lower extremity the most common site of child abuse burns. Abuse always involved the left limb, alone or in association with the right, possibly related to right hand dominance of the abuser grabbing the parallel limb facing him/her—the left—and holding it against the water. The burns were deep second degree (50%) or third degree (50%) (Table 6.6). This study revealed two main ways by which hot tap water resulted in burns: by immersing parts of the body in a hot tub, or by allowing water to run onto the body. When it occurred by immersion, no part of the involved area was spared but there was a sharp and straight demarcation between the burned and the unburned site. If the burn was caused by running hot water, the demarcation was not as straight, because of splashing that occurred, and the other side of the body was spared. According to the study, most of the burns tended to occur by running hot water onto the skin, because the abuser had become frustrated. When it occurred by contact, as was the case in one-third of this study group, the burned surface takes the shape of the hot object used in the abuse. Finding the object assists greatly in confirming or refuting an abuse burn. Therefore contact burns are more easily proven than hot water burns, but they are less common.[36]

In the Ojo et al. study (2007), all occurrences were in children of single young parents who had two to three other siblings. The perpetrator of the abuse in all the cases was the mother's boyfriend, and they all occurred when the mother was away. Thus there was a delay at presentation that ranged between 6 and 48 hours, with trials of different home creams and emollients. The abuse occurred mostly when the children were left in the care of the boyfriend, who was also watching two to three other siblings. The abusers themselves have a pattern. They are unemployed, with no blood relationship to the abused, have excessive need for control, and may have a prior history of abusive behavior. In one-half of families in this series, there was a previous

Table 6.7 Family Characteristics in Abusive Burns

Single young parent
2 or 3 other siblings
Victim is youngest of children
Perpetrator is often mother's boyfriend
Perpetrator unemployed, not related to victim, may have prior history of abusive behavior
Delay in presentation
History of abuse (50%)

history of abuse. This study showed that either gender may be abused, but the victim is always the youngest in the family (Table 6.7).[36]

The location of the burn, though not pathognomonic, can be helpful when ruling out abuse. Face, hands, legs, feet, perineum, and buttocks tend to be predominant sites in abuse. The perineum and buttocks specifically are infrequently involved in accidental burns, and burns in this area are often inflicted as punishment for toilet training accidents. This is consistent with the fact that forced immersions are frequent in the infant and toddler age groups.[23] Burns to extremities bilaterally are between 2.4 and 4.8 times more common in inflicted burns.[51] In contrast, common locations for accidental burns include head, neck, anterior trunk, and arms, reflecting areas likely to be involved in accidental hot liquid spills. Hand burns can be seen in accidents as well, but the more common site is the palm and anterior surface of the fingers, which would be in contact with the hot object while the child is grasping it. When burns are due to abuse, it is the dorsum of the hand that is commonly involved, especially in contact burns. Studies have shown that if there is a delay of greater than 2 hours in seeking medical care for scalds, the injury is more likely to be abusive (Table 6.8).[22]

6.6.2 Water Temperature and Time to Burns

The duration of exposure of the skin to hot water necessary to cause burns has been studied in adults but not children. It is expected that the duration of exposure and heat necessary to cause burns is much less in children and lesser still in infants and toddlers based on an inherently thinner dermis and less capacitance to diffuse the thermal energy causing the tissue injury. In adults, water at 140°F will cause full thickness skin burns in 2 to 5 seconds. At 130°F, it will take 30 seconds, and at 120°F, it will take 2 minutes for full

Table 6.8 Location of Abusive and Accidental Burns

Abusive Burns	Face, hands, legs, feet, perineum, buttocks, dorsum of hand
	Bilateral extremities
Accidental Burns	Head, neck, anterior trunk, arms (spills), palms (contact burns)

Table 6.9 Water Temperature and Time to Full Thickness Burns (Adults)

Temperature	Time
140°F	2 to 5 seconds
130°F	30 seconds
120°F	2 minutes

thickness burns to occur. With most water heaters preset between 130° and 150°F, the maximum water temperature should be obtained from the alleged source for corroboration (Table 6.9).[36]

6.6.3 Immersion Burns

Scalds are the most frequent form of burn abuse. Up to 14% of all pediatric scalds are due to abuse, and more specifically 28 to 45% of scalds due to tap water are abusive. Scalds are typically divided into immersion and splash/spill burns. Forced immersion burns tend to be symmetrical and have clear lines of demarcation, often called tidemarks. They also tend to have a uniform burn depth and commonly involve the buttocks, perineum, and lower extremities. Characteristic features of forced immersion include stocking and glove distribution, zebra stripes, and donut-hole sparing. Stocking and glove burns occur when a child's hands and/or feet are forcibly immersed in hot water, resulting in symmetrical, circumferential, and well-demarcated burns. Zebra stripes are due to sparing of the flexural creases secondary to the body's flexed position in the hot liquid. Donut-hole sparing occurs when the child's buttocks are pressed against the bathtub which is relatively cooler than the water in it.[22] When the child is immersed twice, the "double dunk" injury, the sharp lines of demarcation between burned and unburned skin may not exist.[38] By positioning the child so that the lines of demarcation are parallel, the position of the child during the immersion can be estimated, thus lending credence or doubt to the given history.[38] Paradoxically, forcing a young girl into a bathtub of hot water with the express purpose of disciplining or punishing for toilet accidents may force the legs into abduction as well as flexion at the hips, leaving the intertriginous folds in the groin pulled apart so that the labia majora are scalded as well. Forced immersion burns in boys almost always result in burns of the external genitals.[38] Diapers (both washable and disposable) provide nearly complete protection against scald burns, as a result of the outer barrier layer and inner absorbent layer (Table 6.10).[35]

In contrast to inflicted burns, accidental immersion burns, where a child falls into a container of hot liquid, typically have irregular borders and nonuniform depth as the patient is struggling to escape the hot liquid. This thrashing also causes splash marks which, although they may sometimes

Table 6.10 Characteristics of Abusive Immersion Burns

Symmetrical
Sharp, straight demarcation lines
Uniform burn depth
Commonly on buttocks, perineum, lower extremities
Stocking and glove distribution
Zebra stripes
Donut hole sparing

be found in forced immersion, are more characteristic of accidental immersion. Accidental burns are also rarely full thickness, because they typically involve shorter contact time. Simultaneous scald burns to buttocks, feet, and perineum are highly suspicious for physical abuse.[22]

Children immersed in hot water may struggle and fight to get away from the scalding liquid and so will have splash marks, whereas some young children may jump into a bath with hot water, panic, freeze, and stand still in water, giving themselves a symmetrical, unsplashed burn distribution.[50]

6.6.4 Splash and Spill Burns

Splash and spill burns are scalds resulting when a hot liquid is thrown or poured over a child. They often occur accidentally when a child spills a hot liquid and are not a frequent form of abuse. These burns are generally more superficial than immersion burns because the liquid rapidly cools and the time of contact with the skin is short. Associated splash marks are seen more frequently than in immersion burns. Distinguishing between accident and abuse in this type of a burn can be difficult. Both inflicted and accidental splash and spill burns have irregular margins and variable depth. They both also have a characteristic appearance, in which the largest and deepest part of the burn is at the initial point of contact, usually head or chest, whereas the burn narrows and becomes more superficial as the liquid travels down the body and cools, the "arrowhead pattern."[22,38] Inflicted splash and spill burns are more frequently found on the buttocks and perineum, usually from holding the child under a running faucet. In accidental splash and spill burns, the head, neck, and trunk are commonly involved as the hot liquid is pulled or knocked over from a higher surface and spilled over the child (Table 6.11).[22]

6.6.5 Contact Burns

Certain contact burns have shapes suggestive of the objects used to inflict them. Accidental contact burns are often patchy and superficial, because the

Table 6.11 Characteristics of Abusive Splash and Spill Burns

Burns more superficial
Associated splash marks
Irregular margins and variable depth
Arrowhead pattern
More frequently on buttocks and perineum

child quickly withdraws from the hot object or the falling object brushes across the skin. They may or may not show a clear imprint. Inflicted contact burns are deeper, may be multiple, and have well-demarcated margins. They are commonly due to hot irons, radiators, hair dryers, curling irons, lighters, and stoves (Figure 6.12). Contact burns with uniform depth and well-demarcated margins located on typically protected areas of the body suggest abuse (Table 6.12).[22]

Hair dryers can produce heated air currents up to 110°F temperature, and the heated grill over the end can hold enough heat to inflict full-thickness burns for up to 2 minutes after the dryer had been turned off.[40]

Cigarette burns represent a common form of burn abuse. Inflicted cigarette burns appear as 7- to 10-mm round, well-demarcated burns that have a deep central crater. They heal with scarring, because they extend well into

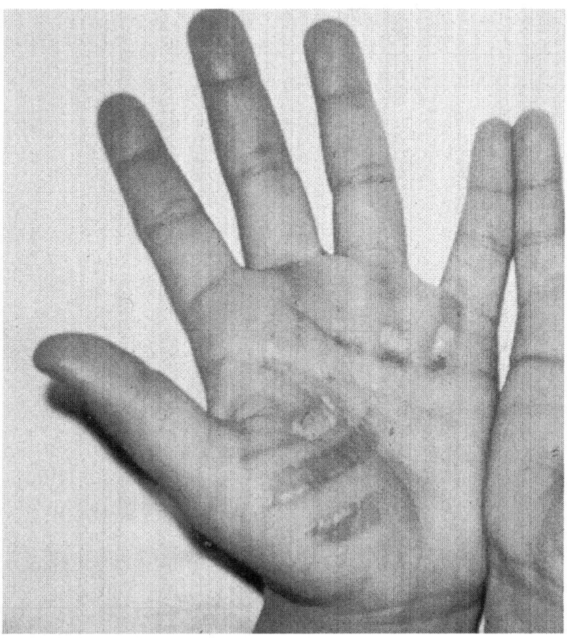

Figure 6.12 Patterned burn due to electric stove.

Table 6.12 Characteristics of Abusive Contact Burns

Shape of inflicting object
Deep burns
May be multiple
Well-demarcated margins
Uniform depth
On protected areas of the body

the dermis. Cigarette burns commonly appear grouped on the face, hands, and feet. When accidental, they tend to be oval or eccentric and more superficial, as the child usually brushes against the cigarette.[22]

6.6.6 Other Types of Burns

There are other forms of abusive burns. Flame burns are often associated with inhalational injury and other concomitant trauma. Flame burns tend to be deep dermal to full thickness. Electrical burns from domestic electricity are low voltage and tend to cause small, deep contact burns at the exit and entry sites (Figure 6.13). The alternating nature of domestic current can interfere with the cardiac cycle, giving rise to arrhythmias. Chemical burns may occur with household chemical products. These burns tend to be deep, as the corrosive agent continues to cause coagulative necrosis until completely removed (Figure 6.14). Alkalis tend to penetrate deeper and cause worse burns than acids.[37] Microwave burns are also recent and fortunately

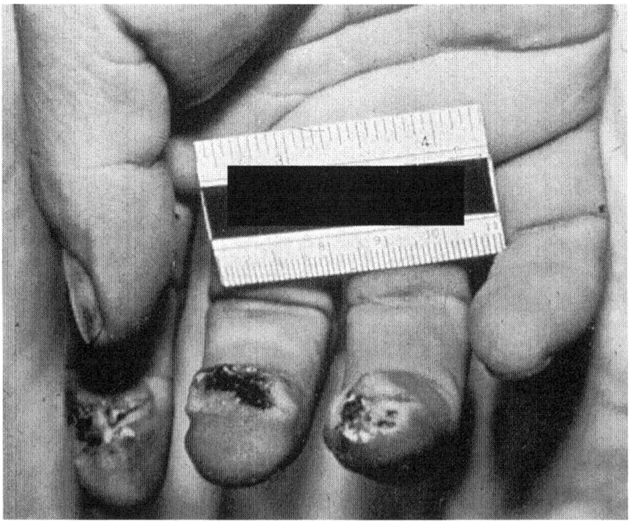

Figure 6.13 Electrical burn from contact with electrical wire.

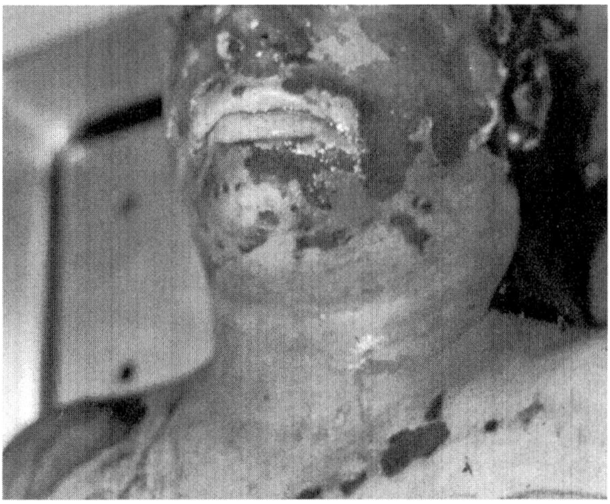

Figure 6.14 Chemical burn from battery acid.

rare causes of child abuse by burning.[41] Because of the characteristic of microwave radiant energy, sparing of subcutaneous fat can occur. The thermal injury is thus confined to the skin and skips down to the muscle, which can be deeply burned. Peculiar skin distributions of burns should alert the physician to the possibility of child abuse by burning in a microwave oven. The diagnosis can be confirmed by a deep biopsy of the burned tissue down to and including underlying muscle.

6.6.7 Investigation of Abusive Burns

Peck and Priolo-Kapel (2002) reviewed the literature on child abuse by burning and presented an algorithm for medical investigators. As is true of many cases of child abuse, an accurate diagnosis of abuse by burning is difficult to establish. The sensitivity of a technique for diagnosing child abuse by burning is proportional to the number of true-positives, that is, abused children reported to Child Protective Services (CPS). On the other hand, the specificity of a diagnostic technique is proportional to the number of true-negatives, who are accidentally injured children correctly identified as not abused. There are two categories of inaccurate diagnosis. False-positives occur when the physician suspects abuse, but the child was injured accidentally (may have been reported to CPS, but CPS was unable to substantiate abuse). False-negatives are abused children who are not reported to CPS. The algorithm begins with the elicitation of a history from the caregiver and examination of the burns. If there is then a concern about child abuse, the subsequent steps include a detailed, chronologic history, a comprehensive physical examination, exhaustive documentation, and communication with CPS and law enforcement.[38]

The pattern of an injury, although not consistent with the history given, is not always readily explainable. In fact, Hammond et al. (1991) found that in the absence of other findings suspicious for abuse (e.g., delay in treatment or injury inconsistent with the child's development or chronologic age), the positive predictive value of the discovery of an injury inconsistent with the history of an accident was only 40%—that is, 60% of those childhood burns for which the physician cannot match the history with the pattern of injury are later found to be because of negligence or accident.[39] For example, a case of neglect where the child was left unattended, and the parent truly has no idea how the child was burned.[38] A delay in seeking medical treatment should be evaluated in the total presentation, taking into consideration any attempts at treatment or advice given by relatives.[53]

Forensic photographs should include a face shot for identification with the patient's medical record number in the photograph. There should be a full body shot, both front and back, to put the burns in context. Photographs at various stages of healing should be obtained, such as at initial presentation and then several days later when the burn depth is unequivocal; the dates should be on the photographs. A scale or ruler should be placed next to the burn to show its dimensions, especially to demonstrate the height of any water line. It is important to photograph the margins of the burns and the burns from all angles. Photographs should include areas of sparing and then the child should be photographed in the flexed position to demonstrate how flexion caused the sparing.[38]

The depth of a burn is often difficult to diagnose in the first 24 hours. Repeated examinations over the next few days are often necessary, particularly to delineate burned from unburned skin.[35]

The next step in the investigation is for the surgeon/physician to obtain specific technical information from those who have personally assessed the alleged crime scene. Technical information in a scald injury, for example, includes the type of liquid, temperature of the liquid, exposure time, volume of liquid, temperature of the hot water heater, water temperature from the faucet, and the material from which the container (sink, tub) is made. When the mechanism of burning is hot tap water, it is important that the water temperature be properly and accurately measured. It is also important to have the investigators contact the homeowner or landlord immediately after the case is reported so that no one is allowed to change the temperature of the water heater. The temperature of the water is critical to corroborate the history. The water temperature measurements should be taken under the same conditions as when the burn injury occurred. For immersion burns, the temperature of the tap water should be taken at different times as the water runs from the spigot, such as every 5 seconds; in addition, the investigator should note the type of water heater, discrepancy between the set water temperature and the actual temperature, measurements of the dimensions of the tub (including

Table 6.13 Investigation of Burns

History from the caretaker
Detailed chronologic history
Examination of the burns
Comprehensive physical examination
Forensic photographs
Scene investigation
Type of liquid
Temperature of the liquid
Exposure time
Volume of liquid
Temperature of the hot water heater
Water temperature from the faucet, at 5 second intervals
Container material and dimensions

how high the child would have to climb from the floor to get into the tub), the distance to the spigot, and the design of the faucet (Table 6.13).[38]

Hampton and Newberger found that child abuse is more likely to be reported for younger children, for children of African-American and Hispanic families, and for children of families with an annual income of $25,000 or less.[48] These children are more likely to present to public hospitals or clinics, where the incidence of physician reporting is also higher; physicians in private practice are less likely to report abuse.[49]

Clark et al. (1997) examined the number of cases of burns due to possible child abuse reported to social services before and after the introduction of a burn profile checklist to the physicians in an urban pediatric emergency department. Before the checklist 3% of burns were reported, and after, 12.1%.[54] The checklist contained 13 associated risk factors for abusive burns: burn attributed to a sibling; unrelated adult seeking medical care for the child; differing historical accounts; treatment delay greater than 24 hours; history of prior accidental injuries; inappropriate affect of the parent; inappropriate affect of the child; history incompatible with the physical examination; burn incompatible with developmental age of the child; mirror image burns; localized burns of perineum, genitalia, buttocks; burn older than the given history; other injuries (Table 6.14).[55]

Allasio and Fischer (2005) preformed a study that looked at the ability of 10- to 18-month-old children to climb into a bathtub. The history that a child climbed into a tub previously filled with hot water is common. A standard bathtub was installed in an examination room at a pediatric clinic. Children were selected if they were between 10 and 18 months old, born at term, and without problems that would interfere with their normal development. Parents encouraged the child to climb into the tub and get toys. Children were allowed 5 minutes to climb, depending on their attention

Table 6.14 Checklist of Associated Risk Factors for Abusive Burns

Burn attributed to a sibling
Unrelated adult seeking medical care for the child
Differing historical accounts
Treatment delay greater than 24 hours
History of prior accidental injuries
Inappropriate affect of the parent
Inappropriate affect of the child
History incompatible with the physical examination
Burn incompatible with the developmental age of the child
Mirror image burns
Localized burns of perineum, genitalia, buttocks
Burn older than the given history
Other injuries

span and tolerance. Of 176 children in the study, 62 (35%) climbed into the tub. One-fourth climbed in head first, and the rest climbed in sideways. The study may have underestimated children's climbing abilities because of the absence of a shower curtain to help with balance and the distracting presence of strangers.[56]

6.6.8 Differential Diagnosis of Burns

The differential diagnosis may be difficult. One example is bullous impetigo, which can present as round, deepithelized or crusted, tender areas that may appear like cigarette burns.[43] Impetigo tends to heal from the center outward, and also responds quickly to appropriate antibiotic treatment. Lesions of bullous impetigo also tend to be grouped and heal without scaring, unlike cigarette burns. Scald abuse must be distinguished from bullous impetigo, cellulitis, epidermolysis bullosa, severe diaper dermatitis, and contact dermatitis.[52] Phytophotodermatitis (solar keratosis from plants) can result in a severe erythematous reaction that mimics a partial-thickness burn.[44] Another example is a burn that is intentionally inflicted for "therapeutic" reasons by a traditional healer. Occasionally, dry pressure injuries caused by infant swings, cowboy boots, or elastic pajama cuffs have been mistaken for child abuse by burning.[45] Car seats can cause confusing burns in hot weather.[46] Finally, there are reports of congenital indifference to pain, which has been mistaken for child abuse by burning (Figure 6.15, Table 6.15).[47]

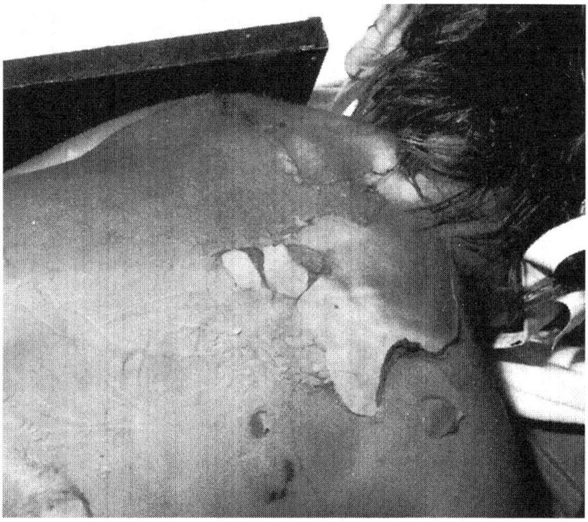

Figure 6.15 Postmortem skin slippage due to heat. Child died of hyperthermia when left in a closed car in summer.

Table 6.15 Differential Diagnosis of Burns

Bullous impetigo
Cellulitis
Epidermolysis bullosa
Severe diaper dermatitis
Contact dermatitis
Phytophotodermatitis
Folk remedies
Dry pressure injuries
Car seat burns in hot weather
Congenital indifference to pain

6.7 Skeletal Injury in Child Abuse

6.7.1 The Skeletal Survey

The skeletal survey should be a routine part of the medical evaluation of physical abuse in infants. Between the ages of 2 and 5 years, the survey should be performed selectively, on the basis of the history and physical examination. Because hidden fractures are rare beyond the age of 5 years, the survey is of little diagnostic value for older children. Thirty-five percent of children that are detected as abused have new or old fractures or both.[42]

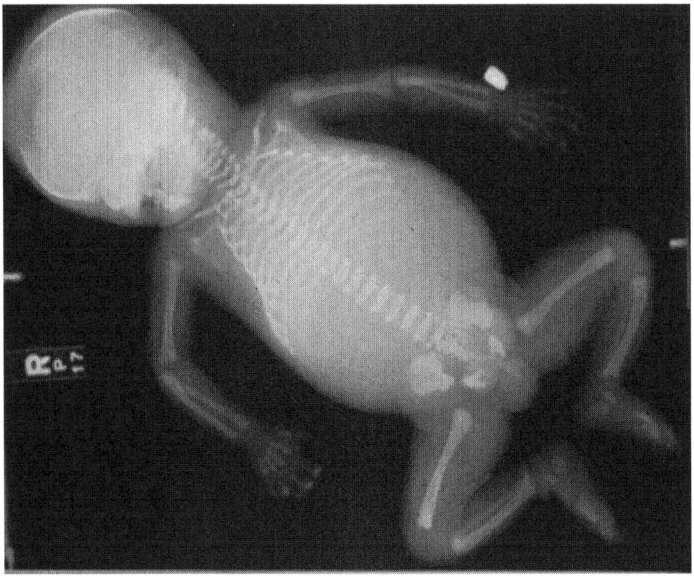

Figure 6.16 Body or baby gram. Note the lack of air in the lungs and intestinal tract in this stillborn.

The body or baby gram (a study that encompasses the entire infant or young child on 1 or 2 radiographic exposures) or abbreviated skeletal surveys have no role in the imaging of the subtle but highly specific bony abnormalities found in child abuse (Figure 6.16). In general, the radiographic skeletal survey is the method of choice for global skeletal imaging in cases of suspected abuse.[57] The standard skeletal survey imaging protocol that has been developed by the American College of Radiology is:

- Anteroposterior views of the humeri, forearms, femurs, lower legs, feet
- Posterolateral and oblique views of the hands
- Anteroposterior and lateral views of the thorax and pelvis including mid and lower lumbar spine
- Lateral views of the lumbar and cervical spine
- Frontal and lateral views of the skull (Table 6.16).[57]

Table 6.16 Standard Skeletal Survey

Anteroposterior views of the humeri, forearms, femurs, lower legs, feet
Posterolateral and oblique views of the hands
Anteroposterior and lateral views of the thorax and pelvis including mid and lower lumbar spine
Lateral views of the lumbar and cervical spine
Frontal and lateral views of the skull

Histologic examination of fractures allows a more precise dating of the fractures, particularly in regard to the early stages of fracture healing.[59]

6.7.2 Metaphyseal Fractures

The classic metaphyseal fracture (CML), corner or bucket handle fracture, extends in a planar fashion through the primary spongiosa (Figure 6.17). The fracture may extend partially or completely across the metaphysis. These fractures are most common in the distal femur, proximal and distal tibia, and proximal humeri and are much less common at the elbow, wrist, and proximal femur. The metaphyseal fracture occurs with torsion and traction of the extremities as the infant is grabbed by the arm or leg. When present in an otherwise normal infant, these findings suggest inflicted injury. It is notoriously difficult to date on radiographs. Sclerosis and subperiosteal new bone formation, features of healing fracture at other sites, are usually absent with CML. Radiologic–histopathologic studies have shown certain subtle indicators of healing in CML. These indicators are the accumulation of hypertrophic chondrocytes at the chondro-osseus junction near the fracture site. They require high-detail images for detection. The differential diagnosis for the

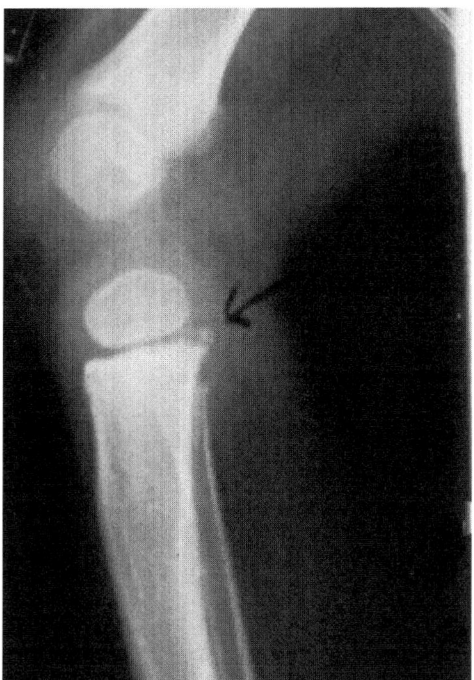

Figure 6.17 Metaphyseal corner fracture in the proximal tibia.

CML includes rickets, birth injury, inherited bone dysplasias, osteogenesis imperfecta, and developmental variants.[58]

6.7.3 Rib Fractures

Rib fractures are the most common fractures noted in infants dying with inflicted injury. Fractures can occur anywhere along the rib arc but are most common near the costovertebral articulations (Figure 6.18). These fractures, as well as fractures near the costochondral junction, are the most difficult to identify radiographically. Fractures at the costovertebral junctions will become more visible on follow-up studies at two weeks; fractures at the costochondral junctions tend to heal with little subperiosteal new bone and tend to become less distinct with time. Most fractures occur with thoracic compression. Radiologic-histopathologic studies support the concept that excessive leverage of the ribs over the transverse processes with anteroposterior compression of the chest results in fractures of the rib head and neck. Although strongly associated with abuse, rib fractures occasionally occur in nonabusive situations: birth injury, cardiopulmonary resuscitation, and accidental rib fractures.[58]

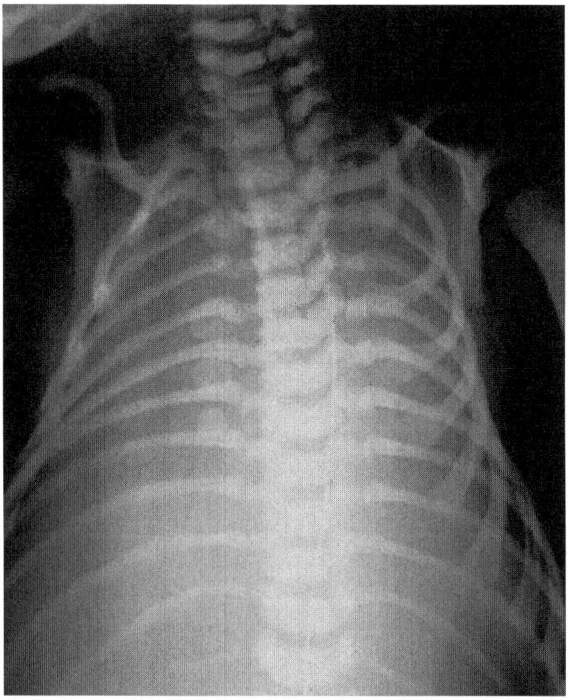

Figure 6.18 Healing rib fractures. Note they are multiple and in a line.

6.7.4 Epiphyseal Separation

In contrast to classic metaphyseal fractures (CML), epiphyseal separation occurs principally through the zone of proliferating or hypertrophic chondrocytes of the physis. They are high-force injuries which, in contrast to the CML, are usually associated with epiphyseal displacement, extensive hemorrhage, and soft tissue swelling, and are accompanied by impressive clinical findings.[58]

6.7.5 Vertebral Body Fracture

A variety of vertebral body fracture patterns has been described in abused infants and children. Although simple compression fractures occur, it is common for vertebral body fractures to involve the cartilage endplate of the vertebral body. Since this is the site of enchondral bone formation, a fracture may result in a growth disturbance, producing vertebral "notching." Severe fracture dislocation has been described at the thoraco-lumbar junction, with dramatic pathologic findings, in the absence of neurologic abnormalities.[58] The proposed mechanism of injury is a combination of axial load, flexion, and rotatory forces.[60]

6.7.6 Long Bone Fractures

Although long bone fractures are commonly identified in abused children and are the most common fracture beyond one year of age, they must be evaluated along with other clinical and imaging findings. Oblique or spiral shaft fracture has little correlation with the presence or absence of abuse (Figure 6.19). Patient age appears to be the most important factor in predicting whether

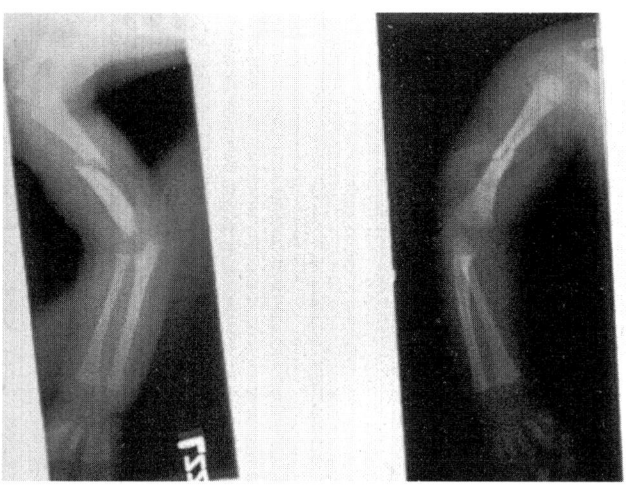

Figure 6.19 Oblique fracture of humerus.

a shaft fracture is accidental or inflicted. Most femoral fractures under one year of age are inflicted. The percentage of fractures due to abuse declines dramatically in toddlers and older children. It is well recognized that a running child may twist and fall, generating sufficient torsional forces to result in a spiral femoral shaft fracture. Femoral fractures may occur in infants who fall down stairs while being held by a caretaker.[58]

As with the femur, most humeral fractures in infants are inflicted. This association diminishes beyond one year of age, particularly with regard to supracondylar fractures that are usually accidental. Rarely, a humeral shaft fracture can occur if an infant is held by one arm and forcefully turned from a prone to a supine position, trapping the other arm beneath the baby.[58]

The toddler's fracture, an oblique or spiral fracture of the mid/distal tibia shaft, is a common accidental injury in infants who have begun to bear weight. As is generally the case with abuse, specific trauma is minimal or absent. Although toddler-type fractures do occur with abuse, an isolated nondisplaced oblique or spiral fracture of the distal tibia in a weight-bearing infant or toddler has a strong correlation with accidental injury.[58]

6.7.7 Skull Fracture

A systematic review of published studies to identify the characteristics of abusive and nonabusive fractures in children and to calculate a probability of abuse for individual fracture types found the probability for skull fractures was 0.30. The most common skull fractures in abuse and nonabuse were linear fractures.[61] Another comparative study found that skull fracture characteristics identified considerably more often in abused children were multiple or complex patterns, depressed, wide, and growing fractures, and associated intracranial injuries including subdural hematomas (Figure 6.20, Figure 6.21).[62]

6.7.8 Periosteal Reaction

Any irritation or disruption to the underlying bone will cause a periosteal reaction and result in new periosteal bone deposition. Periosteal bone formation may be due to either physiologic or pathologic causes.[63] Infants from 1 to 6 months old often normally show symmetric diaphyseal periosteal reaction.[64] Common causes of pathologic periosteal reaction in children include trauma to the underlying bone including trauma from abuse, hypervitaminosis A, prostaglandin therapy, cortical hyperostosis (Caffey's disease), hypertrophic osteoarthropathy, osteomyelitis, leukemia, and syphilis (Figure 6.22, Table 6.17).[63]

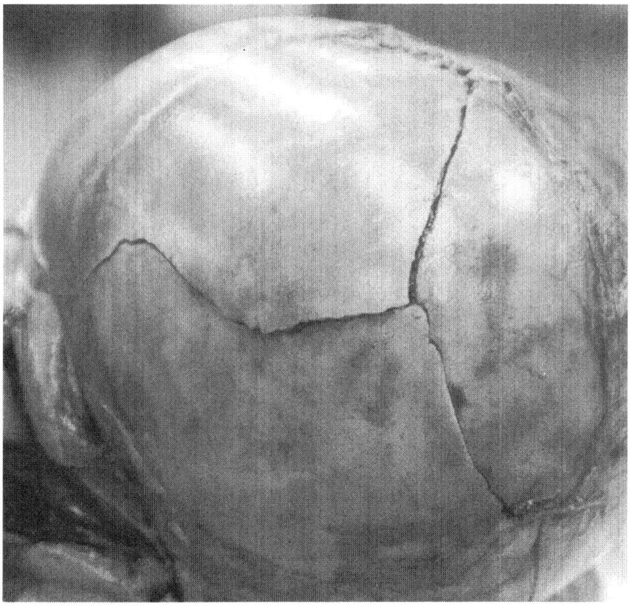

Figure 6.20 Complex skull fracture.

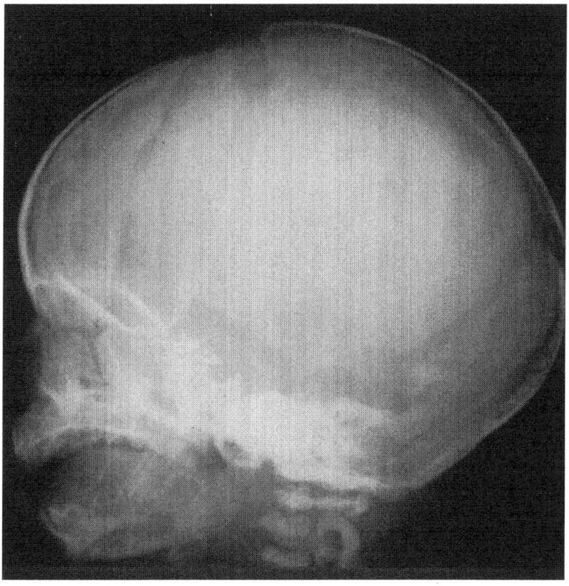

Figure 6.21 Radiograph of widened sutures in a case of child abuse with brain edema.

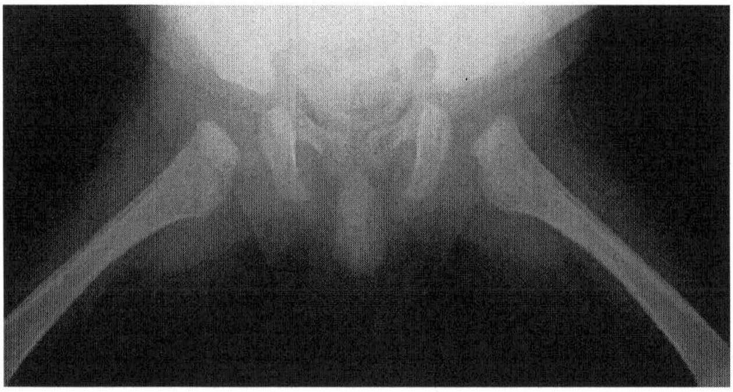

Figure 6.22 Bilateral, symmetrical physiologic periosteal reaction of the femurs.

Table 6.17 Fractures Found in Child Abuse

Fractures Found in Child Abuse
Metaphyseal corner fractures
Rib fractures, especially costovertebral
Epiphyseal separation
Vertebral body fractures
Long bone fractures, especially in infants
Skull fractures, linear, complex, wide, growing

References

1. Lavelle JM, Shaw KN, Seidi T, Ludwig S. 1995. Ten-year review of pediatric bathtub near-drownings: evaluation for child abuse. *Ann Emerg Med* 25:344–48.
2. Wood J, Rubin DM, Nance ML, Christian CW. 2005. Distinguishing inflicted versus accidental abdominal injuries in young children. *J Trauma* 59:1203–8.
3. Labbé J. Cutaneous injuries in normal children. 2008. San Diego International Conference on Child and Family Maltreatment.
4. Pascoe JM, Heldebrandt HM, Tarrier A, Murphy M. 1979. Patterns of skin injury in nonaccidental and accidental injury. *Pediatrics* 64:245–47.
5. Keen JH. 1981. Normal bruises in pre-school children. *Arch Dis Child* 56:75.
6. Ridinger-Tush BA. 1982. Bruising in healthy 3-year-old children. *Mat Child Nursing J* 11:165–79.
7. Roberton DM, Barbor P. Hull D. 1982. Unusual injury? Recent injury in normal children and children with suspected nonaccidental injury. *BMJ* 285:1399–1401.
8. Mortimer PE, Freeman M. 1983. Are facial bruises in babies ever accidental? *Arch Dis Child* 58:75–76.
9. Wedgwood J. 1990. Childhood bruising. *The Practitioner* 234:598–601.
10. Sugar NF, Taylor JA, Feldman KW. 1999. Bruises in infants and toddlers. Those who don't cruise rarely bruise. *Arch Pediat Adolesc Med* 153:399–403.
11. Carpenter RF. 1999. The prevalence and distribution of bruising in babies. *Arch Dis Child* 80:363–66.

12. Labbé J, Caouette G. 2001. Recent skin injuries in normal children. *Pediatrics* 1008:271–76.
13. Downes AJ, Crossland DS, Mellon AF. 2002. Prevalence and distribution of petechiae in well babies. *Arch Dis Child* 86:291–92.
14. Dunstan FD, Guildea ZE, Kontos K, Kemp AM, et al. 2002. A scoring system for bruise patterns: a tool for identifying abuse. *Arch Dis Child* 86:330–33.
15. Maguire S. Mann MK, Sibert J, Kemp A. 2005. Are there patterns of bruising in childhood which are diagnostic or suggestive of abuse? A systematic review. *Arch Dis Child* 90:182–86.
16. Wilson EF. 1977. Estimation of the age of cutaneous contusions in child abuse. *Pediatrics* 60:750–52.
17. Langlois NEI, Gresham GA. 1991. The ageing of bruises: a review of the colour changes with time. *Forensic Sci Intern* 50:227–38.
18. Stephenson T, Bialas Y. 1996. Estimation of the age of bruising. *Arch Dis Child* 74:53–55.
19. Munang LA, Leonard PA, Mok JY. 2002. Lack of agreement on colour description between clinicians examining childhood bruising. *J Clin Forensic Med* 9:171–74.
20. Bariciak ED, Plint AC, Gaboury I, Bennett S. 2003. Dating of bruises in children: an assessment of physician accuracy. *Pediatrics* 112:804–7.
21. Hugues VK, Ellis PS, Langlois NE. 2004. The perception of yellow in bruises. *J Clin Forensic Med* 11:257–59.
22. Kos L, Shwayder T. 2006. Cutaneous manifestations of child abuse. *Ped Derm* 23(4):311–20.
23. Spitz WU. 1980. In *The Medicolegal Investigation of Death,* eds. WU Spitz and RS Fischer, 500–501. Springfield, IL: Charles C. Thomas.
24. Sperber ND. 1981. Bite mark evidence in crimes against persons. *FBI Law Enforc Bulletin* July: 1–4.
25. Kellogg N, American Academy of Pediatrics Committee on Child Abuse and Neglect. 2005. Oral and dental aspects of child abuse and neglect. *Pediatrics* 116:1565–68.
26. Wagner GN. 1986. Bitemark identification in child abuse cases. *Pediatr Dent* 8:96–100.
27. Fisher RS. 1980. In *The Medicolegal Investigation of Death,* eds. WU Spitz and RS Fisher, 22–23. Springfield, IL: Charles C. Thomas.
28. Malecz RE. 1979. Child abuse, its relationship to paedodontics. *J Dentistry Child* 46:193.
29. Naidoo S. 2000. A profile of the oro-facial injuries in physical child abuse at a children's hospital. *Child Abuse Negl* 24:521–34.
30. American Academy of Pediatrics Committee on Child Abuse and Neglect; American Pediatric Dentistry: American Academy of Pediatric Dentistry Council on Clinical Affairs. 2005–2006. Guideline on oral and dental aspects of child abuse and neglect. *Pediatr Dent* 27:64–47.
31. Kittle PE, Richardson DS, Parker JW. 1981. Two child abuse/child neglect examinations for the dentist. *ASDS J Dent Child* 48:175–80.
32. McNeese MC, Hebeler JR. 1977. The abused child: a clinical approach to identification and management. *Clin Symp* 29(5):1–36.

33. Levin AV. 1995. Otorhinolaryngologiic manifestations. In *Munchausen Syndrome by Proxy: Issues in Diagnosis and Treatment,* eds. AV Levin and MS Sheridan, 219–30. New York: Lexington Books.
34. Schlesinger SL, Borbotsina J, O'Neill L. 1975. Petechial hemorrhage of the soft palate secondary to fellatio. *Oral Surg Oral Med Oral Pathol* 40:376–78.
35. Purdue GF, Hunt JL, Prescott PR. 1988. Child abuse by burning: an index of suspicion. *J Trauma* 28:221–24.
36. Ojo P, Palmer J, Garvey R, Atweh N, et al. 2007. Patterns of burns in child abuse. *Am Surg* 73(3):253–55.
37. Hettiarathy S, Dziewulski P. 2004. ABC of burns: pathophysiology and types of burns. *BMJ* 328(7453):1427–29.
38. Peck MD, Priolo-Kapel D. 2002. Child abuse by burning: a review of the literature and an algorithm for medical investigations. *J Trauma* 53(5):1013–22.
39. Hammond J, Perez-Stable A, Ward CG. 1991. Predictive value of historical and physical characteristics for the diagnosis of child abuse. *South Med J* 84:166–68.
40. Prescott PR. 1990. Hair dryer burns in children. *Pediatrics* 86:692–97
41. Alexander RC, Surrell JA, Cohle SD. 1987. Microwave oven burns to children: an unusual manifestation of child abuse. *Pediatrics* 79:255–60.
42. Mead J, Westage D. 1994. *Investigating Child Abuse.* Clino, CA: RC Law & Co.
43. Chadwick DL. 1992. The diagnosis of inflicted injury in infants and young children. *Pediatr Ann* 21:477–82.
44. Hill PF, Pickford M, Parkhouse N. 1997. Phytophotodermatitis mimicking child abuse. *J R Soc Med* 90:560–61.
45. Feldman KW. 1995. Confusion of innocent pressure injuries with inflicted dry contact burns. *Clin Pediatr (Phila)* 34:114–15.
46. Schmitt BD, Gray JD, Britton HL. 1978. Car seat burns in infants: avoiding confusion with inflicted burns. *Pediatrics* 62:607–9.
47. Spencer JA, Grieve DK. 1990. Congenital indifference to pain mistaken for non-accidental injury. *Br J Radiol* 63:308–10.
48. Hampton RL, Newberger E. 1985. Child abuse incidence and reporting by hospitals: significance of severity, class and race. *Am J Public Health* 75:56–68.
49. Warner JF, Hansen DJ. 1994. The identification and reporting of physical abuse by physicians: a review and implications for research. *Child Abuse Negl* 18:11–25.
50. Greenbaum AR, Donne J, Wilson D, et al. 2004. Intentional burn injury: an evidence-based, clinical and forensic review. *Burns* 30:628–42.
51. Heaton PA. 1989. The pattern of burn injuries in childhood. *NZ Med J* 102:584–86.
52. Hobbs CJ. 1989. ABC of child abuse: burns and scalds. *BMJ* 298:1302–5.
53. Rosenberg NM, Marino D. 1989. Frequency of suspected abuse/neglect in burn patients. *Pediatr Emerg Care* 5(4):219–21.
54. Clark KD, Tepper D, Jenny C. 1997. Effect of a screening profile on the diagnosis of nonaccidental burns in children. *Pediatr Emerg Care* 13(4):259–61.
55. Height DW, Bakalar HR, Lloyd JR. 1979. Inflicted burns in children: recognition and treatment. *JAMA* 242:517–20.
56. Allasio D, Fischer H. 2005. Immersion scald burn and the ability of young children to climb into a bathtub. *Pediatrics* 115(5):1419–21.

57. American College of Radiology. 1997. *ACR Standards for Skeletal Surveys in Children.* Resolution 22. Reston, VA: American College of Radiology: 23.
58. Kleinman PK. 1987. *Diagnostic Imaging of Child Abuse.* Baltimore: Williams and Wilkins.
59. OConner JF, Cohen J. 1987. Dating fractures. In *Diagnostic Imaging of Child Abuse,* ed. PK Kleinman, 35–62. Baltimore: Williams and Wilkins.
60. Levin TL, Berdon WE, Cassell I, Blitman NM. 2003. Thoracolumbar fracture with listhesis–an uncommon manifestation of child abuse. *Pediar Radiol* 33:305–10.
61. Kemp AM, Dunstan F, Harrison S, Morris, S, et al. 2008. Patterns of skeletal fractures in child abuse: systematic review. *BMJ* 337:a1518.
62. Hobbs CJ. 1984. Skull fracture and the diagnosis of abuse. *Arch Dis Child* 59:246–52.
63. Ved N, Haller JO. 2002. Periosteal reaction with normal-appearing underlying bone: a child abuse mimicker. *Emerg Radiol* 9:278–82.
64. Pergolizzi R Jr, Oestreich AE. 1995. Child abuse fracture through physiologic periosteal reaction. *Pediatr Radiol* 25:566–67.

Intentional Starvation/ Malnutrition and Dehydration in Children

7

KIM A. COLLINS

Contents

7.1 Lethal Neglect

Pediatric neglect can be defined as the failure of a caregiver to adequately meet a child's basic needs, which include physical safety and protection, food, clothing, shelter, education, medical/dental care, and supervision.[1–4] Neglect, the most common form of child maltreatment, accounts for approximately two-thirds of maltreatment cases, three times more common than physical abuse or battery.[4–10] However, lethal neglect is not common. When neglect is fatal, the form is usually starvation and malnutrition and/or dehydration. Starvation, the deprivation of food and ultimately nutrition, and malnutrition, the lack of proper nourishment for the body's metabolism and survival, can result in death. A child may be fatally neglected by means of dehydration with no signs of starvation or malnutrition. In some cases, the child is both starved/malnourished and dehydrated. The terms active and passive are also used to classify neglect. Active neglect involves a deliberate lack of care or the withholding of necessary components of a child's care. Passive neglect occurs when a caregiver inadvertently does not provide for a child because his/her focus is elsewhere.[2] This determination, based on the intentions and actions of the caregivers, can be difficult to make and relies greatly on the combined efforts of the forensic investigator and the forensic pathologist. A psychiatric evaluation of the caregiver may be needed to assess the possibility of mental illness and the psychosocial dynamics of the caregiver–child relationship.

7.2 The Victim

The typical victim of lethal neglect due to starvation/malnutrition and dehydration falls into one of two categories: (1) infants and nonmobile children who are unable to obtain food or drink; (2) slightly older children who are able to obtain food and drink, although the nutritional content is inadequate. Most victims of lethal neglect are under the age of one year.[2] There is no typical gender, race, or socioeconomic status of the victim. In some cases, the victim is the only abused or neglected child in the family.

7.3 The Investigation

A scene investigation is mandatory in all cases of suspected lethal neglect (Table 7.1). The caregiver should be interviewed immediately. The caregiver often tends to minimize the duration of the child's neglected state.[9] The feeding history (amount and schedule) should be obtained and any remaining formula procured. A thorough investigation will usually show that the history is inconsistent with the physical findings. The manufacturer of the formula can providc information on content and concentration, and the formula can be analyzed for such appropriateness. Any siblings in the household should be separately interviewed. They may report changes in the home dynamics or discriminatory practices against the victim. Neighbors and extended

Table 7.1 The Investigation of Pediatric Starvation/Malnutrition

Interview of caregivers
Feeding history
Formula sample
Manufacturer of formula for content and concentration
Interview of siblings
Interview of neighbors and family
Determination of any changes in household, i.e., financial, new partner, drugs, etc.
Social service records or social history
Medical history
Birth records
Well-baby pediatric clinic records

Table 7.2 The Medical Investigation in Pediatric Starvation/Malnutrition

Medical history
Well-baby pediatric clinic records
WIC records
Charting of body measurements over time
Development over time
Comparison of growth and development with family/social history

family members are also excellent sources of information. A child may have been normal until a specific point in time, when a change took place in the household. Such changes include caregiver drug addiction, new adult partner, financial crisis, or other stressor. However, some victims are isolated, and neighbors or others outside the home never witness the neglect. It is not unusual for a neighbor to have never seen the victim or know he/she even existed. The existence of any social service or comparable agency records or pertinent social history should also be determined.

The medical history is also very important (Table 7.2). The birth records should be obtained to assess gestation at the time of delivery, appropriateness for gestational age, and any neonatal or recent illnesses. Growth records of doctor's office visits will allow the investigator to follow the growth and development of the child over time as well as determine any specific time frames of the neglect and possibly associate a particular caregiver with the deterioration of the child.

7.4 The Postmortem Examination

It is extremely important that a thorough postmortem examination be conducted, including a skeletal survey, complete autopsy, microscopic analysis, and ancillary studies (Table 7.3). It is not common for starved and malnourished children to have components of physical battery; however, the skeletal survey can demonstrate demineralization, osteopenia, osteomalacia, fractures due to demineralization, and rachitic changes (Figure 7.1). A pediatric

Table 7.3 The Autopsy in Pediatric Starvation/Malnutrition

Skeletal survey
Complete autopsy
Comparison of body measurements with prior growth charts
Comparison of body measurements with expected values
Microscopic examination
Ancillary studies
Photographs and diagrams

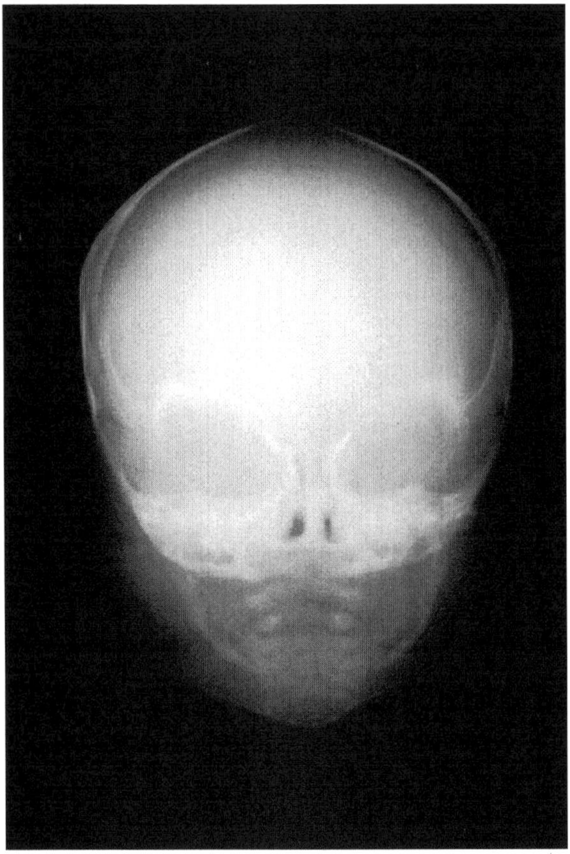

(A)

Figure 7.1 (A) Normal anterior-posterior x-ray of an infant skull. Note the crisp outline of the normally mineralized skull plates extending superiorly to the anterior fontanelle.

radiologist can assist in interpreting some of these subtle radiographic changes secondary to malnutrition. As in all pediatric forensic cases, a "baby gram," i.e., placing the entire body on a single radiographic plate, is unacceptable.

Externally, the body length, crown–rump, head circumference, and body weight are the minimum measurements that must be recorded for assessing starvation/malnutrition and dehydration. The measurements must be compared to standard values and to the child's own growth charts since birth. This chronology is extremely important in assessing abnormal growth and development, supporting the diagnosis of starvation and malnutrition, and ruling out any natural diseases that present with a failure to thrive. If the child was born prematurely, this must be considered when comparing to the standard values. Appropriate growth charts with expected measurements should be obtained, and assistance from a neonatologist may be helpful.

(B)

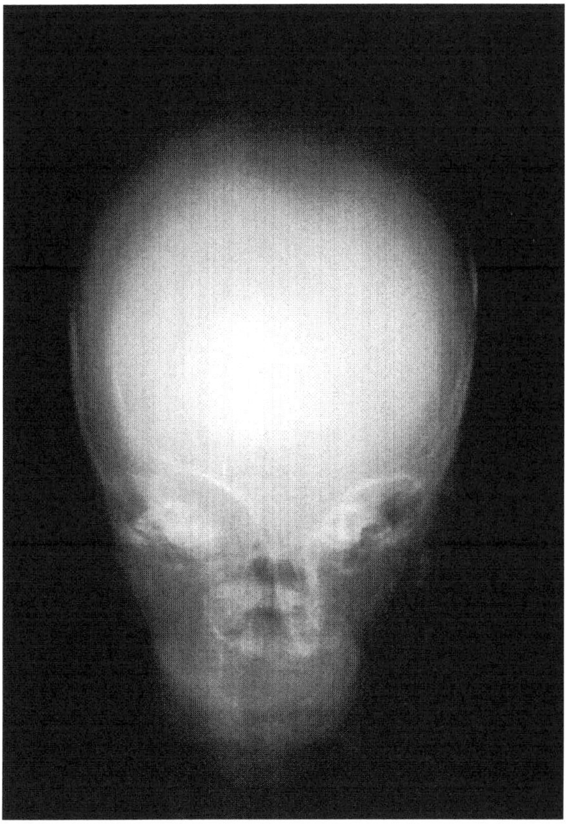

Figure 7.1 (Continued.) (B) Anterior-posterior x-ray of a malnourished infant skull. Compared to image (A), the skull plates are poorly mineralized and seem to fade out or disappear on the film.

Good photographs with backup diagrams are a must in cases of lethal starvation, since the significant diagnostic findings are from the gross examination. Overall photographs depicting the features described below should be taken. Lighting and the flash should be used to help convey the three-dimensional findings at autopsy in a two-dimensional photograph. Some photographs at angles to the body should be taken in order to show the protrusion of bones or sinking of eyes and fontanelles. A color card from a film or photography company can be used in some of the pictures to help illustrate changes in pigmentation or blue pallor of starvation.

7.4.1 The Autopsy

The gross findings are the most remarkable in cases of starvation/malnutrition and dehydration (Table 7.4). Usually, the autopsy provides very subtle

Table 7.4 Gross Autopsy Findings in Pediatric Starvation/Malnutrition

Decreased adipose tissue
Decreased visceral adipose tissue
Atrophied skeletal muscle
Decreased organ weights
Blue pallor of the skin, pale "semi-translucent" skin
Pressure sores
Areas of hypopigmentation
Dental caries
Brittle hair
Alopecia
Protruding occiput
Thin neck
Sunken eyes
Sunken cheeks/decreased buccal fat
Depressed fontanelles
Protruding ribs
Protruding vertebrae
Protruding iliac crests
Winging of the scapulae
"Knobby knees" and joints
Scaphoid abdomen
Wrinkled skin over the joints and extremities
Wrinkled skin and subcutaneous tissue over the buttocks
Thinned walls of the stomach and intestines
Empty GI tract
Distended and filled gallbladder
Dehydrated feces, fecoliths
Sticky serosal surfaces
Tenting of the skin with dehydration
Diaper rash
Secondary infections

or no corresponding microscopic findings. The inadequate intake of calories, nourishment, and/or hydration results in decreased subcutaneous adipose tissue, decreased visceral adipose tissue, atrophy of musculature, and decreased water content in the tissues. The body is underweight for the length (crown–heel), often below the fifth percentile.[11,12] The head appears proportionately large, especially the occiput. This finding is actually due to the decrease in neck adipose tissue and atrophy of neck and shoulder musculature (Figure 7.2). A lateral view with photographs best depicts this illusion of occipital protrusion (Figure 7.3). Scalp hair may be dry, thin, pale, and brittle with areas of alopecia (Figure 7.4). The individual hairs are easily

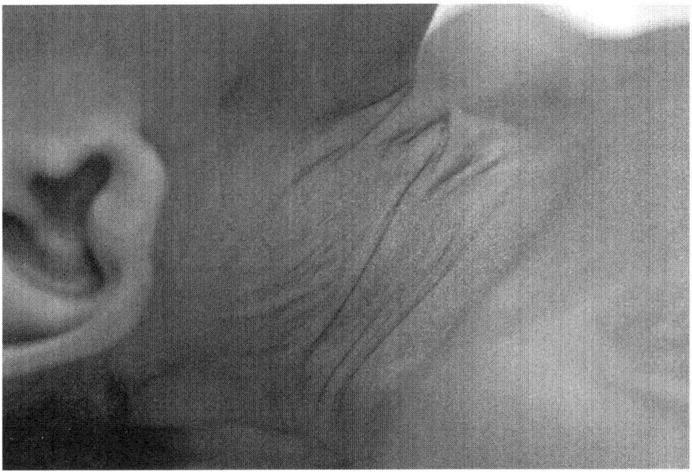

Figure 7.2 The thin neck has atrophied skeletal muscle and adipose tissue with wrinkling of the overlying skin.

plucked from the scalp.[13] The cheeks will be sunken secondary to a loss of the buccal fat pad with accentuation of the zygomatic bone (Figure 7.5). The face will take on a triangular shape with the chin as the apex. A lateral view will also illustrate sunken globes (eyes) (Figure 7.6). This finding is due to decreased orbital adipose tissue as well as dehydration. Likewise with dehydration, the brain parenchyma will shrink, the pressure of the cerebrospinal fluid will decrease, and the fontanelles (especially anterior) will be depressed (Figure 7.7).[14] This depression can be observed and photographed well when

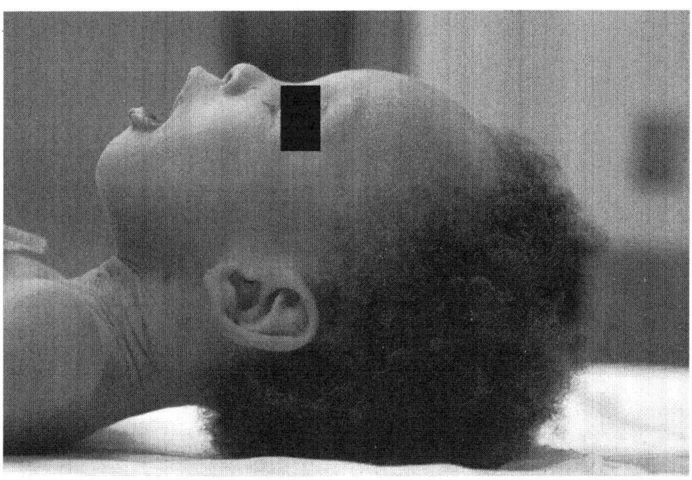

Figure 7.3 The head appears large on the atrophied neck with accentuation of the occiput.

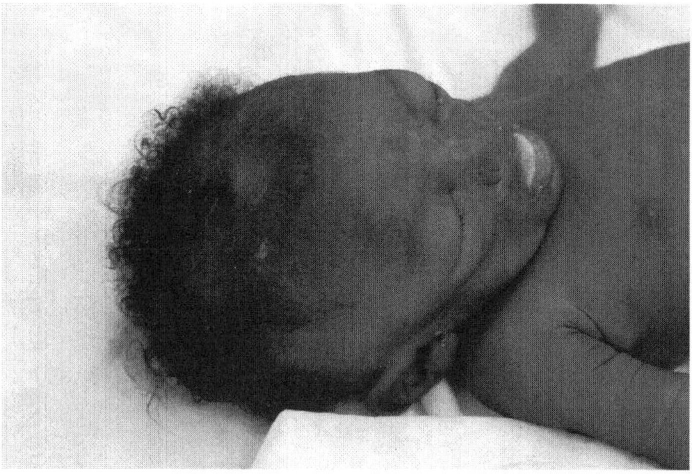

Figure 7.4 Areas of alopecia are evident over the scalp.

viewed laterally. Reflection of the scalp will also allow the pathologist to examine the fontanelles and assess the depression.

Overall, the body is cachetic with a "skeletonized frame" covered by thin, dry skin with possible areas of hypopigmentation. The abdominal panniculus is thin to absent. The skin loses turgor and "tents" when pinched due to a loss of subcutaneous adipose tissue and dehydration. The ribs and vertebral bodies are prominent, occasionally with overlying skin excoriation. The abdomen is scaphoid, and the iliac crests protrude. The scapulas are described as "winging," since they protrude due to atrophy of the muscles,

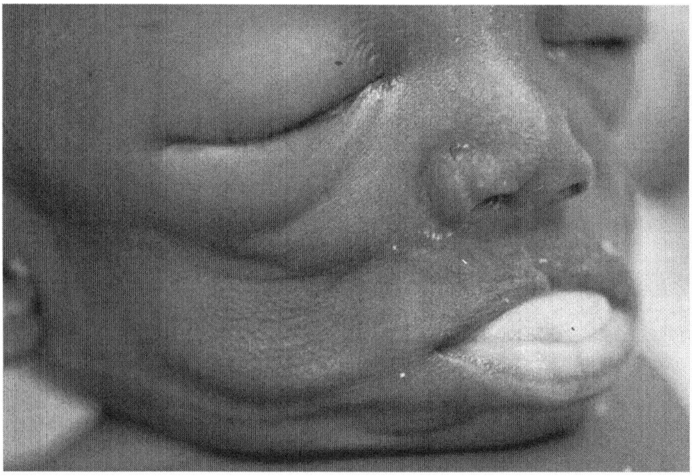

Figure 7.5 The cheeks have lost their normal buccal fat pads and sink within the bony structures of the face.

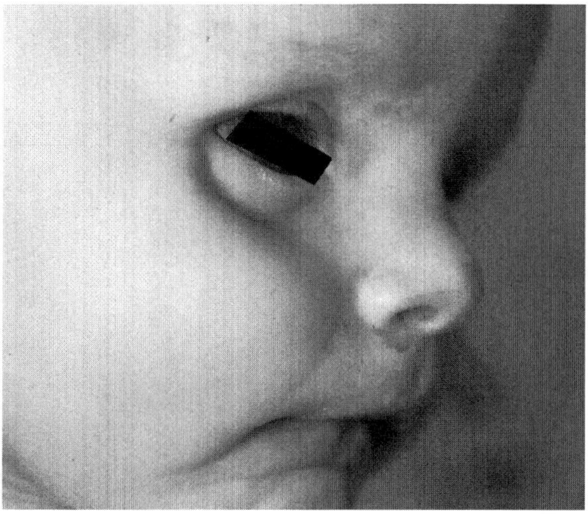

Figure 7.6 With loss of ocular adipose tissue and dehydration, the globes sink within the orbits.

in particular the serratus anterior, trapezius, and rhomboid muscles, which stabilize the scapula. The degree of protrusion is accentuated by the loss of overlying subcutaneous adipose tissue (Figure 7.8). The extremities have decreased skeletal muscle and adipose tissue, leaving the overlying skin to sag and wrinkle (Figure 7.9). The joints are comparatively large and look distorted and "knobby." The buttocks, composed of the gluteus muscle and the gluteal fat pad, are markedly atrophic. The overlying skin is wrinkled and the sacrum prominent (Figure 7.10). Overlying decubitus ulcerations may be present, depending on the resting and often prolonged position of the child and points of pressure. These areas of ulceration are most commonly found over the sacroiliac region, backs of the shoulders, occiput, and heels.

Internally, the aforementioned marked decrease in adipose tissue and atrophy of skeletal muscle is noted. Even deeper (non-subcutaneous) areas have

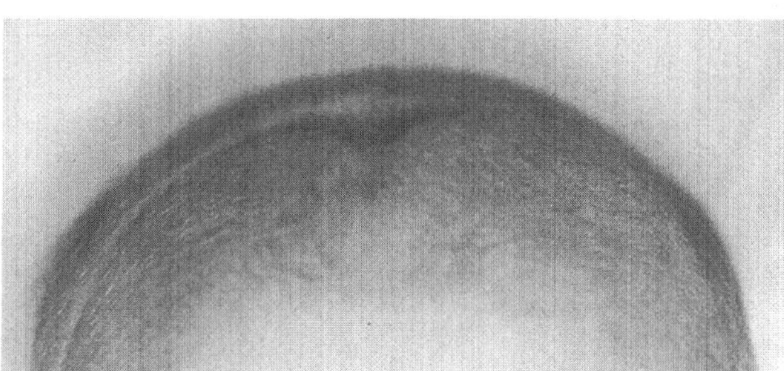

Figure 7.7 Dehydration results in depression of the fontanels and accentuation of the nonfused cranial sutures.

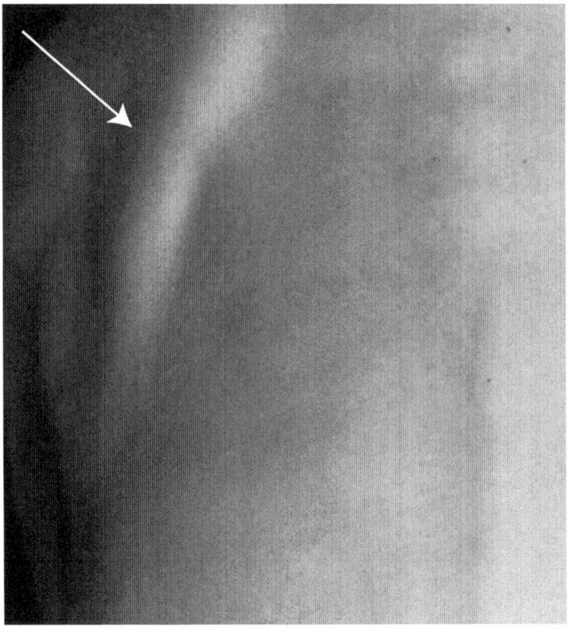

Figure 7.8 Atrophy of the skeletal muscle framework about the scapula results in loss of support and winging of the scapula.

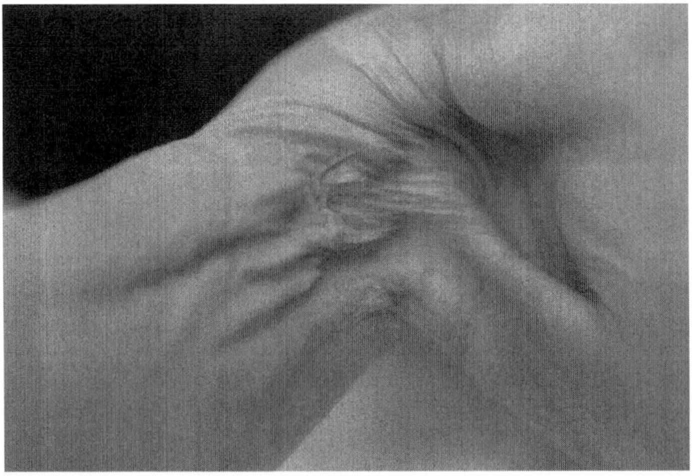

Figure 7.9 The skin covering joints, such as the axillae, sags as the underlying skeletal muscle and adipose tissue has atrophied.

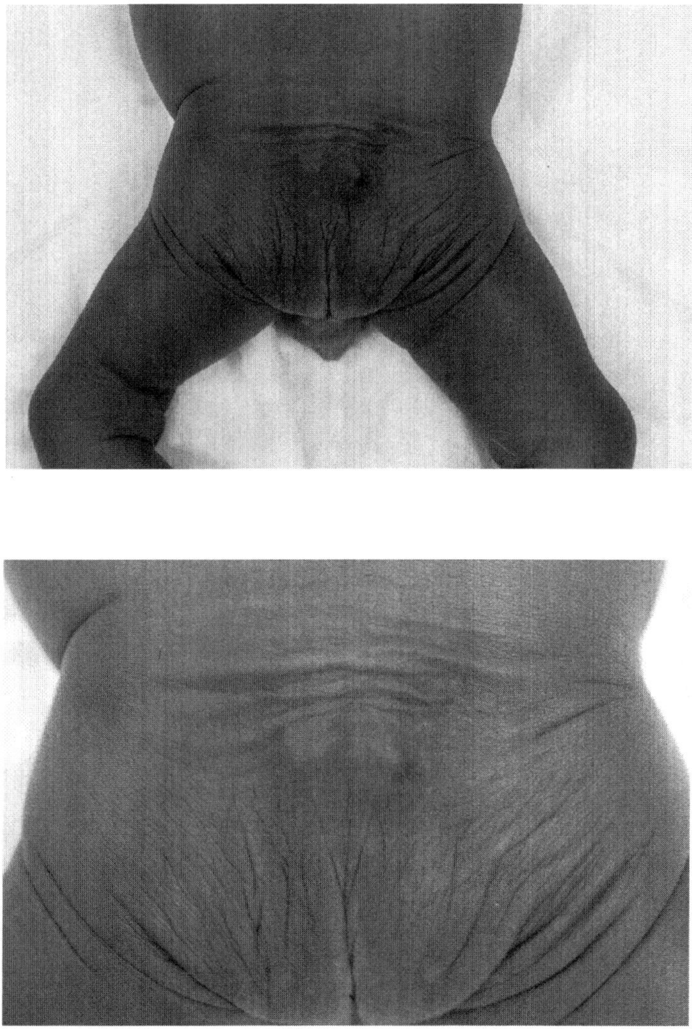

Figure 7.10 Atrophy of the large gluteal muscle and overlying adipose tissue causes flattening of the normal buttock curvature and wrinkling of the skin. The underlying bony structures, such as the pelvis and sacrum, protrude and will eventually erode through the thin cutaneous covering.

loss of adipose tissue, such as the mesentery, omentum, and retroperitoneum around the kidneys. The organs are decreased in weight. The decrease in brain weight, if present, is due to a factor of dehydration and not to atrophy. The luminal viscera such as the intestines will have thinned walls. The liver may be slightly pale and yellow due to steatosis from protein deficiency.[15,16] The gallbladder, which normally secretes bile for digestion, will be unstimulated, and therefore distended with bile. The gastrointestinal system may or may not have any contents depending on the last time that the child was fed or able to obtain

Table 7.5 Microscopic Findings in Pediatric Starvation/Malnutrition

Hepatic microvescicular steatosis
Brown fat transformation
Thymic involution, "starry sky"
Thymic calcification of Hassel corpuscles
Thymic fibrofatty replacement

food. Three volume measurements should be taken and the contents saved: stomach, small intestine, and large intestine. With dehydration, fecal material may be firm and result in fecoliths. Any urine should also be quantified. If a diaper was received with the body, its contents should be documented.

7.4.2 Microscopic Findings

Microscopic findings are sparse and nonspecific (Table 7.5). Three organs that may prove useful are the liver, the thymus, and the adrenals. The liver may demonstrate microvesicular steatosis due to the protein deficiency of malnutrition.[15,16] The physiological response to starvation involves increased muscle proteolysis and adipose tissue lipolysis that supply amino acids and nonesterified fatty acids ("free fatty acids") for gluconeogenesis, oxidation, and ketogenesis.[15] Proposed mechanisms for the accumulation of the intrahepatic lipid are reduced export of lipid and/or increased delivery of nonesterified fatty acids to the liver during starvation.[15] The thymus can show involution with degeneration and calcification of Hassall corpuscles and a depletion of the cortical lymphocytes. The lymphocytes will undergo karyorrhexis, and macrophages infiltrate the cortex. The microscopic result is a "starry sky" appearance. With time, the thymus will show fibrofatty replacement. The adrenal glands can be atrophied and show stress changes typified by a thin, lipid-depleted cortex. Pseudotubule formation can be found in the cortex. If the remaining adipose tissue is examined microscopically, a transformation to higher energy-producing brown fat can be detected.[10] The adipocytes will be granular secondary to increased mitochondria, and the nuclei will be centrally located.

7.5 Ancillary Studies

In cases of suspected lethal neglect, ancillary studies are essential to determine the cause of death and to rule out organic diseases that may cause failure to thrive or dehydration (Table 7.6). These ancillary studies include toxicology, metabolic screening, chromosomal and genetic studies, vitreous

Table 7.6 Ancillary Studies in Pediatric Starvation/Malnutrition

Toxicology
Metabolic screening
Chromosomal and genetic studies
Vitreous chemistry
Microbiology and virology studies

chemistry, and various microbiology and virology analyses. Toxicology should be performed on peripheral blood that has been procured into a gray-top Vacutainer™ containing a preservative.[17] Metabolic screening can also be performed postmortem. The screening methods used include tandem mass spectrometry, immunoassays, and confirmatory molecular analyses. Fresh blood is dropped onto a filter paper card provided by the laboratory. From the dried blood spots, the screen is performed. Some genetic mutations such as the Delta F508 mutation of cystic fibrosis can also be identified by the analysis of dried blood spots. Cytogenetics with karyotyping can be used to diagnose chromosomal abnormalities.[9] The specimens of choice are skin and Achilles tendon; kidney, liver, spleen, and bone marrow may also be sampled. The specimen should be collected within 24 hours after death, best if within 6 hours, and transported in sterile Hank's solution, which is either at room temperature or chilled. Many children with chromosomal abnormalities are more prone to electrolyte disturbances and dehydration mimicking physical neglect. Thus cytogenetic studies aid in alleviating suspicions and in adequately diagnosing the underlying disease resulting in death. Vitreous electrolytes can be analyzed to detect dehydration. Using a needle and syringe, vitreous (2 to 3 mL) is slowly drawn from the globe and placed into a sterile red-top tube. Postmortem levels of sodium and chloride and urea nitrogen reflect premortem values. Potassium rises after death with the increasing postmortem interval. Due to glycolysis, vitreous glucose normally falls after death in a nondiabetic, so a low glucose is insignificant. Dehydration due to neglect is usually hypertonic and can be reflected by an increase in sodium, chloride, and urea nitrogen. However, dehydration (especially isotonic) is also seen in viral gastroenteritis, such as with rotavirus.[14] Rotavirus gastroenteritis can be very dangerous in children. Four methods have been studied over the past several years for detecting rotavirus in fecal samples: latex agglutination, electron microscopy, immunofluorescence, and ELISA. Simple, rapid, and cost-effective manual tests have recently been perfected. Two studies, Dot-ELISA and Rapid Latex, have proven sensitive and specific in detecting rotaviral gastroenteritis.[18,19]

7.6 Secondary Infections

Malnutrition and dehydration depress the immune system so the victim may have secondary infections.[20–24] Secondary infections are due not only to starvation resulting in decreased caloric intake and energy needed to fight infection, but also to malnutrition with the decrease in the protein and amino acid intake.[23,24] Findings from recent studies indicate an important role for amino acids in immune responses by regulating (1) the activation of T lymphocytes, B lymphocytes, natural killer cells, and macrophages, (2) cellular redox state, gene expression, and lymphocyte proliferation, and (3) the production of antibodies, cytokines, and other cytotoxic substances.[23] Adequate intake of vitamins and trace elements is also required for the immune system to function efficiently; a micronutrient deficiency suppresses immune functions by affecting the innate T-cell-mediated immune response and adaptive antibody response. Vitamins and minerals such as B_6, folate, B_{12}, C, E, selenium, zinc, copper, and iron also support cytokine-mediated immune response.[20] Four body areas secondarily infected in the setting of neglect are respiratory system (bronchopneumonia, tuberculosis), skin (cellulitis), urinary tract (cystitis), and central nervous system (meningitis, intracranial abscess, otitis media) (Figure 7.11). Although the immediate cause of death may be a so-called natural disease, the underlying cause of death is the neglect.

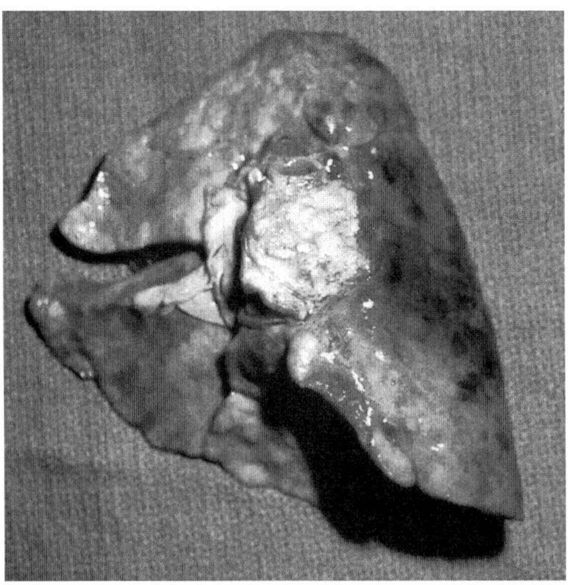

Figure 7.11 Secondary infections are not uncommon in cases of malnutrition such as this case of pulmonary tuberculosis.

7.7 Mimickers

Organic diseases that can result in malnutrition and dehydration must be ruled out in order to confidently classify the cause of death. The aforementioned microscopic and ancillary studies will greatly aid in this task. However, the pathologist must first realize that there are numerous diseases that can mimic starvation/malnutrition and dehydration by neglect.[25] Dehydration can result from entities such as diabetes mellitus, diabetes insipidus, mental retardation, neuromuscular incoordination, chromosomal disorders, metabolic disorders, cystic fibrosis, viral gastroenteritis, and congenital adrenal hyperplasia (Table 7.7).[26,27] Disorders such as oromotor abnormalities, cleft palate, pyloric stenosis, celiac disease, intestinal malabsorption, cystic fibrosis, glycogen storage diseases, carcinoma, congenital heart disease, cerebral palsy, and chromosomal and genetic diseases can produce signs of starvation and malnutrition (Table 7.8).[2,3,28] These entities are more common than lethal child neglect and must be addressed as part of the autopsy and investigation of a suspected starved/malnourished or dehydrated homicide victim.

Table 7.7 Potential Mimickers of Pediatric Dehydration
Diabetes mellitus
Diabetes insipidus
Chromosomal and genetic disorders/mental retardation
Neuromuscular incoordination
Metabolic disorders
Cystic fibrosis
Viral gastroenteritis
Congenital adrenal hyperplasia

Table 7.8 Potential Mimickers of Pediatric Starvation/Malnutrition
Oromotor abnormalities
Cleft palate
Pyloric stenosis
Celiac disease
Intestinal malabsorption
Cystic fibrosis
Glycogen storage diseases
Carcinoma
Congenital heart disease
Cerebral palsy
Chromosomal and genetic diseases

7.8 Conclusion

Lethal starvation/malnutrition and dehydration cases are difficult to investigate. The findings are predominantly gross, the microscopic findings are nonspecific, there is no single pathognomonic finding, and numerous natural organic diseases can present with similar findings. With current technological advances in laboratory medicine, ancillary studies can aid in ruling out these diseases and narrowing the differential diagnoses. Lethal neglect of a child is a homicide.

References

1. Thompson WK, McCarley AL. 2003. Practical consideration in the evaluation and management of child neglect. *Clin Fam Pract* 5:1.
2. Corey TS, Collins KA. 2002. Pediatric forensic pathology. In *Pediatric Pathology,* eds. JT Stocker and LP Dehner, 247–285. Philadelphia, PA: Lippincott Williams and Wilkins.
3. Munkel WI. 1998. Neglect and abandonment. In *Child Maltreatment: A Clinical Guide and Reference,* eds. JA Monteleone and AE Brodeur, 339–46. St. Louis, MO: G.W. Medical Publishing.
4. Cheung KK. 1999. Identifying and documenting findings of physical child abuse and neglect. *J Pediatr Healthcare* 13:142–43.
5. Ellis PS. 1997. The pathology of fatal child abuse. *Pathology* 29:113–21.
6. Frederickson D. 1999. Maltreatment of children. *J Child Fam Nurs* 2:393–401.
7. Meadow R. 1993. Epidemiology. In *ABC of Child Abuse.* London: BMJ.
8. Patterson MM. 1998. Child abuse: assessment and intervention. *Orthop Nurs* 17:49–54.
9. Knight L, Collins, KA. 2005. A 25 year retrospective review of deaths due to child neglect. *Am J Forensic Med Pathol* 26:221–28.
10. Collins KA. 2006. Pediatric forensic pathology. In *Basic Competencies in Forensic Pathology,* ed. JA Prahlow, 135–56. Northfield, IL: College of American Pathologists Press.
11. Kerr MA, Black MM, Krishnakumar A. 2000. Failure-to-thrive, maltreatment and the behavior and development of 6-year-old children from low-income urban families: a cumulative risk model. *Child Abuse Negl* 24:587–98.
12. Wright CM. 2000. Identification and management of failure to thrive: a community perspective. *Arch Dis Child* 82:5–9.
13. Carvalho NF, Kenney RD, Carrington PH, Hall DE. 2001. Severe nutritional deficiencies in toddlers resulting from health food milk alternatives. *Pediatrics* 107:e46.
14. Grisanti KA, Jaffe DM. 1991. Dehydration syndromes. Oral rehydration and fluid replacement. *Emerg Med Clin North Am* 9:565–88.
15. Gan SK, Watts GF. 2008. Is adipose tissue lipolysis always and adaptive response to starvation? Implications for non-alcoholic fatty liver disease. *Clin Sci (Lond)* 114:543–45.

16. Van Ginneken VJ. 2008. Liver fattening during feast and famine: an evolutionary paradox. *Med Hypotheses* 70:924–28.
17. Campbell TA, Collins, KA. 2001. Pediatric toxicologic deaths: a ten year retrospective study. *Am J Forensic Med Pathol* 22:184–87.
18. Kohno H, Akihara S, Nishio O, Ushijima H. 2000. Development of a simple and rapid latex test for rotavirus in stool samples. *Pediatr Int* 42:395–400.
19. Anand T, Raju TA, Vishnu C, Rao LV, Sharma G. 2001. Development of Dot-ELISA for the detection of human rotavirus antigen and comparison with RNA-PAGE. *Lett Appl Microbiol* 32:176–80.
20. Wintergerst ES, Maggini S, Hornig DH. 2007. Contribution of selected vitamins and trace elements in immune function. *Ann Nutr Metab* 51:301–23.
21. Ikeda S, Saito H, Fukatsu K, Inoue T, et al. 2001. Dietary restriction impairs neutrophil exudation by reducing CD11b/CD18 expression and chemokine production. *Arch Surg* 136:297–304.
22. Savino W, Dardenne M, Velloso LA, Dayse Silva-Barbosa S. 2007. The thymus is a common target in malnutrition and infection. *Br J Nutr* 98:S11–16.
23. Li P, Yin YL, Li D, Kim SW, Wu G. 2007. Amino acids and immune function. *Br J Nutr* 98:237–52.
24. Chatraw JH, Wherry EJ, Ahmed R, Kapasi ZF. 2008. Diminished primary CD8 T cell response to viral infection during protein energy malnutrition in mice is due to changes in microenvironment and low numbers of viral-specific CD8 T cell precursors. *J Nutr* 138:806–12.
25. Davis JH, Rao VJ, Valdes-Dapena M. 1984. A forensic approach to a starved child. *J Forensic Sci* 29:663–69.
26. Greig F, Schoeneman M, Kandall SR, et al. 1993. Neonatal hyponatremic dehydration as an initial presentation of cystic fibrosis. *Clin Pediatr* 548–51.
27. Whitehead FJ, Couper RTL, Moore L, et al. 1996. Dehydration deaths in infants and young children. *Am J Forensic Med Pathol* 17:73–78.
28. Copeland AR. 1998. A case of panhypogammaglobulinemia masquerading as child abuse. *J Forensic Sci* 33:1493–96.

Proving Pediatric Poisoning in the Courtroom

8

STEVEN B. KARCH

Contents

8.1 Introduction

Pediatric poisoning is rare. When it does occur, it is usually accidental, the result of a child innocently having ingested a single agent. Very successful public health measures have gradually reduced the frequency of these unfortunate events, although accidental alcohol poisoning remains a problem in teenagers, and occasional cases of accidental methadone and opioid poisoning do occur.[1,2,3] Homicidal poisoning, as opposed to accidental poisoning, is so rare in the pediatric age group that a Medline search, done in preparation for writing this chapter, produced only two "hits." The first was a case review of 709 pediatric deaths, written in 2001.[4] Drugs were found to be the cause of death in 11 cases, only two of which were certified as homicides. One was due to alcohol and one to cocaine. Within the series, cases of accidental poisoning followed a bimodal distribution: Six of the decedents were aged 15 to 17 years, and five were under 4 years in age. No details regarding either of the homicidal deaths were provided. Clinical experience suggests that the bimodal nature of the cases fits a common pattern.

The second Medline hit, a retrospective evaluation of drugs detected in a pediatric postmortem population between the years 1998 and 2002 (n = 730), was recently published.[5] Blacks comprised 54% of cases, males 59%, and 48% were less than one year of age or stillborn. Forty-two percent of deaths were ruled natural, 27% accidental, 13% undetermined, 5% suicide, and 2%

homicide. Only 640 had comprehensive toxicology screening, and 38% were positive for at least one compound. Illicit drugs were found in 26%, ethanol in 11%, and antihistamines in 6%. Eighty-seven cases contained more than one drug. Overall, only 6% of the deaths were thought to be related to maternal drug abuse. However, none of the homicides in the series were considered to be drug related.

Even in India, where viable unwanted female infants are often aborted, poisoning in childhood almost never occurs.[6] In the West, the mode of death in most filicides is usually traumatic.[7] While filicide by poisoning is so rare as to be reportable, death by blunt trauma unfortunately is not. Blunt force trauma is easily recognized, but homicidal poisoning can be an extremely difficult diagnosis to establish with any certainty, not so much because of the science involved, but because of the chaotic legal standards, at least in the United States, used to define homicide. In some states women have been charged with homicide because of allegedly passing a lethal amount of drug to their child by breastfeeding. In others, murder by transplacental drug transmission has been alleged. Such charges raise questions of intention that cannot be reliably answered, at least not by any medical examiner. Intention is a problem for the courts. However, determining the actual cause of death is a matter for physicians to decide, and a large number of factors need to be considered. If these issues are not considered, it may not be possible to reach a diagnosis of intentional poisoning, and the cause of death must remain undetermined.

8.2 Genetic Diseases

Traditionally, drug-death investigations have consisted of three distinct elements: (1) an adequate scene investigation, including history and witness interview; (2) a complete autopsy, which is then followed by (3) comprehensive toxicological testing. The pathologist (the only person in the courtroom who can legitimately opine as to the cause of death) then weighs the findings from all three phases of the investigation and attempts to reach the correct diagnosis. Unfortunately, for several reasons, the traditional method may lead to inappropriate conclusions, largely because the traditional approach was conceived long before the advent of modern molecular biology, the introduction of modern genomics, or the discovery of postmortem drug redistribution. This is why the traditional method is inadequate; no autopsy, at least not one where drugs are considered a possible cause of death, or where there are no obvious physical findings, is ever complete until DNA testing is performed.[8]

8.2.1 Cardiac Conduction Disorders

Mutations affecting electrical conduction in the heart are impossible to diagnose without DNA testing. The latest studies suggest that a large percentage (perhaps nearly a third) of children who die of sudden infant death syndrome/sudden unexpected death syndrome (SIDS/SUDS) carry mutations that lead to a group of disorders collectively referred to as channelopathies. This group of genetic polymorphisms cause abnormalities of the molecular pores that transfer ions into and out of cardiomyocytes.[9] If a child carrying one of these genes died, and happened to be taking any kind of medication, the question of drug involvement would arise even if a comprehensive autopsy was performed. When the office of the chief medical examiner in New York City examined DNA from 42 infants, previously diagnosed as having SIDS/SUDS, channelopathy mutations known to cause long QT syndrome and sudden death were found in 28%.

A position paper published by the American National Association of Medical Examiners (NAME) in 2007 provides detailed information on the protocols to be used in SIDS/SUDS investigation. It suggests dividing these cases into six different categories. In all but one, it is assumed that the autopsy is complete.[10] Given what is known today, autopsies of all SIDS/SUDS decedents are incomplete because mutational analysis is not performed. By definition, then, nearly one-third of SIDS/SUDS cases are now misclassified.

Even the most comprehensive autopsy of a child with SIDS/SUDS cannot be considered complete because the correct diagnosis cannot be made with a microscope, but only by DNA resequencing. A paper published in 2008 illustrates the problem: A pair of identical male monozygotic twins, 138 days old, died within one hour of each other. A detailed autopsy and extensive histological and toxicological testing, far exceeding the requirements set by NAME, did not disclose a cause of death. However, DNA extracted from the tissue blocks obtained from both twins was found to contain the same heterozygous nonsense SCN5A mutation (W822X), one of the rarest forms of Brugada polymorphisms, and the cause of death was certified as natural.[11]

More than one parent has been convicted of murder because of juries that erroneously accepted Meadow's law ("One [case of SIDS in a family] is a tragedy, two is suspicious and three is murder unless there is proof to the contrary").[12] If any drug had been detected, even in only modest amounts, it might very well have been considered the cause of death. If drug concentrations were high, the temptation to classify the death as drug-related would have been particularly hard to resist. The issue is further complicated by the fact that genetic polymorphisms are not confined to the heart. Genetic variations in the hepatic P450 system can alter the way individuals metabolize drugs.

8.2.2 Toxicogenetics

Either mother or child may not be able to metabolize drugs normally, which means that the presence of toxic drug concentrations, in the living or the dead, does not necessarily imply that a toxic dose of drug has been administered, either intentionally or unintentionally. Another recently published case report illustrates this part of the problem. A newborn died from morphine poisoning. All of the classical symptoms were present, and there was no doubt about the diagnosis. The mother had been taking a prescribed codeine/acetaminophen mixture while breastfeeding her newborn. A postmortem blood sample taken from the mother disclosed a morphine concentration of 70/ng/mL, and her milk had a morphine concentration of 87 ng/mL. The possibility that the mother was a narcotic abuser was considered, but the idea was rejected when the physicians recalled that a small percentage of codeine is converted to morphine. Several of the physicians suspected, and later were able to confirm, that the mother was an ultrarapid metabolizer. She had multiple duplications of cytochrome P450 2D6. Instead of converting the normal 5% to 10% of codeine to morphine, her body was converting nearly all of it,[12a] and her infant died as a result. As recently as five years ago she might have been charged with drug abuse and infanticide.

Another earlier case report emphasizes the same point. A 9-year-old boy with a history of multiple developmental disorders was being treated with methylphenidate, clonidine, and fluoxetene. He developed status epilepticus and died shortly after being brought to the hospital. Foul play was suspected, the other children were removed from the household, and murder charges against the parents were contemplated, all because the postmortem fluoxetene concentrations were so high. It was assumed that the parents had administered an overdose. Samples of the decedent's liver were tested for P450 abnormalities and it was determined that the child had no functional CYP2D6. Therefore he could not synthesize fluoxetene's main metabolite, and a toxic amount of fluoxetene accumulated. When the genetic defect was discovered, the investigation was dropped.[12b]

Before the death of any child can be classified as drug-related, certain questions must be answered.

1. Where did the drugs come from?
2. Did the mother abuse drugs while she was breastfeeding?
3. If the mother was a drug abuser, was the same drug detected in both mother and child?
4. Was the presence of these drugs clearly the cause of death, or are serious alternative explanations possible?

Genetic aberrations are not the only alternative explanation for a positive drug test. If there are drugs in the environment—for example, a mother and child living with a drug dealer, or drugs found in a child who is living in a house that is being used as a methamphetamine laboratory—then those drugs will inevitably be found in the child.[13]

Does the mere detection of a drug prove that the infant died from some effect of the drug? In some cases, probably yes. High opiate concentrations in a drug-naïve child can be presumed to have caused death via respiratory depression. However, not all drugs found in dead children are respiratory depressants, and many drugs are only detected as incidental findings. Still other drugs can "unmask" a previously undiagnosed channelopathy.[14] If a drug is known to produce specific symptoms (such as an anticholinergic syndrome), and if those symptoms are present and no other cause is apparent, then the presence of the drug should be considered a possible cause of death. If symptoms are lacking, the drug may well be an innocent finding.

8.3 The Courts and the Scientific Method

Since 1993, when the Daubert ruling was enacted, judges have been required to act as gatekeepers (Daubert, 2005; Melnick, 2005) who exclude unreliable evidence and unreliable experts from the courtroom.[15,16] In theory, it should no longer be possible for a prosecutor to claim that mother–child drug transfer can lead to the death of the child without first providing scientific evidence to support that accusation. Acceptable evidence consists of more than one expert witness's own scientific opinion, published case reports, or reports to the FDA; reliable scientific evidence consists of peer-reviewed, controlled scientific studies. The Daubert decision also requires that the evidence be relevant and reliable. In the case of alleged pediatric poisoning, the opinion of a nonphysician should be irrelevant, since only physicians can determine the cause of death. In order to be considered scientifically reliable, four criteria must be met:

1. The conclusion reached must have been based on a method that has been tested and found reliable.
2. The method used has been published in the peer-reviewed literature.
3. The method used has an error rate, and that error rate must be known. For example, the error rate for methamphetamine urine screening tests is very high, partly because the test cross-reacts with many amphetamine-related drugs, including cold remedies that, although they exert different effects, share similar molecular structures.
4. The method is widely accepted within the scientific community.

The second and third criteria are unarguably correct and easy to understand, but the first and fourth criteria are problematic: Judges are ill equipped to specify which method is relevant and which scientific communities possess the relevant knowledge. The Daubert decision should have had enormous impact on the number of women charged with having caused the drug-related deaths of their children by drug transfer (breast milk or transplacental), but it has not. Nor has it had much effect in cases of intentional poisoning.

The recent negligent conviction of a daycare provider for murder illustrates the problem (*State of Montana v Sabine Bieber*).[17] The accused was found guilty of having administered a lethal dose of diphenhydramine-containing cold medication to a one-year-old. It was alleged that she had given the medication to keep the child sedated and easier to manage. The child never displayed any symptoms of anticholinergic poisoning that one might expect after ingesting a lethal dose of an anticholinergic drug like diphenhydramine, but instead ate his lunch and took a nap. He was found dead a few hours later. The autopsy revealed no obvious cause of death. The state retained a clinical toxicologist, who wrote, "The concentrations clearly exceed those expected in children given 'therapeutic' doses and are consistent with reports in other pediatric fatal overdoses." The problem here is that no forensic pathologist or toxicologist would ever suggest that postmortem drug concentrations bear any predictable relationship to drug concentrations measured in the immediate antemortem period.[18,19,20] Since they treat only the living, it cannot be presumed that "clinical toxicologists" are aware of the issues faced by pathologists and postmortem toxicologists. Because toxicologists are not, as a rule, physicians, they cannot express an opinion as to the cause of death, but they can say that the drug levels are "consistent" with toxicity. The bizarre aspect of *Bieber* was that the child had no symptoms of poisoning; the postmortem drug concentrations may have been "consistent" with poisoning, but there was no evidence of poisoning. It is extremely unlikely that a judge would have any idea of the differences between clinical toxicologists, who are generally unacquainted with the problems inherent in analyzing autopsy material, and postmortem toxicologists, who know the inherent limitation of the process. On the other hand, it is the responsibility of the judge to make sure that the jury understands the differences between "consistent with" and "caused."

8.4 Problem Poisonings

8.4.1 Stimulant-Related Drug Poisoning

The diagnosis of stimulant-related drug poisoning, which kills thousands in the United States every year, is problematic in children. Unlike opiates, which kill naïve drug users by respiratory depression, leaving no specific anatomic markers, stimulants do leave markers in adults, such as acute, widespread contraction band necrosis and myocardial micro-hemorrhages. However, pediatric myocardium, especially at birth, is resistant to the effects of catecholamines. The birthing process is associated with massive surges of catecholamines, but the beta-receptors are downregulated, making the myocardium resistant to catecholamine cardiotoxicity.[21,22,23] Several case reports suggest that there may be a relationship between intra-utero cocaine exposure and fibromuscular dysplasia of the coronary arteries.[24] However, the relationship has never been confirmed in a clinical study, and no charges against mothers have ever been brought for this finding.

8.4.2 Ethanol Toxicity

Severe toxicity from ethanol can be fatal, and should an adult provide alcohol to a child, depending on the laws of the state, murder charges could be filed. Poisoning is manifested as coma, and it occurs at lower blood alcohol concentrations in young teenagers than in adults. Coma, vomiting, and hypothermia are the most common symptoms in young teenagers intoxicated by alcohol. The biochemical disturbances in children 11 to 16 years of age with alcohol intoxication resemble those of adults, with mild respiratory acidosis and mild hypokalemia. As with cocaine, the young are, in some ways, protected from the deleterious effects of alcohol, because preschool-age children are reported to eliminate ethanol twice as fast as do adults. Unlike adults, where no correlation exists between blood concentrations and symptoms, in children the effects of ethanol on the state of consciousness are directly proportional to the blood alcohol concentration. Among small children there is also less significant risk of hypoglycemia, which is why deaths from alcohol poisoning are quite uncommon, though intoxication is not.[25] While multiple organ disease is likely to be seen in the alcohol-related deaths of adults (liver, brain), no unique lesions are seen in children.

References

1. Kivisto JE, Mattila VM, et al. 2008. Secular trends in poisonings leading to hospital admission among Finnish children and adolescents between 1971 and 2005. *J Pediatr* 153:820–24.
2. Kintz P, Villain M, et al. 2005. Methadone as a chemical weapon: two fatal cases involving babies. *Ther Drug Monit* 27:741–43.

3. Ali J, Sima B, et al. 2008. Opium as a fatal substance. *Indian J Pediatr* 75:1125–28.
4. Campbell TA, Collins KA. 2001. Pediatric toxicologic deaths: a 10-year retrospective study. *Am J Forensic Med Pathol* 22:184–87.
5. Naso C, Jenkins AJ, et al. 2008. A study of drug detection in a postmortem pediatric population. *J Forensic Sci* 53:483–90.
6. Bandyopadhyay S, Singh A. 2003. History of son preference and sex selection in India and in the West. *Bull Indian Inst Hist Med Hyderabad* 33:149–67.
7. Bourget D, Grace J, et al. 2007. A review of maternal and paternal filicide. *J Am Acad Psychiatry Law* 35:74–82.
8. Pelissier-Alicot AL, Gaulier JM, et al. 2003. Mechanisms underlying postmortem redistribution of drugs: a review. *J Anal Toxicol* 27:533–44.
9. Tang G, Bieschke E, et al. 2008. Comprehensive molecular genetic testing for cardiac channelopathy genes in 42 cases of sudden infant death and sudden unexplained death in the city of New York revealed high mutation rate, Abstract G34. Annual Scientific Meeting of the American Academy of Forensic Sciences. Washington, DC, American Academy of Forensic Science.
10. Corey TS, Hanzlick R, et al. 2007. A functional approach to sudden unexplained infant deaths. *Am J Forensic Med Pathol* 28:271–77.
11. Turillazzi E, La Rocca G, et al. 2008. Heterozygous nonsense SCN5A mutation W822X explains a simultaneous sudden infant death syndrome. *Virchows Arch* 453:209–16.
12. Karch SB, Wong S. 2009. A letter from America: the ghost of Dr. Griggs 2008; 15(1):7–15. *J Forensic Legal Med* 16(2):106–7.
12a. Madadi P, Ross CJ, Hayden MR, Carleton BC, Gaedigk A, Leeder JS, Koren G. 2009. Pharmacogenetics of neonatal opioid toxicity following maternal use of codeine during breastfeeding: A case-control study. *Clin Pharmacol Ther* Jan; 85(1):31–5.
12b. Wong SH, Wagner MA, Jentzen JM, Schur C, Bjerke J, Gock SB, Chang CC. 2003. Pharmacogenomics as an aspect of molecular autopsy for forensic pathology/toxicology: Does genotyping CYP 2D6 serve as an adjunct for certifying methadone toxicity? *J Forensic Sci* Nov; 48(6):1406–15.
13. Smith FP, Kidwell DA. 1996. Cocaine in hair, saliva, skin swabs, and urine of cocaine users' children. *Forensic Sci Int* 83:179–89.
14. Weiner RB, Weiner SD, et al. 2008. Removing the mask. *Am J Med* 121:113–16.
15. Daubert. 1993. 509 U.S. 579.
16. Melnick RL. 2005. A Daubert motion: a legal strategy to exclude essential scientific evidence in toxic tort litigation. *Am J Public Health* 95 Suppl 1:S30–34.
17. Tuttle G. 2005. Bieber's 1st prosecutor praises jury. *Billings Gazette*. Billings, Montana.
18. Karch SB. 2003. Is post-mortem toxicology quackery? *J Clin Forensic Med* 10:197–98.
19. Drummer O, Forrest AR, et al. 2004. Forensic science in the dock. *BMJ* 329(7467):636–37.
20. Ferner R. 2008. Post-mortem clinical pharmacology. *Br J Clinl Pharmacol* 66(4):430–43.

21. Schulpis KH, Margeli A, et al. 2006. Effects of mode of delivery on maternal-neonatal plasma antioxidant status and on protein S100B serum concentrations. *Scand J Clin Lab Invest* 66:733–42.
22. Vlachos DG, Schulpis KH, et al. 2008. The effect of the mode of delivery on the maternal-neonatal erythrocyte membrane acetylcholinesterase activity. *Clin Biochem* 41:818–23.
23. Foerster K, Groner F, et al. 2003. Cardioprotection specific for the G protein Gi2 in chronic adrenergic signaling through beta 2-adrenoceptors. *Proc Natl Acad Sci U S A* 100:14475–80.
24. Thomas KR, Thomas SP, et al. 2007. Fibromuscular dysplasia in association with intrauterine cocaine exposure. *Cardiovasc Pathol* 16:313–16.
25. Lamminpaa A. 1994. Acute alcohol intoxication among children and adolescents. *Eur J Pediatr* 153:868–72.

Timing of Death and Injuries in Infants and Young Children

9

KAREN J. GRIEST

Contents

9.1 Determination of Time of Death

9.1.1 Introduction

There are two reasons to determine time since death in homicide cases:

1. The time since death can give the police an estimate of the time of an assault.
2. It can verify a given history.[1]

Specific to children's cases, time of death is used to determine if a child was born alive or died/was killed after birth.[2,3]

The time of death determination must be reliable to be of use. Determining time of death, however, is difficult, and complete accuracy is impossible. Only a determination of a range of time is possible: the most probable earliest and latest time of death. The most reliable determinations of time of death will involve using more than one indicator. Determining a time of death of less than one hour, even in recent deaths, is not possible using anatomical or environmental indicators.[3]

The postmortem interval is defined as the time elapsed from death until discovery and medical examination of the body. The longer the postmortem interval, the wider will be the range of probable time since death. The longer the postmortem interval, the more probable that associated or environmental evidence will provide more reliable information about time of death than anatomical changes.[3]

Three sources of information should be used to determine time of death:

1. Information from the body itself
2. Information from the environment around the body
3. History of the circumstances of death, normal habits, and movements of the victim, i.e., the police investigation[3]

Information from the body can be used because there are changes that occur after death that progress in a predictable manner over time. Each change has its own progression over time and its own factors that influence that progression. These postmortem changes are physical changes of the body itself (algor and livor mortis), physicochemical changes (rigor mortis), supravital reactions (metabolic changes), autolysis, and putrefaction (bacterial changes) (Table 9.1).[1]

All studies on time of death estimation have been performed on adult bodies. Infants and young children are smaller, have a larger surface area-to-mass ratio, smaller muscles and muscle mass, and thinner skin, and retain some primitive responses not present in adults. Therefore time of death estimation in infants and young children is uncertain and difficult. Postmortem changes used to determine time of death and how they present in infants and young children are given in Table 9.2.[3]

9.1.2 Algor Mortis (Body Cooling)

Body cooling is the most dependable factor in the determination of time of death for the first 24 hours postmortem. Body temperature changes can only be used in cool and temperate climates, since in tropical climates there may be only a minimal fall in body temperature postmortem, and in extreme

Table 9.1 Anatomical Factors Used in Time of Death Estimation
Algor mortis
Livor mortis
Rigor mortis
Supravital reaction
Mechanical excitability of muscle
Pharmacological excitability of the iris
Autolysis
Putrefaction
Adipocere formation
Mummification
Maceration
Vitreous humor potassium and hypoxanthine
Stomach contents
Postmortem animal damage

climates the body temperature may even rise. Body cooling should be correlated with other indicators of time of death.[1,3]

Body core temperature should be measured when using algor mortis to determine time of death. This can be done per rectum or with an intrahepatic or subhepatic (adults) temperature measurement via an abdominal stab. Direct skin, oral, or axillary temperatures should not be used. The benefits of taking the rectal temperature at the scene must be weighed against preservation of evidence in possible sexual assault cases. No instrument should be inserted in the rectum until trace evidence is obtained. The use of a chemical thermometer 10 to 12 inches long with a range of 0 to 50 degrees Celsius is best. Thermocouple probes with a digital or printed readout can also be used.[1,3]

The body core temperature should be recorded as early as possible. The environmental temperature should also be recorded, as well as the environmental conditions. Any change in the environment should also be noted. For instance, infants and young children are often given cardiopulmonary resuscitation (CPR) and transported to the hospital even if there are no signs of life.[1,3]

Table 9.2 Why Time of Death Determination in Infants Differs from That of Adults
Smaller size
Larger surface area-to-mass ratio
Smaller muscles and muscle mass
Thinner, finer skin
Retention of some primitive responses

Table 9.3 Algor Mortis in Time of Death Determination

Advantages	Most dependable in the first 24 hours
	Reliability increases when combined with other time of death indicators
	Nomograms that allow for environmental factors and body size
Disadvantages	Useful only in cool and temperate climates
	Requires core temperature measurement
	Rectal or abdominal/hepatic stab
	Requires a chemical thermometer or thermocouple probe
	Variable body temperature during the day in children
	Average higher body temperature in infants and early childhood
	Nomogram starts at 20 kilogram body weight

The normal oral temperature in adults fluctuates between 35.9°C (96.7°F) and 37.2°C (99°F). The rectal temperature is 0.3°C to 0.4°C (0.5°F to 0.75°F) higher than the oral temperature.[3] Temperature regulation in infants and young children is less well controlled than in adults. The average rectal temperature is higher in infancy and early childhood, usually not falling below 37.2°C (99.0°F) until after the third year of life. At 18 months, 50% of children will have rectal temperatures of 37.8°C (100°F) or higher. Body temperature in individual children may vary as much as 3°F or 4°F during the day. Rectal temperatures may approach 101°F in normal children, particularly in the late afternoon after a full day of activity. Anxiety may also elevate body temperature (Table 9.3).[4]

The initial body temperature may be lower than normal due to hypothermia, shock, cardiac failure, or massive hemorrhage. The initial body temperature may be higher than normal due to heat stroke, sepsis, fever, or pontine hemorrhage (Table 9.4).[3,5]

After death, heat loss from the body is due to convection, conduction, radiation, and evaporation. The first two are the most important. Evaporation may be a significant factor if the body or clothing is wet (Table 9.5).[3]

Table 9.4 Factors That Influence Initial Body Temperature

Lower than Normal	Hypothermia
	Shock
	Cardiac failure
	Massive hemorrhage
Higher than Normal	Heat stroke
	Sepsis
	Fever
	Pontine hemorrhage

Table 9.5 Methods of Heat Loss

Convection	Transfer of heat energy by movement of currents
Conduction	Transfer of energy through matter from particle to particle
Radiation	Electromagnetic waves that directly transport energy through space
Evaporation	Transfer of energy when a liquid becomes a gas

Body cooling is predominantly a physical process, but does not closely follow Newton's law of cooling. Newton's law of cooling states that the rate of cooling of a body is determined by the difference between the temperature of the body and that of its environment. Newton's law applies to small inorganic bodies. The human body has a large mass, irregular shape, and is composed of tissues with different physical properties. When temperature is plotted against time, cooling of an adult human body follows a sigmoid curve. There is an initial maintenance of body temperature which is mainly dependent on the body weight and the body's low thermal conductivity. This initial plateau, or "temperature plateau," usually lasts from one-half to one hour, but may last up to 5 hours. This is followed by a relatively linear rate of cooling. Finally, there is slowing of the cooling rate as the body approaches the environmental temperature. Assessment of time of death by cooling is only possible on the linear part of the curve. It is not accurate during the temperature plateau or as the body temperature approaches the environmental temperature (Figure 9.1).[1]

Other factors that influence the rate of body cooling are as shown in Table 9.6.

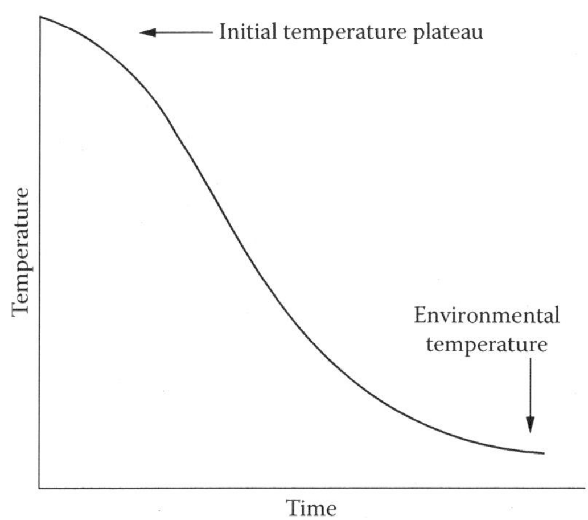

Figure 9.1 Graph of body cooling over time.

Table 9.6 Factors That Influence Rate of Body Cooling

Factors
Air movement
Air humidity
Wet clothing
Water, still versus flowing
Warm versus cool water
Body mass and mass-to-surface ratio, infant versus adult
Body position, flexed versus extended
Clothing and body coverings

1. *Environmental conditions (temperature, wind, air humidity, rain or wetness).* Any air movement accelerates cooling through convection. Cooling is also more rapid in humid rather than dry air; moist air is a better conductor of heat. The air humidity will affect cooling by evaporation when the body or clothing is wet. Water is a better conductor of heat, so a body in water will cool more rapidly than one on land. For a given temperature, cooling in still water is about twice as fast as in air, and about three times faster in flowing water. Obviously, a body will cool faster in cool water than warm water.
2. *Body mass and mass-to-surface ratio.* The greater the surface area of the body relative to its mass, the more rapid will be heat loss from the body. Infants have a large surface-to-mass ratio and therefore lose body heat very rapidly.
3. *Position of the body (extended or flexed).* The more surface area of the body exposed to the environment, to the atmosphere, as in an extended body position versus a body with the extremities flexed against the trunk, the quicker the cooling. In the fetal position only 60% of the total surface area effectively loses heat.
4. *Clothing or coverings.* Clothing and coverings over the body insulate the body from the environment and slow cooling. Cooling of a naked body is twice as fast as a clothed body. Infants and young children are often undressed by emergency medical personnel during resuscitation efforts.[1,3]

The best known and most used method for calculating time of death from body temperature is the nomogram of Henssage (Henssage, 1988). The nomogram corrects for environmental temperature, requires deep rectal temperature measurement, and assumes a normal temperature at death of 37.2°C. Henssage's nomogram is based on a formula that approximates the sigmoid cooling curve. Henssage produced two nomograms, one for ambient temperatures above 23°C and the other for ambient temperatures below 23°C. Within each of these two nomograms is a differing allowance for the effect of environmental temperature on the rate of cooling as well as an allowance for the effect of body weight. There is a protocol for application of the nomogram method which should be strictly followed to assure accuracy. Henssage has also developed a computer program based on the nomogram. The nomogram starts at 20-kilogram body weight and therefore is of no use in infants and children until they reach a weight of 20 kg. Henssage also derived empiric corrective factors to allow for conditions that increase or delay body cooling compared to standard conditions (lying in water, wind, body coverings). A complete presentation of the nomograms and protocol can be found in the published works of Henssage. Even in the best of circumstances, the resulting time since death gives a range of ±2.8 hours about the mean value. By combining the temperature method with other methods, it will be possible to verify and perhaps refine the time-of-death determination.[1,3,6]

9.1.3 Livor Mortis

Livor mortis, lividity, or hypostasis is dark purple discoloration of the skin (and internal organs) resulting from gravitational pooling of blood in the veins and capillary beds following cessation of the circulation. Blood seeks the lowest levels in the vascular system under the influence of gravity when blood pressure ceases. Livor mortis begins immediately after cessation of circulation. It is present in all bodies, but may be subtle.[1,3,7]

Livor mortis is able to develop because the blood remains liquid in the vascular system. Within 30 to 60 minutes of death in most bodies, the blood becomes permanently incoagulable due to release of fibrinolysins mainly from small caliber vessels and from serous surfaces, e.g., the pleura. Clots may persist when the mass of clot is too large to be liquefied by fibrinolysins. In some deaths due to infection and cachexia, the fibrinolytic effect may be absent, leading to the presence of abundant clots in the heart and large vessels. The fluidity of the blood is not characteristic of any special cause of death, but some investigators believe that the blood remains liquid longer in asphyxial deaths.[3]

As a result of continued oxygen consumption by the tissues after death, the early pink to red color of livor mortis becomes a blue to purple.[3]

The development of livor mortis is too variable to serve as an isolated indicator of time of death. It is most useful to the forensic investigator due to its color and distribution. Normally, lividity has a purple or reddish-purple color. Lividity may be pink on the sides of bodies that are exposed to the air, while the lividity at the back and in other areas near the ground will remain purple. Carbon monoxide poisoning will give lividity a cherry red color, because carboxyhemoglobin does not dissociate readily. Methemoglobin formed in the blood during life (e.g., potassium chlorate, nitrates, aniline poisoning) gives livor mortis a chocolate brown color. Cold exposure and areas of the body covered by moist clothing give livor a pink color. Cyanide poisoning creates a lividity that is pink, bright scarlet, or violet.[1,3,7]

Lividity usually first becomes apparent 20 to 30 minutes after death as dull red patches or blotches that deepen in intensity and coalesce over time. Some lividity may appear shortly before death in individuals dying of terminal circulatory failure. The appearance of lividity may be delayed in persons who have chronic anemia or massive terminal hemorrhage. In infants, lividity appears to develop more quickly than in adults due to their thin, fine skin.[3,7]

Blanching of postmortem lividity by thumb pressure indicates that the lividity is not fully fixed. After 10 to 12 hours, the lividity becomes "fixed," and repositioning of the body will result in two patterns of lividity, because some of the original lividity distribution will remain. The primary pattern of lividity will disappear and a secondary pattern will appear more quickly if the body is moved within the first 6 to 8 hours after death, but a secondary pattern of lividity can develop after 24 hours if the body is moved. A double pattern of lividity indicates that the body has been moved after some advanced time (many hours) after death. The fixation of lividity over time is due to hemoconcentration of intravascular erythrocytes due to transcapillary plasma extravasation and constriction of blood vessels by cooling, congealing body fat.[1,3,7]

Pressure on the skin will prevent filling of the vessels after death and will result in a lack of livor mortis in that area. Thus areas of the body pressed against the underlying supporting surface will be pale compared with the surrounding skin livor. A supine corpse will have contact pallor over the shoulder blades, buttocks, calves, and heels. Firm-fitting clothing will also create areas of contact pallor (e.g., the elastic of underwear, bras, and belts). Any firm object beneath the body will also create contact pallor in the shape of that object (e.g., the arm of the deceased beneath the body or the blanket pattern against skin). Thus lividity will show the position of the body after death and objects that are in contact with the body at the time of death (Table 9.7, Figure 9.2, Figure 9.3).[1,3,7]

In areas where there is heavy accumulation of lividity, the blood may rupture small vessels leading to the production of punctate purple-black hemorrhages between one and several millimeters in diameter. The larger

Table 9.7 Livor Mortis in Time of Death Determination

Advantages	Livor color may indicate cause of death
	Livor distribution may indicate body repositioning
	Will indicate position of the body after death
	May indicate objects in contact with the body
Disadvantages	May be inconspicuous
	Wide range of apparent time of onset and of fixation

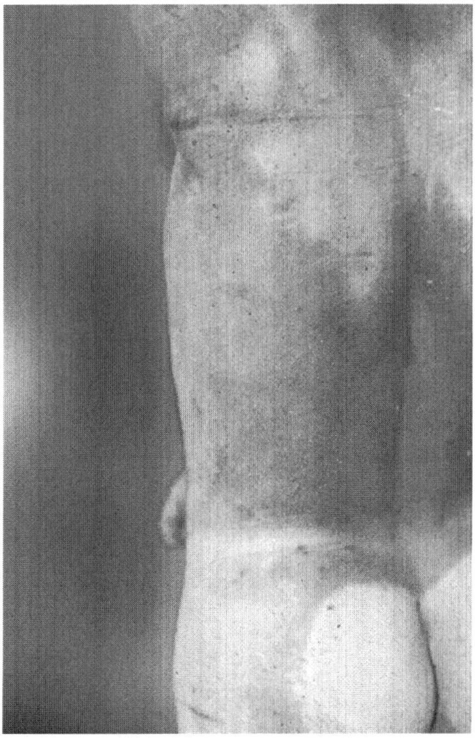

(A)

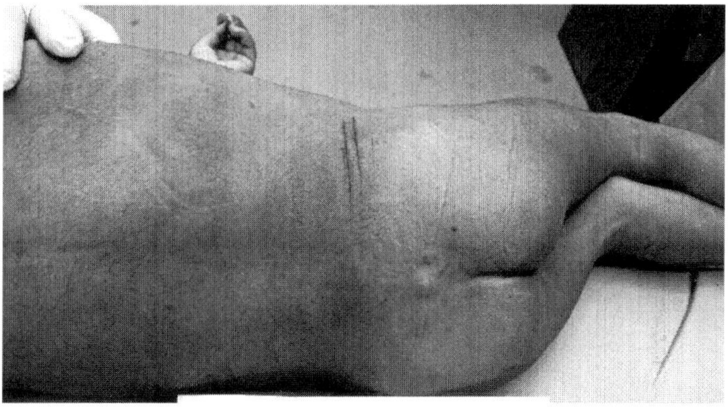

(B)

Figure 9.2 (A) Livor mortis in an adult showing posterior contact blanching. (B) Livor mortis in a child showing posterior contact blanching. The livor mortis is less distinct than that of the adult in (A). There are linear scratches on the back and side of the child.

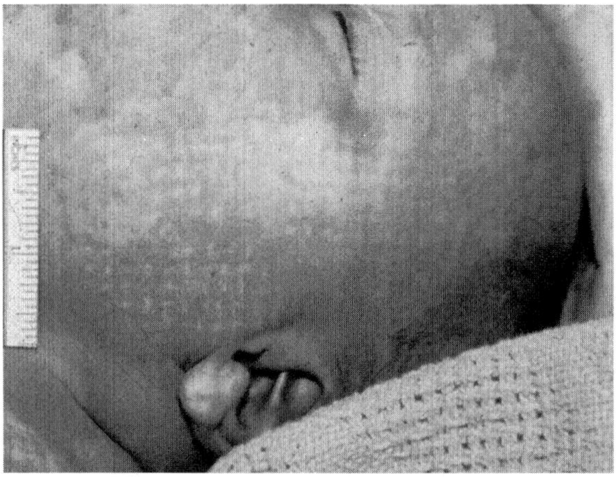

Figure 9.3 Livor mortis showing pattern of the blanket that the infant was lying on.

of these hemorrhagic spots are called "Tardieu spots." This type of postmortem bleeding must be distinguished from premortem petechial hemorrhages (Figure 9.4).[3,7]

In death due to heart failure, there may be vascular congestion in a distribution superior to the heart (e.g., shoulder, neck, and head). This congestion closely resembles livor mortis and must be distinguished from it.[3]

Differentiation of lividity from bruising can be made by incising the skin. In bruising, the hemorrhage will be present in the tissues; in livor mortis, the blood is confined to the vascular system. Microscopic examination may help distinguish the two. As putrefaction progresses, red blood cells hemolyze, and the hemoglobin diffuses into the surrounding tissues. At that point in decomposition, it may be impossible to distinguish lividity from a putrefying bruise.[3]

9.1.4 Rigor Mortis

Immediately after death there is total muscular relaxation, flaccidity, due to loss of tone. This is followed by generalized muscle stiffening, rigor mortis. After a variable period of time, rigor mortis will pass, leading once again to flaccidity.[1,3,7]

Soon after death, the muscles become anoxic, and oxygen-dependent processes cease. Intracellular ATP is then produced by anaerobic glycolysis, which results in production of pyruvic and lactic acids. As muscle glycogen stores are depleted, the pH falls to around 6, the level of ATP falls below a critical level, and rigor mortis rapidly develops. Normally ATP inhibits the activation of actin–myosin linkage in the muscle cells; with the depletion of ATP, these linkages are irreversibly formed. Individuals who have become exhausted before death or who are starved before death have low glycogen levels, and in those cases, rigor may develop rapidly.[1,3]

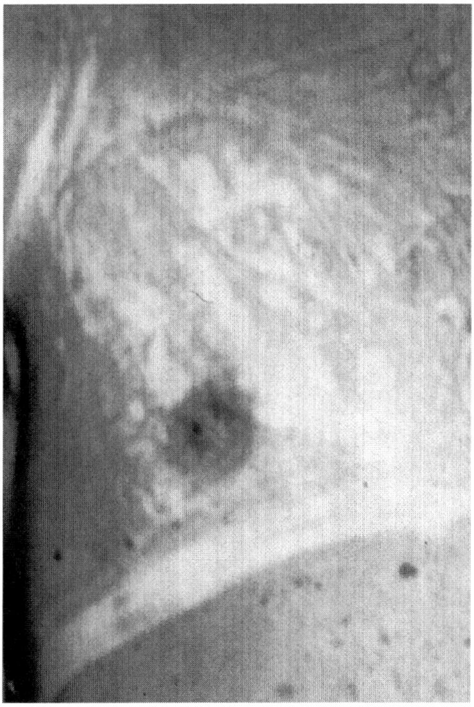

Figure 9.4 Livor mortis showing pattern of clothing that was on the body. The rounded areas on the lower and lateral chest are Tardieu spots.

When rigor becomes fully developed, the joints of the body become fixed. The flexion or extension of the joints during rigor mortis depends on the position of the body at death. Muscle shortening does not occur during rigor mortis unless the muscles are under tension, so rigor should not cause any significant change in the body position after death. Movement of the corpse after rigor mortis develops can occur if the body is in a precarious position, for instance balanced at the edge of a couch. The fingers are often flexed after death supposedly because the tendons shorten as they cool. If the body is moved before the onset of rigor mortis, the joints will become fixed in the new position. If the parts of a body in full rigor are not being supported by their surroundings (e.g., on the floor with the knees flexed and an arm suspended in midair as if the body had been in an armchair at death), the body was obviously moved.[1,3,7]

Rigor mortis involves both voluntary and involuntary muscles. Rigor mortis of the heart must be distinguished from myocardial hypertrophy, and the flaccidity that develops in the heart after the passing of rigor must be distinguished from myocardial dysfunction. The muscles of the iris are also involved with rigor mortis, which can lead to irregular and unequal pupil size. The postmortem pupil size cannot be used to interpret their antemortem state. Rigor mortis of the arrectores pilorum muscles of the skin hairs may result in "goose flesh" or "cutis anserine." Contraction of the walls of the seminal vesicles by rigor can cause discharge of seminal fluid at the glans penis.[3,7]

Normally, rigor mortis develops in a predictable sequential fashion. It is first apparent in the small muscles of the eyelids, lower jaw, and neck. It is next observed in the limbs, beginning with the small distal joints of the hands and feet, progressing to the larger proximal joints of the elbows, knees, shoulders, and hips. In fact, rigor develops simultaneously in all muscles, but completely involves the smaller muscles more rapidly than the larger. Generally, rigor mortis passes in the same order as it develops. Forcible bending of a joint fixed by rigor will tear the muscles and "break" the rigor. If the rigor mortis was fully developed, no rigor will reappear in the involved muscles. If not fully developed, rigor may develop again to a greater or lesser degree, depending on when the rigor was broken in its progression. Reestablishment of rigor mortis may be seen up to 6 to 8 hours postmortem and, in cold environments, up to 12 hours postmortem.[1,3,7]

During autopsy examination, when spreading the buttocks to examine the anus, rigor mortis and the breaking rigor mortis in the muscles of the anal sphincter may give the anal opening an irregular, wide appearance that has been mistaken for sexual abuse in children (Figure 9.5).[8]

There is a wide range of time of onset and duration of rigor mortis. If the muscles are depleted of glycogen (premortem exercise, convulsions, electrocution), rigor mortis will develop more quickly in those muscles. The ambient temperature also influences the onset and duration of rigor. The higher the environmental temperature, the faster the onset and progression of rigor mortis. In temperate climates, rigor will start to disappear approximately 36 to 48 hours postmortem. If the environmental temperature is high, or in cases of septicemia, the accelerated development of putrefaction may cause rigor to pass off in 9 to 12 hours. In cold environments, rigor may persist for several weeks. Below 10°C, in general, rigor mortis will not develop at all. Resolution of rigor mortis is due to protein degradation from autolysis and bacterial activity.[1,3,7]

Rigor mortis can only give a rough estimation of time of death and should not be used in isolation. A compilation of the timing of rigor mortis reported in the literature (1811–1969) in 28 total texts showed that there was no lower limit for the beginning of rigor, and its onset had an upper limit of 7 hours. Its time of maximum development ranged from 6 to 10 hours, its duration from 29 to 85 hours, and its complete resolution from 12 to 140 hours (Table 9.8).[1,3,7]

The intensity of rigor mortis is determined by the deceased's muscular development. Thus it is less intense in children and in the aged. In addition, its onset and complete resolution appear to be quicker in infants, young children, and in older adults. Complete rigor has been reported in infants dying of sudden infant death syndrome (SIDS) within 2 hours of their having been put to bed. An early onset and resolution of rigor is also found in those dying of septicemia and wasting diseases (Table 9.9).[1,3,7]

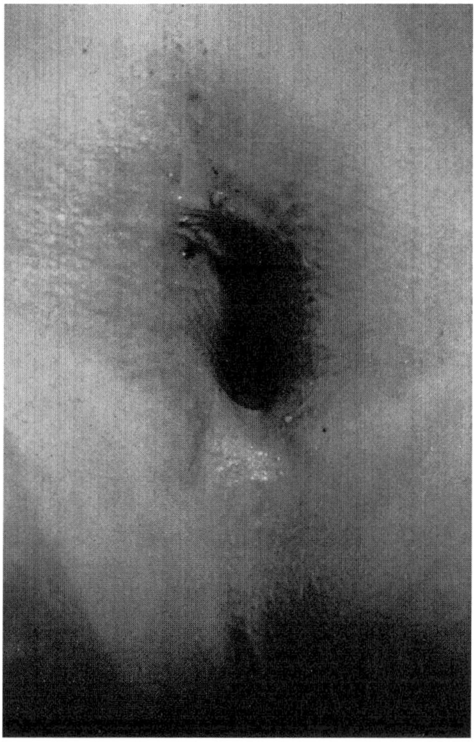

Figure 9.5 Wide, irregular postmortem anal opening.

Table 9.8 Rigor Mortis in Time of Death Determination

Advantages	Indicates repositioning of the body after death
Disadvantages	Wide range of apparent onset, total development, and passing
	Influenced by environmental and individual factors

Table 9.9 Factors That Influence the Development of Rigor Mortis

Premortem exercise
Convulsions
Electrocution
Cachexia
Septicemia
Muscular development
Ambient temperature

Exposure of the body to intense heat will cause coagulation of the muscle protein with stiffening of the tissues. Heat stiffening will cause shortening of the muscles, resulting in the characteristic pugilistic posture of burned bodies. Heat stiffening should not be confused with rigor mortis. Freezing of a body will cause stiffening of the muscles, which also should not be confused with rigor mortis. Rigor mortis will not develop until the body is thawed.[3]

9.1.5 Supravital Reactions

Supravital reactions are the reactions of tissues on postmortem stimulation. After cessation of circulation, tissues continue to live for a period of time that is tissue specific. The duration of supravital reaction time in the tissues is not the same as the resuscitation time. The resuscitation period of skeletal muscle at normal temperature is 2 to 3 hours, while the supravital electrical excitability of skeletal muscle may last up to 20 hours postmortem.[1]

In determining time of death, the supravital reactions of use are mechanical and electrical excitability of skeletal muscle and pharmacological excitability of the iris. All experimentation in this field has been on adults. How this translates specifically for infants and young children is unknown.[1]

9.1.5.1 Mechanical Excitability of the Muscle

The mechanical excitability of the muscle can be examined by hitting it with the back of a knife. Data exist for the biceps brachii muscle. There are three phases of mechanical excitability: contraction of the whole muscle (up to 1.5 to 2.5 hours postmortem), reversible idiomuscular spasm (4 to 5 hours postmortem), and weak idiomuscular spasm (8 to 12 hours postmortem).[1]

9.1.5.2 Electrical Excitability of Skeletal Muscle

With electrical excitability of skeletal muscle there is a strong contraction of the muscles in the early postmortem period, and the excitation will spread to surrounding muscles. As the postmortem period increases, the contraction will become weaker and become more confined to the area excited. Finally, only a fascicular twitching will be elicited.[1]

Muscles of the face have been studied, i.e., orbicularis oris and orbicularis oculi. Simulation is induced by current impulses of 30 mA, of 10 ms duration, repeated at a rate of 50 ps.

Factors that may increase the duration of electrical excitability are hematoma or emphysema in the area of excitation and hypothermia. Factors that decrease the duration time are long terminal or agonal episodes.

9.1.5.3 Pharmacological Excitability of the Iris

The iris muscle is reactive to electrical or pharmacological stimulation for a longer period than skeletal muscle. To perform pharmacological stimulation,

0.5 mL of a solution of norepinephrine, tropicamide, atropine, or acetylcholine is injected into the subconjunctiva. A positive reaction will be seen within 5 to 30 minutes. The pupil will become larger with the injection of atropine, tropicamide, or norepinephrine, or smaller with acetylcholine. The reaction lasts for at least one hour.[1] A recent study indicates that pupil pharmacological reactivity as a method for assessing the time since death in the early postmortem period is questionable.[19]

9.1.6 Putrefaction and Autolysis (Postmortem Decomposition)

Putrefaction is the postmortem destruction of the soft tissues of the body by bacteria and enzymes (bacterial and endogenous). Autolysis is the breakdown of tissues resulting from endogenous enzymes alone. Putrefaction results in color changes, gas formation, and liquefaction of tissues.[1,3,7]

Bacteria are an integral part of the process of putrefaction. Some commonly found bacteria in putrefaction are those that are typically found in the respiratory and intestinal systems: anaerobic spore-bearing bacilli, coliform organisms, micrococci, diphtheroids, and proteus organisms. Anaerobic organisms predominate. The majority of the bacteria are from the bowel, with a predominance of *Clostridium welchii*. Septicemia and other premortem infections will hasten the evolution of putrefaction. Ambient temperatures greatly influence the development and progression of putrefaction. Putrefaction is optimal at temperatures between 70°F and 100°F (21°C to 38°C). It is retarded at temperatures below 50°F (10°C) or above 100°F (38°C).[1,3,7]

Other factors influence the development of putrefaction. Obese bodies putrefy more quickly than lean bodies. Blood provides a channel for spread of bacteria; therefore exsanguination will delay putrefaction. Widespread infection, congestive heart failure, and anasarca will promote putrefaction. Putrefaction tends to be more rapid in children than adults, with the exception of unfed newborns who have no bacteria in their intestines. Warm temperatures promote putrefaction, so heavy clothing or coverings that retain body heat, warm rooms, and electric blankets will increase the onset of putrefaction. Intense heat will produce "heat fixation" and inactivate autolytic enzymes with a consequent delay in decomposition. Injuries to the body promote decomposition by providing an entryway for bacteria, and blood is an excellent medium for bacterial growth (Table 9.10).[1,3,7]

The rate of decomposition after burial will depend on the depth of the grave, the warmth of the soil, soil drainage, and the permeability of the coffin. Decomposition may be slowed with restriction of air, deep burials, and clay soil, but will not be stopped. In well-drained soil, an adult body will skeletonize in about 10 years, a child's body in about 5 years.[3]

The first visible sign of putrefaction is normally a green discoloration of the skin in the lower right side of the abdomen, in the region of the cecum

Table 9.10 Factors That Influence Putrefaction

Retard	Environmental temperature below 50°F
	Environmental temperature above 100°F
	Lean body
	Exsanguination
	Newborns never fed
	Intense heat
	Deep burials in well-drained clay soil
Advance	Septicemia
	Other premortem infections
	Obese body
	Congestive heart failure
	Anasarca
	Infancy (except newborns)
	Warm temperature
	Heavy clothing or covering
	Injuries to the body

where the bowel contents are more fluid and contain abundant bacteria. Occasionally the green discoloration will first be noted in the periumbilical region or the left lower abdomen (Figure 9.6). The green discoloration is due to the production of sulfhemoglobin. The green discoloration will then encompass the entire abdominal wall, followed by the flanks, chest, limbs, and face. As putrefaction progresses, the superficial veins of the shoulders,

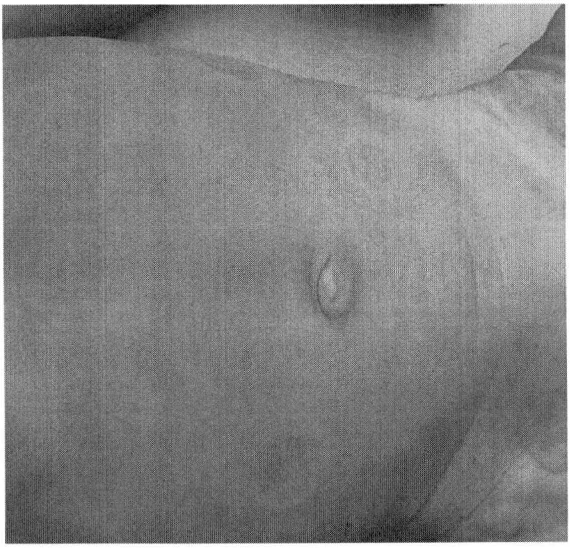

Figure 9.6 (see color insert following page 80) Green discoloration of skin at umbilicus and in left lower quadrant of abdomen.

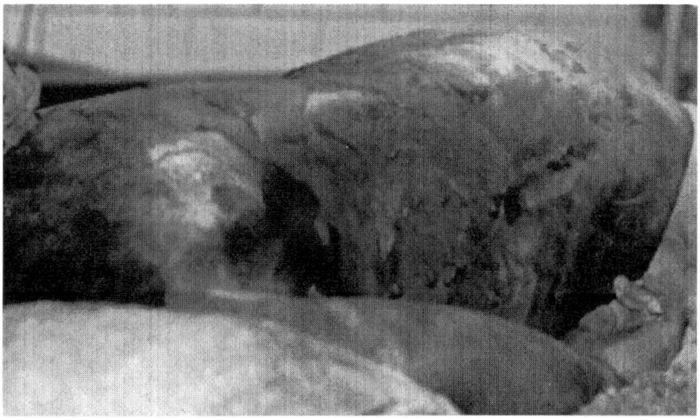

Figure 9.7 Advanced putrefaction with dark green generalized discoloration and swelling of the body. There is skin slippage with yellow, parchment-like drying of the underlying tissues.

upper chest, abdomen, and groins will appear as a purple-brown network described as "marbling." The skin at this point of decomposition has a dusky reddish green to purple black, glistening appearance and slips off in large sheets with light contact. Under the skin slippage, the epidermis is shiny, moist, and pink. It can dry to a yellow parchment-like tissue. Skin blisters varying in size from less than 1 cm to 20 cm in diameter will then develop. The blisters contain a dusky, sanguinous fluid and putrid gases (Figure 9.7, Figure 9.8, Figure 9.9, Figure 9.10).[3,7]

Putrid gas forms in the stomach and intestines, causing the abdomen to distend and become tense. The gases cause purging of putrid blood-stained

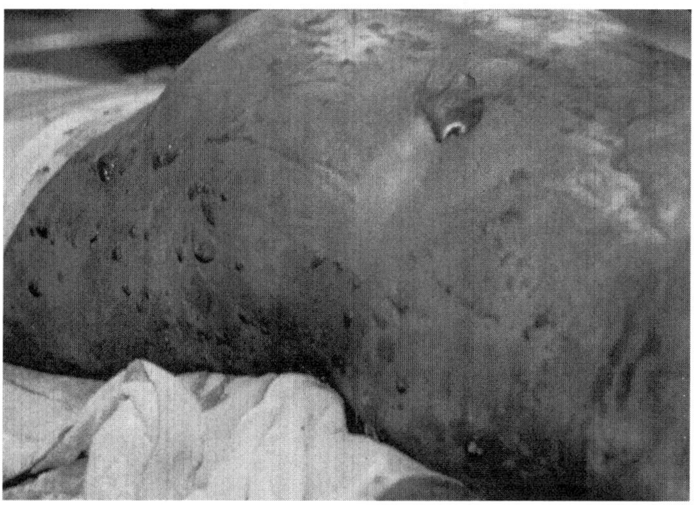

Figure 9.8 Advanced putrefaction with blister formation. There is generalized dark green discoloration and swelling of the body.

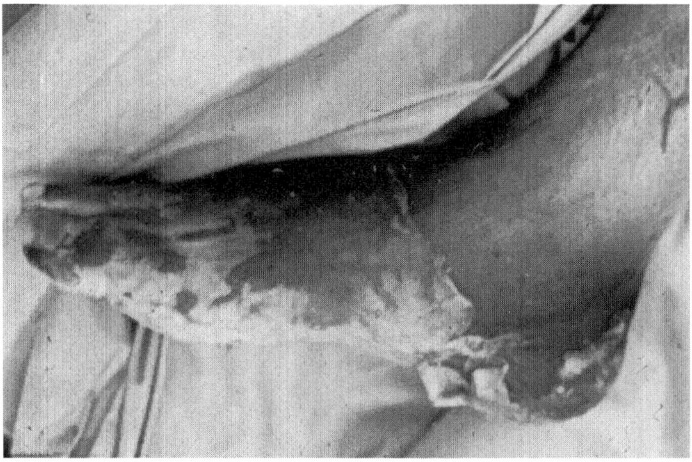

Figure 9.9 Skin slippage due to putrefaction. There is yellowish white mold formation on the skin of this coffin-buried body.

fluid from the nose, mouth, vagina, and rectum. Gas forms within the tissues, which become bloated and crepitant. There is bloating of the face, scrotum, penis, labia, and breasts. The gases are composed of hydrogen sulfide, methane, carbon dioxide, ammonia, and hydrogen. The foul odor is caused by some of the gases and mercaptans.[3,7]

The putrefied dusky green-purple bloated face has eyelids swollen tightly closed, swollen lips, swollen distended cheeks, and a protruding distended tongue. The head and body hair is loose and is easily removed in large clumps. The fingernails and toenails detach, often with the skin of the hand or foot in a "glove" or stocking" formation called "degloving." The neck, trunk, and limbs are also turgid and swollen. As the putrid gases escape, there is collapse

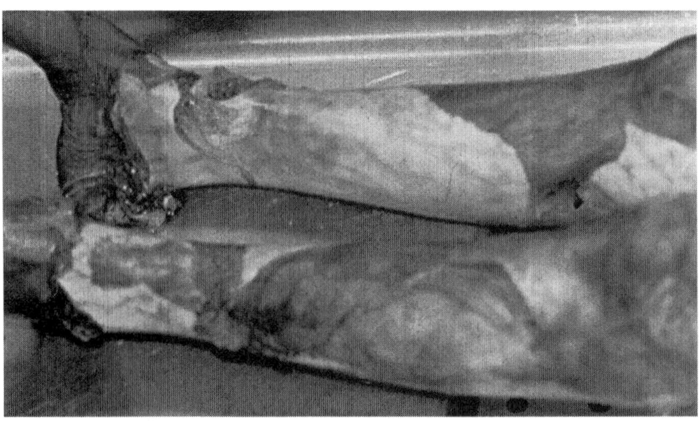

Figure 9.10 Skin slippage due to heat from house fire, note soot on body. This skin slippage must not be confused with putrefaction.

of the decomposing soft tissues. When the putrefactive fluids have drained and the soft tissues have shrunk, the rate of decay will slow.[3,7]

The internal organs also show the effects of advanced decomposition. The gastric mucosa and intestines take on a brownish purple color. The mucosa of the airways becomes a deep red, as do the endocardium and vascular intima. The heart becomes flabby and a deep brown red. The liver develops a honeycomb appearance from gas formation and a dusky red color. The kidneys also become dusky red. The spleen becomes mushy. The brain becomes riddled with holes from gas formation, and then liquefies. The lungs are filled with sanguinous fluid, appear dusky red, and are friable. The sanguinous fluid diffuses into the pleural cavities. Diffusion of bile pigments stains the adjacent liver, duodenum, and transverse colon. The liver, spleen, and kidneys also finally liquefy within their capsules. The more dense fibromuscular organs such as the prostate and uterus remain recognizable late into decomposition, aiding in sex recognition.[3]

In general, in temperate climates, the earliest putrefactive changes of the anterior abdominal wall occur between 36 and 72 hours postmortem. Progression to gas formation occurs at approximately one week, but there is considerable variation in the timing of putrefaction. The temperature of the body after death is the most important factor determining the rate of putrefaction. If the temperature remains above 80°F (26°C) after death, putrefaction becomes apparent after 24 hours and gas develops within 2 to 3 days.[3,7]

Perforation of the fundus of the stomach or lower esophagus into the left pleural cavity or abdominal cavity may occur within a few hours of death. This is due to autolysis rather than bacterial putrefaction. It is uncommon and most frequently found in deaths from cerebral injuries and terminal pyrexias.[3]

9.1.7 Adipocere

Saponification or adipocere formation is a modified form of putrefaction characterized by the transformation of fatty tissue into a yellow-white, greasy substance with a sweetish rancid odor. Once formed, it can remain unchanged for years. A warm, moist, anaerobic environment favors adipocere formation. Adipocere development is the result of hydrolysis of body fat with the release of fatty acids, which, being acidic, subsequently inhibit putrefactive bacteria. Putrefactive bacteria, *C. welchii* being the most active, are important in the initial formation of adipocere. The adipocere is mixed with the mummified remains of muscles, fibrous tissues, and nerves (Figure 9.11).[3,7]

Under ideal conditions of damp and warmth, adipocere may appear to the naked eye after 3 to 4 weeks. However, usually it takes months to form, and extensive adipocere is not seen before 5 or 6 months after death, maybe years.[3,7]

The medicolegal importance of adipocere lies in its ability to preserve the body and injuries.[3]

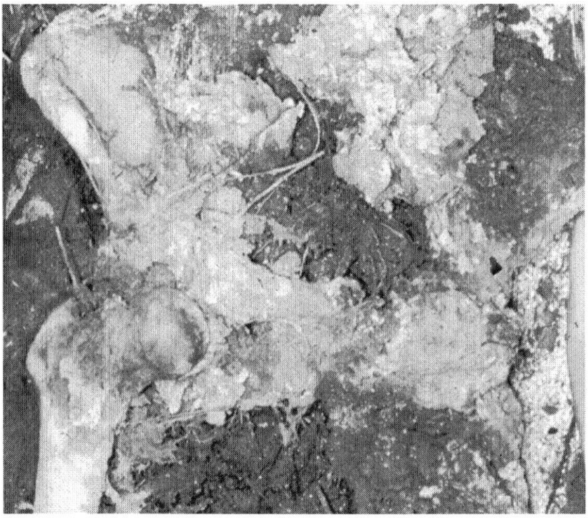

Figure 9.11 Yellow-white adipocere formation in pelvic region of nearly skeletonized body.

9.1.8 Mummification

Mummification is a modified form of putrefaction in which there is dehydration or desiccation of the tissues. The body shrivels and becomes a leathery mass of skin and tendons covering bone. The internal organs are often decomposed or may be dry preserved. Skin shrinkage produces large splits that can mimic injuries. These splits are often seen in the groins, around the neck, and at the armpits.[3,7]

Mummification develops in conditions of dry heat, especially where there are air currents (e.g., a desert or dry, warm house). Newborn infants, being small and sterile, mummify easily. Complete mummification can occur by the end of a few weeks under ideal conditions, but is quite variable.[3,7]

The medicolegal importance of mummification lies in the preservation of tissues and injuries.[3]

9.1.9 Maceration

Maceration is a special form of decay unique to fetuses who die *in utero* and remain in the amniotic sac for at least several days before delivery. It is aseptic autolysis of the fetus. Normally the changes of maceration take approximately one week to develop.[3]

The body is flaccid, the head flattened, with mobility of the skull, and the limbs may be easily separated from the body. There are large, moist skin bullae which rupture to disclose a reddish-brown epidermis. The skin slips

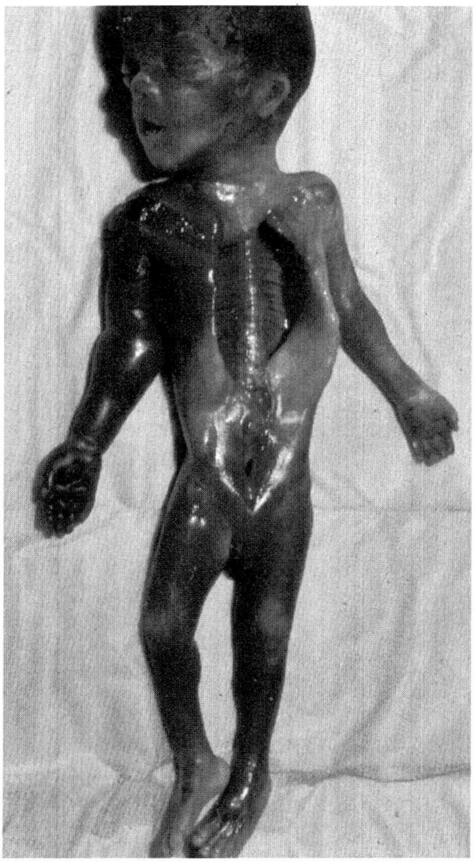

Figure 9.12 Maceration with generalized dull red color. The interior walls of the trunk, shown here post autopsy, are also a generalized dull red.

easily. The epidermis, wall of the trunk, and all organs have a uniform dull, red-brown color (Figure 9.12).[3]

9.1.10 Vitreous Humor

Of the many elements studied in vitreous humor, potassium and hypoxanthine have proved useful in determining postmortem interval. Both the postmortem concentration of potassium and hypoxanthine increase in the vitreous humor over time.[1,9–11]

Vitreous potassium has been studied as a marker in determining time of death by a number of researchers with varying results. Using potassium concentration to estimate the time since death, different authors determined different 95% confidence limits. The confidence limits varied from ±9.5 hours up to ±40 hours in postmortem times up to 100 hours, and from ±6 hours up to ±12 hours in postmortem intervals up to 24 hours. In addition, simultaneous sampling from both eyes showed that the potassium concentration in one eye can differ by up to 10% from the mean value of both eyes.[1,9,10]

It has been found that by excluding cases of possible antemortem electrolyte disturbances (cases with vitreous urea levels above 100 mg/dL), the accuracy of potassium concentrations versus time since death improved. The relationship between potassium concentration and time after death up to 120 hours becomes linear, but the 95% confidence limits are ±22 hours.[1,10]

Newer methods of sampling vitreous humor have also improved the accuracy when using potassium concentrations. Using capillary zone electrophoresis and pretreatment before analysis has improved the accuracy of estimation of time since death, as have several different statistical approaches.[11,14]

Several studies indicate that the level of vitreous potassium rises at a much faster rate over time in infants than it does in adults. Graphs prepared for adults to determine time of death using potassium concentration do not work for young children. To date, no studies have developed a graph for infants alone.[11]

Hypoxanthine (Hx) is formed by hypoxic degradation of adenosine monophosphate (AMP) and may be elevated due to antemortem hypoxia, but also increases after death. A study of postmortem time and temperature on vitreous humor Hx and potassium levels showed that the spread of the potassium levels measured shortly after death was much greater than the corresponding Hx levels. The vitreous humor concentration for both Hx and potassium increased in a fairly linear fashion over time. The slopes for both Hx and potassium were steeper with increasing temperature. Hx seemed to be better suited for the determination of time of death in cases without antemortem hypoxia, especially in the first 24 hours after death.[11] Accuracy was improved if sampling from both eyes was combined.[15]

9.1.11 Stomach Contents

For estimating the time since death, the volume of the last meal and transportation distance into the small intestine must be known. The state of digestion and transportation rate of food from the stomach into the duodenum depend on many antemortem factors which contribute to the great intra- and inter-individual variability of gastric emptying (i.e., liquid diet, hunger, hyperglycemia, drugs, stress, diabetes mellitus, acute abdomen, etc.). Time of death estimation based on stomach contents should be made only with great caution. Other indicators of time of death should be taken into consideration.[1]

Digestion continues after death due to enzymatic activity. Thus the state of digestion is of little value in estimating the time of death. The stomach contents themselves can have value. Movement of food from the stomach into the duodenum does not occur after death. Gastric emptying has been studied and quantified within the last decade using various methods: radiology, intubation–aspiration, radioisotopes, ultrasound, absorption kinetics of orally administered solutes, and ferromagnetic traces.[1]

In the normal individual, liquids leave the stomach much faster than solids. Gastric emptying follows an exponential function for liquids; solids show a linear emptying pattern. Mixed meals show an exponential emptying pattern. Emptying time itself depends on the volume and composition of the last meal. Carbohydrates, proteins, and lipids leave the stomach in this order. The following gastric emptying times are given in the literature: 1 to 3 hours for a light, small-volume meal; 3 to 5 hours for a medium-sized meal; 5 to 8 hours for a large meal. In normal individuals, prior to upper gastrointestinal endoscopy a 6-hour nil per mouth period ensures that initially every stomach is empty irrespective of food type, and that often a 4-hour period will ensure that the stomach is empty.[1]

In cases of raised intracranial pressure and continued survival in hospital, gastric emptying may cease for several days.[1]

According to one study, at autopsy, if 50% of the volume of the last meal (mixed food) is found in the stomach, the last food intake was about 3 to 4 hours prior to death, with 98% confidence limits not shorter than 1 and not greater than 10 hours. When 90% of the last meal is found in the stomach, the last food intake was probably within the hour prior to death, with 98% confidence limits not more than 3 to 4 hours. If only 30% of the last meal is found, the last food intake was around 4 to 5 hours previous to death, with 98% confidence limits not shorter than 1 to 2 and not longer than 10 to 11 hours prior to death.[1]

In newborns, because the fetus swallows *in utero,* there may be a small amount of material in the stomach.[16] On occasion, this material may be white. Caution should be used when using stomach contents to determine if a newborn was fed and thus born alive. An analysis for milk proteins in the stomach contents can be used if there is any doubt (Figure 9.13).

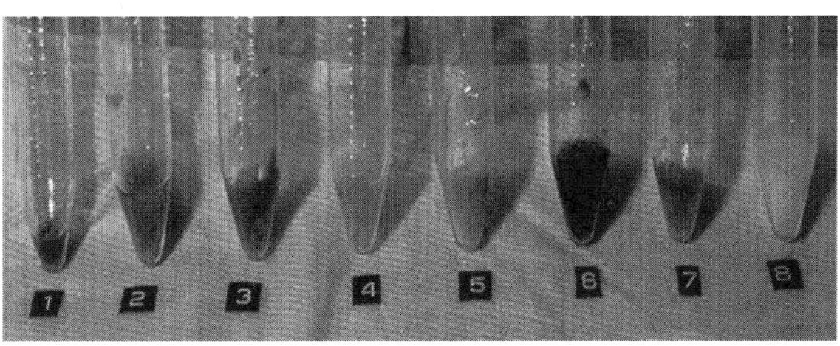

Figure 9.13 Various stomach contents retrieved from stillborn infants. The contents of tube 8 are white.

9.1.12 Postmortem Animal Damage

After death, ants, roaches, and beetles can rapidly cause superficial damage of the skin. When dry, these insect bites can look like abrasions (Figure 9.14).[3,7]

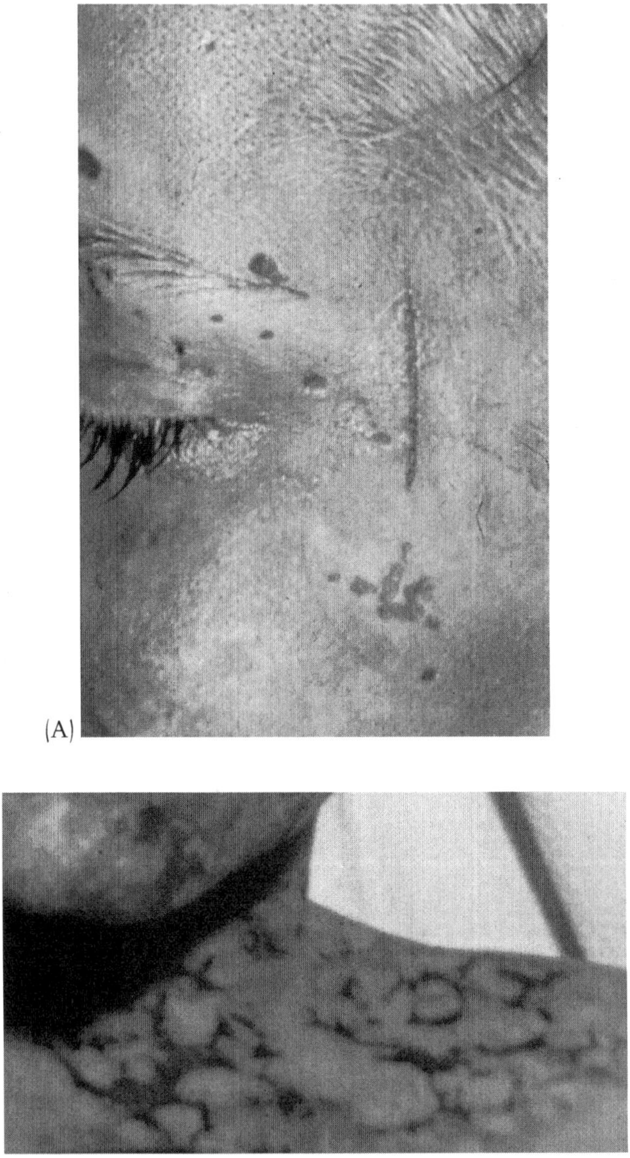

(A) (B)

Figure 9.14 (A) Postmortem ant bites. There is also a linear abrasion next to the eye due to postmortem trauma. (B) Postmortem ant bites. The bites are in the distribution of the underlying skin vasculature.

Rodents cause more severe damage. The size of the rodent can be estimated from the size of the bites. The edges of the bites will be sharp and will show the configuration of the teeth.[3,7]

Cats, canines, and foxes produce severe destruction of soft tissue with ragged margins showing the arrangement of the teeth. These animals as well as birds and rodents can widely scatter bones and soft tissues from bodies that remain outdoors.[3,7]

Maggots and carrion beetles will invade and destroy a body. Initially maggots can cause rounded holes in the skin. Maggots, pupae, flies, and beetles can be used as an aid in determining time of death by forensic entomologists.[3,7]

9.2 Wound Age Estimation

9.2.1 Introduction

The postmortem interval may be preceded by a long survival period. Survival period is defined as the time from injury or onset of a terminal illness to death. The survival period will be determined by an evaluation of the injuries and the victim's response to the injury. At autopsy, the extent of inflammatory response to injury as well as the extent of healing can be used to give an estimation of the survival period.[3,17]

9.2.2 Age Estimation in Human Skin Wounds

There are several morphological, cellular changes during the healing process that can be detected microscopically. Their detection can determine the minimal wound age, but their absence is less reliable. Negative findings may be due to sampling problems or interindividual variation. The ages of individuals studied in the cellular detection of wound healing ranged from 15 to 94 years.[17]

There is, in general, faster wound healing in younger people and in wounds on the head. However, there is considerable interindividual variability. There are no relevant differences found in wound healing by wound type (laceration, surgical or stab/cut wounds).[17]

Microscopic timing of wounds must be based on unambiguous detection of reactive changes in a sufficient number of specimens from each skin lesion. Cells normally present in blood can drift passively into an area of bleeding. Therefore granulocytes, macrophages (without phagocytized particles), and lymphocytes must be present in relevant numbers outside the area of bleeding before they can be regarded as a vital reaction. Only clear evidence of neutrophils outside the area of bleeding should be regarded as the earliest reactive change detectible on routine histology. In the Betz study

(1994), polymorphonuclear granulocytes (PMN) were first observed in skin wounds after approximately 20 to 30 minutes. These results are similar to other study reports. Neutrophils were observed by Betz (1994) in all wounds investigated at age 15 hours or more. This suggests, but cannot prove, that if neutrophils are absent, the wound is less than 15 hours old. PMNs were still present in granulation/scar tissue of wounds with post infliction times of up to a few months, but in reduced numbers.[17]

Eosinophilic granulocytes are not found to be a reliable predictor of wound healing time due to difficulty in detection and irregular appearance of these cells.

In the literature, initial detection of macrophages ranges from 2 to 24 hours. In the Betz study (1994), macrophages were found outside the area of bleeding at the earliest 3 to 4 hours after wound infection, but negative results were found up to 3 days after injury. A clear infiltration of macrophages generally indicates a wound age of at least 1 to 2 days, and negative results suggest a wound age of less than 3 days.[17]

With increasing postinfliction intervals the number of granulocytes decreases, and the number of macrophages increases. The ratio between these two types of cells in wounds can be used for wound age determination. Macrophages predominate after 12 to 24 hours or more postinfliction survival (in some wounds). In the Betz study (1994), a preponderance of macrophages appeared in a wound at the earliest 20 hours postinfliction and in all wounds at 12 days or more. The relationship between the number of granulocytes and macrophages can help differentiate between wounds that are a few hours old from those some days old.[17]

The presence of macrophages with different incorporated particles can also help determine the age of a wound. Lipid-phagocytosing macrophages appear at the earliest 3 days after wound infliction and can be seen regularly in lacerations aged 5 days or more. Similar results have been seen in other studies. Negative results may be due to the lack of mechanical release of lipids during wounding.[17]

Erythrophagocytosis (phagocytosis of red blood cells) is one of the major findings during wound healing. Before phagocytosis, erythrocytes will attach to the surface of macrophages. The detection of three or more erythrocytes attached to a macrophage is called "rosette formation." These rosettes can be formed accidentally in lesions less than 9 hours old; therefore they cannot be used in wound age determination. Erythrophages were found at the earliest 3 days after wound infliction in the Betz study (1994). Erythrophages were found in many wounds aged between 6 days and a few months, showing that only positive results prove a minimum wound age of approximately 2 to 3 days.[17]

The appearance of hemosiderin and siderophages was closely correlated with erythrophages. Hemoglobin of extravasated erythrocytes is degraded intracellularly by the microsomal hemooxygenase of macrophages. Iron deposits were detected at the earliest 3 days after wound infliction. Multiple other authors report the same finding. The iron-free pigment hematoidin occurs following hemoglobin degradation and can be distinguished with Prussian blue staining from the blue hemosiderin deposits by its yellow color. In the literature, there is variability of the earliest reported appearance of hematoidin in a skin wound, from 3 to 43 days. In the Betz series (1994), hematoidin was first detected 8 days after wound infliction and was found in a wound aged 1.5 months. This pigment is a rare finding, so only positive results can be used and indicate a wound age of at least approximately one week.[17]

Lymphocytes are mainly involved in chronic inflammatory processes. Betz found that only the appearance of typical spot-like lymphocytic infiltrates outside the area of bleeding could be reliably used, because relevant numbers of lymphocytes could be found in areas of bleeding in postmortem injuries or wounds with short postinfliction times. Valid lymphocytic infiltrates outside the area of bleeding indicate a wound age of at least approximately 8 days. However, such infiltrates occur irregularly and can be present up to a few months postinfliction.[17]

With H&E staining, the development of a granulation tissue containing numerous spindle-shaped fibroblastic and migrating endothelial cells occurred in the Betz study at the earliest 3 to 5 days after wound infliction, indicating a survival time of at least a few days. Numerous fibroblasts and endothelial cells must be present to unambiguously identify this stage of healing.[17]

In routine histology, the beginning of epidermal migration can be detected by the presence of large flat and "clear" epidermal cells at the wound edge. In the Betz study, these cells appeared at the earliest about 2 days after injury. The completion of reepithelialization, though easy to detect, depends on the size of the defect. Betz found that complete reepithelialization occurred in surgically treated and primary healing human skin wounds at the earliest 5 days after injury and is regularly found in lesions aged 21 days or more. Migrating keratocytes were clearly detectable in every wound aged 7 days or more (Table 9.11).[17]

Enzyme histochemistry has been studied with, at present, variable results and application to forensic timing of wounds. The activity of nonspecific esterases, acid phosphatase, and other enzyme histochemistry studies indicate a minimum postinfliction interval of a few hours when they are exclusively positive, but if negative are of no practical meaning due to their frequency.[17]

9.2.3 Timing of Early Changes in Brain Trauma

The early changes resulting from brain trauma were studied by Anderson and Opeskin (1998). In their study, injury occurred from motor vehicle accidents (MVA), gunshot wounds, blunt instrument injuries, and falls. The patient's

Table 9.11 Age Estimation in Human Skin Wounds Using Cellular Reactions

Cell Type	Time of Histologic Appearance
Polymorphonuclear granulocytes	20–30 minutes to months
Macrophages	1–2 days to months
Lipid-phagocytosis	At least 3–5 days
Erythrophagocytosis	At least 2–3 days
Hemosiderin pigment	At least 3 days
Hematoidin pigment	At least about a week
Lymphocytes	8 days to months
Granulation tissue	At least 3–5 days
Epidermal migration	7 days or more

ages ranged from 2 to 88 years. All cases demonstrated subarachnoid and parenchymal hemorrhages.[18]

Eosinophilic neurons were noted in many cases surviving greater than 1 hour after injury and increased in frequency and severity with time. They were most commonly seen in areas of contusion, the hippocampus, and the arterial boundary zones of the cerebral cortex. Neuronal incrustation was seen from 3 to 48 hours postinjury in areas of contusion. Axonal swelling and spheroids were seen in the white matter in areas of laceration and hemorrhages at 1 hour postinjury in many cases, and continued through all time periods. Glial swelling was seen in the subpial and subependymal regions and around hemorrhage from very early to 48 hours postinjury. Polymorphonuclear leukocytes (granulocytes) were present in the tissues at all time periods, with increasing frequency over time. Granulocytes were also found surrounding corpora amylacea in cases with survival times greater than 1 hour. Axonal swelling, eosinophilia of neurons, and incrustation of neurons were noted at earlier time periods than previously reported in the literature. Edema was present in nearly all cases but was not considered in timing injury because histologic evaluation of edema is difficult.[18]

Three categories of granulocyte response were noted:

1. Pavementing—“sticking” of granulocytes to the endothelium of small vessels, usually adjacent to areas of hemorrhage.
2. In the tissue—usually adjacent to hemorrhage.
3. Surrounding corpora amylacea—usually noted adjacent to hemorrhage (e.g., in the subpial position adjacent to subarachnoid hemorrhage, around parenchymal hemorrhages, and within parenchymal hemorrhage). In some subpial examples, this was the only location where granulocytes were found. They were seen in persons ranging in age from 29

> to 83 years old. Because the number of corpora amylacea increases with age, this change was most commonly seen in the elderly.[18]

Granulocytes and axonal changes were present in only some of the blocks of tissue showing contusion or hemorrhage in any individual case. This suggests that the more blocks of tissue examined, the more likely reactive changes will be found.[18]

Any attempt at timing of histologic changes in postmortem brain injury is difficult because of autolytic changes, prolonged resuscitation attempts with increased or decreased blood flow through the damaged brain, and hypoxia related to the brain and other injuries sustained at the same time. However, there are changes in the short-term survivors of physical injury that can be used to date injuries.[18]

Dark neurons have pyknotic nuclei; the cytoplasm appears condensed, stains darkly, and frequently shows small vacuoles at its edge. The dendrites are usually more obvious, and the cell is frequently elongated and irregular in shape. It appears that, although dark neurons may be artifacts in some cases (from postmortem handling of the brain), they are seen more commonly in cases of brain trauma. In the Anderson and Opeskin study, dark neurons were present at all time periods during the first 48 hours; therefore they are of no use in the timing of brain tissue.[18]

Eosinophilic neurons are a prominent feature in areas of physical damage and in zones of secondary hypoxic change. As confirmed by other researchers, this change is seen early. They appeared to follow a progressive course with time. Eosinophilic refers to a gradation of change. Initially, the nuclei of eosinophilic neurons are pyknotic; the cytoplasm shows a loss of Nissl's staining and mild eosinophilia. Later, the nuclei appear less dark and more homogeneous, and the cytoplasm appears more eosinophilic. Perineuronal spaces are dilated. Eventually nuclear staining is lost, and the cytoplasm is brightly eosinophilic. Eosinophilic change was noted especially in areas of contusion, adjacent to deeper hemorrhages, and in areas affected by hypoxia such as the hippocampus and boundary zones of the blood supply. Eosinophilic neurons were noted in one-half of the cases surviving greater than 1 hour, and increased in frequency and severity with increasing survival time.[18]

Incrustation of neurons was noted in a small percentage of cases in areas of contusion and were seen in survival times of greater than 3 hours, and thereafter were seen in a few cases in each time period up to 48 hours postinjury. Incrustation refers to neurons showing small, 2- to 4-μm basophilic nodules on the surface of the cell body and dendrites. Using electron microscopy, these nodules are electron-dense zones surrounded by what appear to be dilated astrocyte processes. Incrusted neurons were noted especially in areas of contusion.[18]

Most of the damage to axons takes place at the same time as physical impact. The separation of swellings cut longitudinally from spheroids is artificial and depends on the direction of cutting. Axonal swelling and spheroids were seen in the white matter close to both large and small lacerations and hemorrhages in about one-half of cases in the first hour and continued throughout all time periods. Garvey's silver axon stain was excellent for demonstrating these changes, even though they were also visible using H&E stain. BAPP staining was not useful in short survival times because it takes a few hours before its accumulation in damaged axons is demonstrated.[18]

Axonal swelling and spheroids can occur in nontraumatic brain hemorrhage, infarction, and other areas of local destruction of brain tissue. Axonal swelling and spheroids in the Anderson and Opeskin study were confined to areas of hemorrhage and laceration, were not a feature of other areas of the brain, and were not seen to the same degree of abnormality in any nontraumatized brains.[18]

Eosinophilic swelling of glial cytoplasm is a very early change in posttraumatic brain injury. Eosinophilic swelling of glial cytoplasm has been seen in nontraumatic cases, especially those in which there has been hypoxia, subarachnoid hemorrhage, or both. Eosinophilic cytoplasmic swelling of glia is most prominent in the subpial and subependymal glia of the brain stem, the subependymal regions of the third and lateral ventricles, and around parenchymal hemorrhages. Initially, the cells show clear or pale eosinophilic cytoplasm, but with increasing time the cytoplasm shows deeper staining with eosin, PAS, LFB, GFAP, HSP-70, and BAPP. The exact nature of these cells is uncertain. Most have small, round nuclei and resemble oligodendroglia or microglia; however, it is clear that a moderate proportion of the cells are astrocytes, as shown by the presence of GFAP-positive processes. Astrocytes are normally the predominant type of cell in the subpial and subependymal zones.[18]

Neutrophil polymorphonuclear leukocytes (granulocytes) are the first blood-borne leukocytes to appear in the damaged tissues. Granulocytes were initially seen in small numbers around vessels adjacent to hemorrhages and were seen on a few occasions in the first hour after the trauma. In experimental situations following injury of tissues, direct viewing of vessels in rabbit ear chambers showed that there was initial pavementing of granulocytes in vessels; escape of polymorphs into the tissues took 2 to 9 minutes. Early escape of granulocytes into tissues is also an occasional feature in surgical biopsy specimens that have taken a moderate time, often less than 1 hour, to procure.[18]

In the present study, one interesting finding was the presence of granulocytes surrounding corpora amylacea. This was seen especially in subpial zones adjacent to subarachnoid hemorrhage, and raises the question of whether chemotaxis plays a part in this phenomenon.[18]

Foamy macrophages in tissues were infrequent in the first 48 hours postinjury, and this finding is in keeping with many other reports of timing over longer periods. Foamy macrophages were noted from 19 hours.

Table 9.12 Age Estimation in Human Brain Injury Using Cellular Reactions

Cell Type	Time of First Appearance Postinjury
Eosinophilic neurons	From 1 hour
Neuronal incrustation	From 3–48 hours
Axonal swelling and spheroids	From 1 hour
Glial swelling	From very early to 48 hours
Polymorphonuclear leukocytes	From 1 hour
Foamy macrophages	At least 48 hours
Iron-containing macrophages	More than 48 hours

Iron-containing macrophages were not seen in the first 48 hours of survival time (Perls' stain) (Table 9.12).[18]

Autolysis of the internal granular layer is considered to be a postmortem change.[1]

References

1. Madea B, Payne-James C. 2003. Time since death. In *Forensic Medicine: Clinical and Pathological Aspects,* eds. J Payne-James, A Busuttil, W Smockk, 91–114. London: Greenwich Medical Media.
2. Spitz WU. 1980. Investigation of deaths in childhood. In *Medicolegal Investigation of Death,* eds. WU Spitz and RS Fisher, 470–74. Springfield, IL: Thomas
3. Pounder DJ. 1995. Postmortem changes and time of death. Dept. of Forensic Medicine, University of Dundee. Unpublished.
4. Hoekelman RA. 1974. *A Guide to Physical Examination,* ed. B. Bates, 325–26. Philadelphia and Toronto: J.B. Lippincott.
5. Gilbert-Barness E, Debich-Spicer DE. 1995. Pediatric forensic pathology. In *Handbook of Pediatric Autopsy Pathology,* eds. E Gilbert Barness and DE Debeich-Spicer, 471–98. Totowa, NJ: Humana Press.
6. Henssge C, Madea B. 2007. Estimation of the time since death. *Forensic Sci Int* 165:182–84.
7. Fisher RS. 1980. Time of death and changes after death. In *Medicolegal Investigation of Death,* eds. WU Spitz and RS Fisher, 12–38. Springfield, IL: Thomas.
8. McCann J, Reay D, Siebert J, Stephens BG, et al. 1996. Postmortem perianal findings in children. *Am J Forensic Med Pathol* 17:289–98.
9. Coe JI. 1989. Vitreous potassium as a measure of the postmortem interval: an historical review and critical evaluation. *Forensic Sci Int* 42:201–13.
10. Madea B, Rodig A. 2006. Time of death dependent criteria in vitreous humor—accuracy of estimating the time since death. *Forensic Sci Int* 164:87–92.
11. Rognum TO, Hauge S, Øyasaeter S, Saugstad OD. 1991. A new biochemical method for estimation of postmortem time. *Forensic Sci Int* 51:139–46.

12. Lange N, Swearer S, Sturner WQ. 1994. Human postmortem interval estimation from vitreous potassium: an analysis of original data from six different studies. *Forensic Sci Int* 66:159–74.
13. Tagliaro F, Bortolotti F, Manetto G, Cittadini F, et al. 2001. Potassium concentration differences in the vitreous humour from the two eyes revisited by microanalysis with capillary electrophoresis. *J Chromatogr* A 924:293–98.
14. Blumenfeld TA, Mantell CH, Catherman RL, Blane WA. 1979. Postmortem vitreous humor chemistry in sudden infant death syndrome and in other causes of death in childhood. *Am J Clin Pathol* 71:219–23.
15. James RA, Hoadley PA, Sampson BG. 1997. Determination of postmortem interval by sampling vitreous humour. *Am J Forensic Med Path* 18:158–62.
16. Widström AM, Christensson K, Ransjö-Arvidson AB, et al. 1988. Gastric aspirates in newborn infants: pH, volume and levels of gastrin- and somatostatin-like immunoreactivigy. *Acta Paediatr Scand* 77:502–8.
17. Betz P. 1994. Histological and enzyme histochemical parameters for the age estimation of human skin wounds. *Int J Leg Med* 107:60–68.
18. Anderson R, Opeskin K. 1998. Timing of early changes in brain trauma. *Am J Forensic Med Path* 19:1–9.
19. Orrico M, Melotti R, Mantovani A, et al. 2008. Pupil pharmacological reactivity as method for assessing time since death is fallacious. *Am J Forensic Med Path* 29:304–8.

Index

U

V